David Knoff is a speaker and specialist in remote leadership, management in isolation, Antarctic operations, resilience and mental health strategies and practices. He has worked for fifteen years in international relations with the Australian Government, as an officer in the Australian Army and as Station and Voyage Leader for the Australian Antarctic Program. David lives in Melbourne. *537 Days of Winter* is his first book.

davidknoff.com

537
DAYS OF WINTER

DAVID KNOFF

affirm
press

First published by Affirm Press in 2022
This edition published in 2023
Boon Wurrung Country
28 Thistlethwaite Street
South Melbourne VIC 3205
affirmpress.com.au

10 9 8 7 6 5 4 3 2

This book is a work of non-fiction based on the author's conversations, experiences and memories. The author acknowledges that some creative licence has been used. Places and timings have sometimes been rearranged. In certain instances, names have been changed and individual 'characters' have played the role of multiple people. While accurate when possible and faithful to the truth of the story, some elements have been altered or amalgamated.

 A catalogue record for this book is available from the National Library of Australia

ISBN: 9781922992284 (mass market paperback)

Cover design by Luke Causby/Blue Cork © Affirm Press
Cover image by Damien Everett
Typeset in Minion Pro by J&M Typesetting
Printed and bound in China by C&C Offset Printing Co., Ltd.

*For my father, Bruce, who travelled the world but never got the
chance to visit Antarctica or see his kids grow up.
For my family – Pam, Penny & Luke, Michael & Bianca,
Emily & Annabelle.*

Contents

Foreword   ix

Maps   xii

Preface   xv

Part I   **Summer**

Chapter 1   Hitting the Ice Running   3

Chapter 2   The Case of the Dropped Burrito   31

Chapter 3   What's COVID Got to Do with It?   57

Part II   **Winter**

Chapter 4   The Sound of Silence   79

Chapter 5   Woah, We're Halfway There?   103

Chapter 6   The Bombshell   125

Chapter 7   When the Novelty Wears Off   137

Chapter 8   Quitting Is Not an Option   167

Chapter 9   The Last Days of Sea Ice   201

Chapter 10   A Christmas Miracle   209

Part III   **Summer II: The Sequel**

Chapter 11   The Waiting Game Sucks   241

Chapter 12   What Do You Mean, Yet?   263

Chapter 13   Home   281

Image Credits   299

Acknowledgements   301

Foreword

For more than seventy years, the Australian Antarctic Division and its predecessor, the Australian National Antarctic Research Expedition, have provided the platform for some of the most important and exciting research undertaken by Australia. By unlocking the secrets of the Antarctic, we are able to learn so much about our planet – its past and its potential future. That the program has been so successful can be attributed directly to the men and women who have accepted the many challenges that working in the Antarctic presents. This book, *537 Days of Winter*, pulls back the curtain on life in an Antarctic station under both normal and abnormal circumstances.

Governors-general of Australia have held a close relationship with the Australian Antarctic Division for many years. Two governors-general have visited Australia's Antarctic stations. Given this vice-regal relationship, my visit to the division's headquarters at Kingston and my interest in leadership, my curiosity was piqued when David sent me an advance copy of his book accompanied by a request to write a foreword. Once I had read *537 Days of Winter*, I realised that it was an essential book to read about leadership. I accepted his request with pleasure.

Expeditions to the Antarctic are normally of twelve months' duration. For David and his twenty-three companions, their expedition began on that premise. David writes in a very readable and honest style his account of life on their station, about their arrival and their early trials and achievements. He pays particular attention to the pressures that he experienced as the expedition leader. Almost subliminal in this story is the knowledge that after twelve months, the expeditioners would all be home for Christmas. The outbreak of the COVID-19 pandemic was to disrupt this assumed truth.

As the pandemic spread across the globe, the closing of borders and the shutting down of international travel being among many national responses, the isolation of the Antarctic spared David and his team from the pandemic's physical and mental health impacts. But the pandemic contained a 'bombshell'. Eventually it became clear that the team could not be relieved after twelve months and that they would be required to stay for another summer season. This news placed the team under severe stress. Life at the station after this news is the heart of David's story. In telling his story, he illuminates for us an experience that all leaders face: the 'loneliness of command'.

From the bombshell of the pandemic to the drama of an engine fire on MPV *Everest* on the eventual return journey, David tells a remarkable story of emotional turmoil, feats of courage in difficult weather conditions and the challenge in leading twenty-three people in extraordinary circumstances in perhaps the harshest environment on earth. It is a very personal story, laying bare his frustrations, uncertainties and concerns. It is a story for everyone in a leadership position, for all will travel on this journey.

My advice is to read this book and urge others to do so. David's story reminds us of the strength of our human will and our ability to overcome the most difficult challenges. This book will hopefully excite others to take on the challenges of leadership in our country.

His Excellency General the Honourable
David Hurley AC DSC (Retd)
Governor-General of the Commonwealth of Australia

Map 1: Australia to Antarctica.

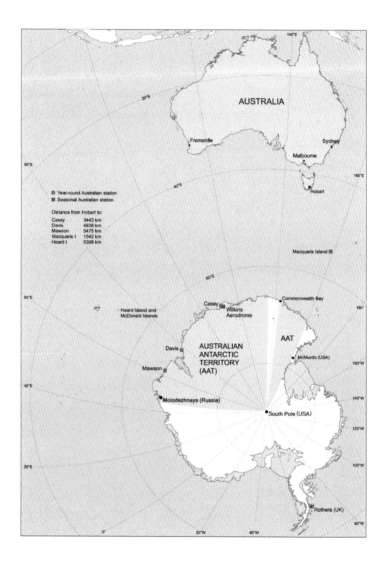

Map 2: Davis Station Operating Area.

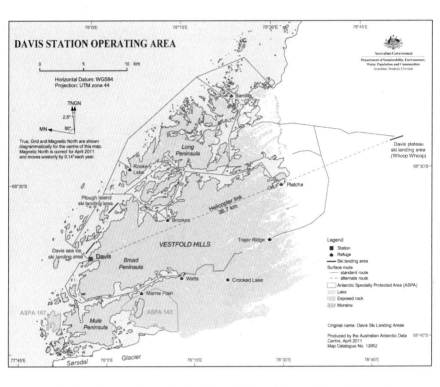

Note that the coastal route depicted from Davis station to Whoop Whoop is open water from around January to March and covered by sea ice from April to December.

Preface

Based in the Tasmanian city of Kingston, just outside Hobart, the Australian Antarctic Division (AAD) is responsible for managing the Australian Antarctic Territory and Australia's two sub-Antarctic islands of Macquarie Island and Heard Island. The AAD's main role is to manage Australia's three permanent Antarctic stations, Casey, Davis and Mawson, which are accessible only in the summer months, when warmer weather allows access to the Antarctic continent. The AAD also manages the station at Macquarie Island on behalf of the Tasmanian Government.

From 1990, Australia relied on the purpose-built icebreaking ship the RSV *Aurora Australis* and over thirty years the shipping schedule became routine and well timed with the melting of the Antarctic sea ice over summer. After 2006, *Aurora*'s schedule was supplemented by regular flights to the Wilkins Aerodrome, 60 kilometres inland from Casey station, to carry expeditioners back and forth between Hobart and Wilkins via a long-range Airbus A319, adapted for Antarctic operations. The four-hour flight is also a critical part of emergency capabilities, should the need arise to evacuate someone back to Australia for medical treatment.

During the summertime, smaller fixed-wing aircraft and helicopters are used to move teams of scientists, expedition teams and visitors between stations and vessels over vast distances, enabling a dynamic and fast-paced season. In the winter, access to

Antarctica by air or sea is almost impossible, with thick pack ice blocking maritime access, hurricane-strength winds, temperatures as low as minus 50 degrees Celsius and near-total darkness.

The Australian Antarctic Program includes all those who work and conduct research at Australia's stations and on AAD voyages, even though many of the participants are in non-scientific roles, such as engineers, doctors, tradesmen, pilots and aircrew. They are collectively known as expeditioners in recognition of the unique challenges and work required to operate and survive in the harsh Antarctic wilderness.

During the summer of 2019–20, over 118 expeditioners visited and worked at Davis research station, many flying in via Wilkins and across to Davis to stay for as little as two weeks. The station itself is spread over about a square kilometre and features summer accommodation buildings, the main wintering accommodation building, two diesel powerhouses, helipads and a hangar, the operations building and multiple science laboratories, as well as a warehouse, vehicle workshop, communications satellite, wharf, boatshed and science storage areas. In many ways, Antarctic stations resemble small towns and are well equipped with gyms, saunas, cinemas and libraries for the community to enjoy when not working.

At Australian stations, wintering expeditioners are seasonal contractors who have signed up for a single year before returning to their lives back home. The wintering teams' job is to maintain the station infrastructure during the dark winter months and to monitor remote scientific instruments. The bulk of the scientific work is conducted during the summer months by glaciologists, geologists, marine biologists and many other scientists from universities across

Australia who join the program to complete their fieldwork. Some return multiple times; others only ever get one chance to visit Antarctica for their research.

On 25 October 2019, the wintering team of the Davis station's 73rd Australian National Antarctic Research Expedition (ANARE) sailed south on one of the final voyages of the *Aurora* for a routine summer and winter in Antarctica. We were scheduled to return on Australia's new icebreaker, the RSV *Nuyina*, which was being built in Romania and was due to arrive in Hobart by late 2020. What happened across the world that year as the COVID-19 pandemic unfolded would dramatically change that plan.

This is a true story. Names and characters have been changed and amalgamated for literary efficiency and privacy, but the narrative remains true to the situations we faced and both the good and bad reactions we all had along the way. The sequence of events is accurate and chronological where practical, with a few minor variations that do not impact the overall outcome. Using my personal notes and diaries to assist my memory, I have tried to recount events as accurately as possible. Where differing opinions or alternative narratives exist, I have included them where appropriate. I am humbly aware that I made mistakes along the way and that, with hindsight, there were better ways to achieve success on occasions, but if you're able to sit around and have such discussions with everyone home safely, then I'll take feedback, criticism and opinions anytime.

David Knoff
Station leader, Davis research station
73rd ANARE

It is not the critic who counts; not the man who points out how the strong man stumbles, or where the doer of deeds could have done them better. The credit belongs to the man who is actually in the arena, whose face is marred by dust and sweat and blood; who strives valiantly; who errs, who comes short again and again, because there is no effort without error and shortcoming; but who does actually strive to do the deeds; who knows great enthusiasms, the great devotions; who spends himself in a worthy cause; who at the best knows in the end the triumph of high achievement, and who at the worst, if he fails, at least fails while daring greatly, so that his place shall never be with those cold and timid souls who neither know victory nor defeat.

—Theodore Roosevelt, 23 April 1910

Part I

SUMMER

Chapter 1

Hitting the Ice Running

Day 16: 9 November 2019
Temperature: -6.1°C to 0.1°C
Station population: 93

'There it is, Dave! Our home for the next year,' Doc said.

We were perched high above the decks of Australia's iconic icebreaker, the RSV *Aurora Australis,* watching *Aurora's* bow crunch into the edge of the 'fast ice' – so called because it is fastened to land. In this case, the fast ice extended from Davis about 5 kilometres out to sea, blocking access to our intended anchorage: about halfway between us and the coloured buildings of Davis station, which looked like Lego bricks in this distance. It had been a two-week voyage across the Southern Ocean, through giant seas and then, as we got closer to our destination, the floating pack ice and fields of icebergs that surround Antarctica, but we had arrived.

The ship ground to a halt in the nearly 2-metre-thick ice and the engines reversed, creating a whirlpool in front of us as the captain backed her up for another run.

'Hold on for round two,' I said to Doc as the captain engaged forward drive and we lurched into the fast ice once more. The steel hull screeched as the ship's bow rose up onto the ice and a gaggle of penguins went scrambling as a loud *crack* could be heard below us as the ship broke through the ice and came to rest on the water.

'This is going to take a while,' said Doc.

Bing-bong. A call came over the PA – it was for me: 'Can we get the ingoing station leader to the bridge, please?'

When I got to the bridge the voyage leader was waiting for me. 'It'll take all night to break through this ice to get close enough to station for resupply to commence,' the voyage leader said, loud enough to be heard above the captain on the radio marshalling his crew for another run at the ice. 'Grab your gear and head to the heli-deck. We'll fly you and a few others ashore this afternoon and start cargo tomorrow.'

As I returned to my room to collect my bags, I ran into my cabinmate, Paul, who had recently been appointed captain of the RSV *Nuyina*. Paul was on the voyage to familiarise himself with Australian standard operating procedures for a station resupply voyage. He had taught me more in two weeks about icebreakers and polar operations than I'd thought possible.

'See you in November with the new ship,' I said as we shook hands.

'You can count on it,' said Paul, smiling cautiously. 'See you then and have a good season.'

There aren't too many perks to being a station leader, but being first ashore is one. I rugged up in about 10 kilograms of Antarctic survival gear for the quick flight and headed down to the ship's heli-hangar, which opened out onto the back deck and helipad. It was a lovely day, hovering around zero degrees but sunny enough to feel the warmth of the sun.

For flights, every expeditioner wears their full survival kit, consisting of a merino wool thermal underlayer, a polar-fleece mid layer and a Gore-Tex-style outer layer or heavyweight goose jacket, plus a few options for beanies, gloves and boots, depending on the situation. What you aren't wearing is carried in one bright-red survival bag, figuratively attached to your hip wherever you go in Antarctica. I was sweating underneath the layers but, if the helicopter went down or we had to land anywhere other than the intended destination, at least I'd be warm.

I've always loved flying, and even though it was only a five-minute ride in the Squirrel B3 helicopter over the ice and towards Davis station, I was grinning from ear to ear. Even after studying it for months on maps and in briefings, I was still impressed by the scale and size of the station. The buildings were scattered between gravel roads, with banks of snow separating them. I looked out at the bright-green accommodation building in the middle and wondered which of the windows would be my home for the year. I then squinted against the glare of the helicopter's windshield to the rooftop of the yellow operations building, adorned with antennas and cameras, where a lone figure was hurriedly making his way down the stairs and along the road towards the helipads to greet us.

Flying above the fast ice, I looked past the hills towards the Antarctic Plateau, which looked like a giant cloud on the horizon, and remembered a similar moment four years earlier that led me here. It was 2016 and I was flying over Baghdad in a Blackhawk helicopter and wondering about my future. After a decade of seeing the worst side of humanity in conflict zones and war-ravaged landscapes, I'd decided it was time to refocus my life and join Australia's Antarctic Program.

Now, as we flew over the parades of penguins and spectacular icebergs, I knew this new chapter in my life would be exactly the change I'd been looking for so I could focus on the more positive side of humanity – its pursuit of science and adventure.

As we touched down, I was met by the outgoing station leader, Simon, whom I'd met a year earlier in Melbourne.

'Welcome to Davis! Boy, it's good to see you here,' he said as the pilots took off again.

'It's good to be here, finally,' I said, studying Simon's face. It was clear this experience had changed him. I wondered what I would look like after a year down here.

There was no time to catch up, though, as we got straight down to the business of planning the resupply and handover of the station. This was the busiest and most complex time of the year, and Simon would remain in overall command right up until the last minute of handover. There was a very clear difference between his outgoing team, who walked around in T-shirts and knew where everything was, versus my team, all rugged up and wandering around starry-eyed. Naturally, we worked closely together for the next two weeks as my team learned the ropes and got ready to take over.

With the *Aurora* now at anchor, and solid ice surrounding it like a wharf, the resupply was in full swing. Those who hadn't been flown in now disembarked down the gangway and were driven ashore. The station population had reached maximum capacity: ninety-three people who were there for summer, plus daytrippers from the resupply team based on the ship who came ashore to help during the day.

Between getting everyone ashore, conducting the briefings, transferring a year's worth of cargo and then refuelling the station, it was hard to find time to sit down and talk one on one with Simon to ask him all the questions I had about the realities of being an Antarctic station leader. After I'd followed Simon around for a few days, we grabbed a ute and went for a drive off station along Dingle Road, which snakes its way north and into the Vestfold Hills that surround the station. The road makes for a good 5-kilometre run, walk or bike ride, depending on the conditions.

Today the conditions weren't suitable for the ute, and we quickly got bogged in snow. We returned to the station to upgrade to one of the tracked Hägglunds vehicles, which cope better in the soft summer snow.[1] The downside of the Hägglunds was that we were sitting on top of a very noisy diesel engine and, along with the noise of the tracks bouncing over rocks, it was hardly the best place for 'a quiet word'.

Eventually, we had a chance to talk with the engine off. I had many questions to ask: 'How did you manage alcohol? How did you deal with troublemakers? How did you deal with conflicts? Who did you trust? Who can't you trust? What did you get wrong? What would you do differently? Who did you turn to for help?'

'Mate,' Simon began before I had the chance to say anything, 'you can forget anything written in a management textbook about how to deal with what happens down here while you're all living and working together through the winter. The smallest things become massive, people will be at each other's throats, you'll be pulling your hair out – even the best feel the effects of the darkness and isolation.'

It seemed like Simon was glad to be able to vent for the first

---

[1] Thankfully we didn't get bogged badly enough to require radioing back for a 'white shovel', the code for assistance.

time in a while.

'How'd you keep yourself sane?' I asked, knowing that if the station leader isn't running well, the whole system is doomed.

'Get a good support network of previous or current station leaders to talk to,' Simon answered, 'because none of the problems you'll face are unique or new. Seek help, and don't let it wear you down when you think it's not going perfectly, because it never does.'

* * *

Simon was pushed for time as he managed the resupply and we got ready for the summer. As I trailed him, I felt somewhat overwhelmed by the complex aviation, maritime, industrial and scientific operations all working in unison around me. There was never a quiet moment during an Antarctic summer, as many of the expeditioners returned nearly every season to continue their research. Running the station and keeping my finger on the pulse without micromanaging or slowing things down would be a delicate balance, as would safety and expectation management; I knew we'd all want opportunities to get out and enjoy the environment and not just work the whole time.

The summer expeditioners would have a brief window to get as much done as possible in the warmer months, and they could manage a frantic pace knowing they'd only be there a short time. But those of us in the winter team would have to ensure we could keep up a steady pace for twelve months. Right from the start, I looked at the two groups differently, from a management and personality point of view. Almost anyone can work together for a few months in summer, but an Antarctic winter is a different story.

* * *

The handover ceremony was a low-key occasion marking the completion of the 72nd ANARE team's winter and the beginning of the 73rd's season.[2] We gathered in the upstairs living quarters, where about one hundred people were squeezed into the area. Simon presented the wintering medallions to his team and the official 'Key to Davis' to me, along with the station leader's VHF portable radio.

I'll never forget the odd look of joy on Simon's face as he handed me the radio. It gave me a sense that this was the real burden of the role; that, from now on, twenty-four hours a day until I handed over the key to my successor, I was in charge, on call, the person ultimately responsible.

Although it sounds dramatic, this is true for everyone on an Antarctic station, regardless of your role. At any point you may be required to assist in an emergency situation or with an aspect of community life that needs your help. During resupply, it was commonplace to see some of Australia's leading scientists helping unload containers of frozen food or peeling fresh produce to be frozen for the months ahead. During the summer season we would maintain about a fifty–fifty split of scientists to non-science

---

[2]   The Australian National Antarctic Research Expedition (ANARE) gives a historic delineation of each season, used since the beginning of Australia's permanent stations on the continent in the modern age. This nomenclature has endured through the various iterations of the Australian Antarctic Division's place within government bureaucracy and creates a sense of historical connection with those who came before us.

participants, who included the operations team, chefs, plumbers, electricians, carpenters, plant operators and mechanics, and the safety auditors and environmental inspectors, who visited for sometimes as little as a few weeks. Science would always be the priority, and I knew it would be challenging to manage the expectations of field teams as they sought to maximise their time sampling everything from mosses to rocks, soil, lake sediments, ice cores, sea ice, marine debris, penguins and even the Antarctic air, to better understand the planet we live on and how it is changing. Many of these field teams would work well into the night and on any day of the week if the weather allowed, but the station tempo was based on a typical work week to ensure a balance between work and rest.

To me, working unusual hours was standard. My friends often say I've never had a 'real job' working nine to five for 'the man'. All of my professional experience has been in immersive jobs, working twenty-four-hour days. It didn't matter what your workplace agreement said you got paid to do, because you had a higher sense of purpose and duty to do whatever was required. I quickly learned this wasn't necessarily true for everyone else's professional experience at Davis, so I knew that building a sense of team and purpose would be essential.

* * *

Following handover of the station and as the *Aurora* turned north and headed back to Hobart, we stood on the balcony and along the rocky and icy banks of the station to farewell the ship with the traditional lighting of flares, to which the ship replied with a long blow of its horn. Thankfully this all happened on a nice sunny afternoon, so I opened the bar for the first time and we enjoyed a drink and some snacks before getting a good night's sleep, knowing that tomorrow the season proper would start.

* * *

Walking into the station leader's office for the first time without Simon, I took stock of my surroundings. The view was spectacularly distracting: the office window looked out across the bay towards a horizon of icebergs and islands. Nearer to my window was the station flagpole and every morning I'd raise the Australian flag – a brand new flag I'd put up to signify the start of the 73rd ANARE – before starting work.

From the window I could also see the 'street sign' monument, with distances marked to various capital cities and stations around the world. My home town, Melbourne: 5210km. The sea ice was still solid and I could see that the gap where the *Aurora* had been parked was now serving as an easy way for penguins to access the open water as they leaped in and out – a distracting view indeed!

The office itself was a drab purple colour and featured a bookshelf of old station logbooks and standard operating procedures for everything from aviation to hazardous chemical storage. In the centre of the room were three 'comfy' green leather chairs and a coffee table. An invitation to the station leader's office to sit in the 'comfy' chair was the equivalent of being called to the principal's office at school, and not something expeditioners wanted to happen to them. I wondered how often I'd have to close the door and counsel bad behaviour or mediate disputes.

The walls were adorned with maps of the Vestfold Hills, the 400-square-kilometre rocky area surrounding Davis and forming the main station operating area, as well as colour-coded charts for wind speeds and the corresponding operating restrictions when they crossed certain thresholds. I looked at the whiteboard and the fortnightly planning system Simon had used. I planned to keep his systems for now and would adjust it later, once I knew what I was doing. I'd left Australia weeks before, but this was my real day one.

I'd been to Antarctica twice before, but this was my first time as the station leader. The station was a strange but perfect mix of the features of my two most influential professions before the Antarctic Program. The layout of the station and facilities were similar to that of a modern military Forward Operating Base (FOB); I'd spent a year in one in 2016, embedded with coalition forces and flying back and forth between northern Baghdad and the Australian embassy in central Baghdad, except all the buildings here were brightly coloured so you could find them in a blizzard. But the organisational structure of the AAD and station was similar to that of an Embassy or government taskforce. Everyone knew their roles well and could operate independently, but ensuring they were all working towards the same goals and communicating well would be my biggest challenge.

On an Antarctic station, you and your team are on your own, so if anything goes wrong, there is no fire brigade, no police rescue, no cavalry to save the day except for the team on station, who need to be trained up and ready to fill these roles. Therefore, before anyone headed out into the wilderness – the unforgiving landscape of Antarctica – we needed to set up and exercise the Incident Management Team and establish its search and rescue (SAR) capability. Throughout the voyage to Davis, the core leadership group and I had been planning how we would get through the checklist and requirements efficiently so we could 'hit the ice running'.

The Incident Management Team was chaired by me and comprised the leadership team members plus a few others filling additional roles such as notetakers and watchkeepers. This would ensure continuity, as an incident response can drag on for days and weeks. The overall crisis management system is brilliantly simple in the way it scales up, and comprises three main levels:

1. The Incident Response Team is a small team of first responders at the actual incident site, including doctor, or field specialists as required.
2. The Incident Management Team (IMT) coordinates the station or voyage response to a critical incident, separating responses and managing station continuity. It involves everyone on station pivoting their role to support the response.
3. The Crisis Management and Recovery (CMR) team is based in Kingston, Tasmania, and involves almost the whole Australian Antarctic Division, as well as elements from Canberra, and is coordinated between the stations and other nations with Antarctic stations and assets that may be able to assist.

Antarctica is a complex operating environment and the AAD was no stranger to managing critical incidents. In the last decade alone, the *Aurora* had broken its mooring lines while resupplying Mawson station and run aground, a helicopter had crashed into a glacier near Davis station and, in a separate and tragic incident, a helicopter pilot had died after falling down a crevasse.

On my first day as station leader, I gathered my leadership team in the operations room and laid it out cold. 'I know many of you have sat in this very room when things have gone wrong. Antarctica is an unforgiving and dangerous location in which to operate and simply exist. The smallest incident can be fatal when it incapacitates you in the bitter cold. Hypothermia and frostbite can occur in minutes if you are not properly protected from the elements. So don't let the sunshiny days breed complacency.'

I looked around the room. I could sense minds wandering to the darkest moments of Antarctic history. The walls of the operations building were adorned with photos of medical evacuation scenarios involving foreign planes being loaded with casualties.

I felt a sudden wave of empathy for previous station leaders who had to deal with the life-or-death situations Antarctica had thrown at them. I hoped I would never have to face such a moment during my time down south. Despite the professionalism and experience on station, in a crisis, you're it. It can take days or weeks to get any additional support to a station during an emergency, if there even is someone nearby who can help.

It was a slightly different story with the search and rescue team. The four field training officers[3] on station during the summer were

---

[3] Field training officers (FTOs) are responsible for all aspects of field training and are experts in Antarctic-specific risks and capabilities. Their backgrounds vary from being mountaineers and adventure training teachers to heli-ski guides, along with ex-special forces types and others who had made careers in Antarctica. They're all

the immediate response team to any field incident. I felt confident in their skills and experience, but in winter we would only have one FTO left, so we selected six members from the winter team to support him and be trained in advanced search and rescue techniques. One of my mottos became 'lead the team you've got, not the team you want', as I struggled to select the perfect combination of experience for the winter search and rescue team.

The excitement and enthusiasm of the six members we settled on indicated they expected their training to be a Hollywood-style version of helicopters, rappelling, ice axes, ropes and fun, when the reality was often long, repetitive days of training in basic systems of rescue and developing familiarity with equipment and procedures. For every moment of excitement, there would be hours of learning the basics.

Expectation management would be one of the biggest challenges of the summer, but it was often the workaholics and martyrs who caused the friction, not the expeditioners who were there to enjoy the experience.

* * *

Walking back from my office one evening to track down some scientists, I entered the main 'cold porch'[4] of the living quarters (LQ), which acted as the buffer between the inside and outside, hung my jacket on a hook and clumsily tried to take my boots off by stomping

---

different, but somehow all the same.

[4]   Each building had a small room to manage the transition between the freezing cold of outside and the interior. This 'cold porch' was often overcrowded with an array of boots, jackets, shovels, rubbish bins, fire extinguishers and lost property.

on the heel with the other foot. I overheard one expeditioner turn to another and remark, 'Oh, that's great you went on a boat trip. I just don't have time for things like that.' The other expeditioner was grinning ear to ear after an evening of cruising around the icebergs and penguin colonies in an inflatable rubber boat. I followed them in and pulled the aggrieved expeditioner aside.

'Mate, I just heard what you said. Leave it with me and I'll get you covered tomorrow night so you can do an iceberg cruise. Everyone should get a chance by the end of the season.' I expected this to be music to his ears.

'No, it's okay. I don't really want to do one,' he replied.

'But you just said you wish you had time? We can make it work, just say the word,' I replied. Soon I realised he just liked complaining and acting busy. This was still just a workplace, after all, with all the usual gripes and complaints, just with more penguins than back home.

Staring at the crowded mess on the lower level of the LQ, I joined the back of the queue that snaked around and looked at the room – there was barely enough room to walk between the tables. It reminded me of a scene from a prison movie, with rival gangs sitting at different tables: the scientists, the tradies, the pilots, the old guys, the round-trippers and the misfits who bridged the gaps.

'Thanks, chefs!' I said to the trio of summer chefs loitering around the kitchen as I piled my plate with another delicious meal. The competitive nature of the chefs certainly helped the meal quality, as they seemingly outdid themselves every night. Tonight: Danish meatballs.

It was a daily challenge to keep up with what was happening in the station community while I was busy running the place, and early on in the summer I was reassured that a decision I'd made months earlier to select my deputy station leader from the wintering team was the right one.

The deputy plays a critical role in the running of an Antarctic station and is an important part of the community. Two candidates from the wintering team put their hands up; a third candidate from the summer team had me toying with the idea of having both a summer deputy and then a winterer, but after taking advice from a few wise retired station leaders I went for the same deputy, Rhonda, the wintering chef, from Day 1 to Day 537, and never regretted my decision for a second.

'How's everything going?' I asked her as I cleaned my plate and added it to the tray of dirty dishes.

'Fantastic!' she said. 'This is always the best time of the year, while we're all new.'

Rhonda was well known in the Antarctic program, having completed multiple winters at Australian and New Zealand Antarctic stations. A no-nonsense chef from New Zealand, she'd spent her life running kitchens at mining camps and Antarctic stations. From the beginning, Rhonda had been the obvious choice for deputy, but she was reluctant to apply until she'd had a chance to assess me.

This cheeky but calculated approach was exactly what I wanted. I needed a deputy who was not after the status or extra pay, but was motivated by wanting the group to succeed and would complement my leadership style while offering an alternative to it, acting as a check and balance for my decisions and helping me plan for the season.

Back in Hobart before we left, as we concluded the week-long firefighting training with the Tasmanian Fire Service, covered in soot and saturated with water from fighting fires all day during exercises and assessments, I quietly asked Rhonda, 'Do you still want the job you applied for?'

'I'd be delighted,' Rhonda replied with a smile as we shook hands, and that was that. The two of us would be the core leadership team for the journey ahead, but, on station, the chefs and the kitchen were the heart of morale and community.

I later approached one of the unsuccessful candidates to offer some feedback, to which he simply replied, 'No need for feedback – good choice.'

* * *

The most exciting and adventurous thing down south is to get out into the field. The Australian program gives everyone a chance to head into the field during their time but, before you do, you have to complete Antarctic-specific survival training or field travel training with one of the field training officers. With up to ninety-three expeditioners on station at any one time during the summer and only four FTOs, it was a juggling act to get everyone trained.

As the summer progressed, the sea ice gradually decayed and around mid-December it became unsafe for travel. The priority was to get the winter team trained on the sea ice before it closed, and then we'd get as many of the summer team as possible through the one-night on-land survival training to give them some freedom to get off station on the weekends. People generally understood the priorities and were happy enough to wait their turn, but there were always those who felt an injustice had been served.

Enter Fred. We all had our 'Fred' moments, and no one was perfect. Ultimately, we all react differently to challenges but Fred was the one expeditioner who took it to the next level. When I said one thing, Fred did another. When the community voted for a pizza night, Fred wanted stir-fry. When the rules said drive safely at 30 kilometres per hour, Fred drove at 40. Fred was an expert on everything and accountable for nothing. He was the first to ask questions out of hours, yet took offence when asked to work on his day off. We've all worked with someone like Fred, and despite most workplaces having rigorous selection processes and screening in place – from Amsterdam to Antarctica – there is always a Fred.

I was staring out the mess window across the sea ice, pondering the day ahead while waiting for my toast to pop up, when Fred saw his opportunity.

'Why am I in the last group to be trained?'

'Morning, Fred, how are you?' I replied.

'I just think I should be in an earlier group. It's important, and I'll be a good field leader,' he continued, clearly having rehearsed this conversation.

'Fred, my toast is still in the toaster on its journey from bread to toast to breakfast. Swing by my office later and we can talk about it,' I offered.

'I'm busy all morning,' replied Fred, insistent on getting an answer right there and then.

My toast popped up and I grabbed it gingerly, buttering it and adding a thin but perfect amount of vegemite. As I did so, I explained the process to Fred. 'It's simple, everyone who has an operational need goes first, and then we'll assess who is going to be a field leader based on how the training goes. Field leadership is more about attitude than completing the training.'

I was bemused that someone demanding something for their own benefit would approach me in such an abrupt manner and have zero awareness of the fact it was seven o'clock in the morning and I was in the middle of making breakfast.

'Well, okay, but I've been a field leader before,' replied Fred.

'And I'm sure you'll demonstrate those skills when you get out in the field here, and then we can assess if I sign you off as one this season.' I ended it there, as it was time for me to start eating my toast and get on with the morning. Fred at least seemed to understand the situation and was satisfied there was a pathway for him to achieve his goal.

This exchange left a strange seed of uncertainty in my mind about the expectations and motivations of the team. I had a sense that their approach to the Antarctic program was as much about some of them getting what they saw on the brochure as it was about achieving the aims of the program. I'd spend many hours discussing this topic with various team members. Was it a millennial thing? Was it an education and professional experience thing? Should I call their parents and blame them? Or was it simply humans being humans and looking out for number one?

I also needed to get myself on field training and suitably experienced to lead fieldtrips, ideally before the sea ice decayed and eventually broke out. The decision to open and close access to the sea ice falls to the station leader. I'm no scientist and had limited experience with sea ice, but it's actually quite intuitive – when it starts to look bad, it's time to close. With a bit of luck, I was able to join the last training group in early December, along with Doc and two other lads from the winter team – Jimbo the plumber and Lewis the head mechanic – led by our trusty wintering training officer, Jarrod.

For the first time, I handed the reins to Rhonda, who'd be in charge while I was off station. In the event that something serious happened, a helicopter could return me within thirty minutes, but I still went through everything with Rhonda, from current field parties to emergency procedures. This became a good habit every time I left station to make sure there were no surprises, and also to prevent anyone from trying the old 'Knoffey approved it before he left' trick.

You can't just walk out the door in Antarctica and wander off. The weather is unpredictable, the temperatures are always freezing and there are limited resources for rescue, should you get into trouble. Before we left, we spent an hour or so loading up the gear and equipment we needed to survive. We then briefed everyone on the trip plan, made sure our rosters were covered and finally turned our fire tags to 'red' on the station muster board in the mess, which indicates to the team that you're off station.

This time we'd be heading out on quad bikes. Quad bikes were a controversial topic at the time; a government-wide policy was pushing for their replacement and a recent announcement confirmed they would be phased out of the program. The area around Davis is well known for its good access to sea ice and vast frozen fjords and lakes to explore and, since sled dogs were replaced in 1992, quad bikes were the most popular vehicles to get around on.

We were all smiles as we motored off on a sunny day onto the sea ice at the approved 30 kilometres per hour. It was a strange sensation to ride along over the frozen ocean, knowing that later in the season, after the sea ice had melted, we'd have to use boats to access the same area.

Our destination that night was Bandits Hut, about 30 kilometres north of station along the coastal sea ice, navigating through icebergs and islands all locked together by the frozen ocean. Along the way we stopped to learn about the environment from Jarrod, who pointed out various ice anomalies and hazards to look out for around the grounded icebergs and leads.[5] We also enjoyed stopping to take photos of penguins and seals. Who says you can't have fun on a training trip?

After a long day's ride we made it to Bandits, which was perched on a rocky island surrounded by icebergs, much closer than the station to the Antarctic Plateau. Bandits is considered the best of the field huts scattered around the Davis operating area. With a spectacular view from the helipad just behind the hut and a comfortable layout for four people (with a fifth on the floor this time), the huts were five-star accommodation in my book. Complete with a gas stove and oven, a kettle and a generator, these huts had been built around the hills over the years and were a brilliantly simple construction of freezer panel walls and wooden bunk beds.

---

[5] Near the coast there were dozens of 'grounded icebergs', which are much like frozen islands when firmly resting on the sea-floor. The general rule was to keep at least the height of the berg away from it, to be safe in the event of a rollover. A break in the sea ice is referred to as a 'lead'. Sometimes the break is only a few centimetres and not an issue; other times it might be wide enough to swallow the quad bike whole. They also refreeze, so you might be on 2-metre-thick ice and suddenly find yourself on a refrozen lead only 10 centimetres thick!

As we unpacked the gear and got settled, a radio call from Davis changed my plans for a warm cup of tea and a biscuit.

'Bandits party, Bandits party, this is VLZ Davis,[6] can you tell Dave to be ready at the helipad in about fifteen minutes? He needs to do a reconnaissance flight over the Sørsdal Glacier with the senior FTO,' came the familiar voice of the comms operator. We'd been trying to do this flight over the glacier for a few nights now and just hadn't had the right weather, so I was half expecting this call to come in. In the coming weeks, a team of scientists planned to visit the Sørsdal Glacier to study crevassing, and this flight was an important part of selecting the site and understanding the terrain conditions. These flights were in the late evening to take advantage of the low angle of the sun, which reflected off the surface to make identifying dangerous crevasses easier. As I was required to sign off on the overall risk of travelling to the area known for crevassing, it was important for me to see it firsthand but, work requirements aside, the spectacular sunset and clear conditions made it a beautiful night for flight.

Glaciers are living, breathing beasts, one of nature's truly spectacular works of art. I've seen them all over the world, from the Antarctic Peninsula to northern Pakistan, but this would be my first time flying over an Antarctic glacier to consider the operational risks. Crevasses form as glaciers move across the rocks far below the surface, creating icy canyons on the surface of the glacier. You'd think a giant crack in the ice would be easy to spot, but nature has a cruel way of slowly bridging these gaps with snow, forming what

---

6   VLZ Davis is the historic call sign of the station, much like a ship's designation or an airport code, e.g. VLV Mawson, VLZ Davis, VNJ Casey and VNAA for the *Aurora Australis*.

looks like a solid, continuous surface – but when you step on it, you fall right through. The tragic incident of the helicopter pilot who'd fallen down a crevasse was still fresh in the minds of many on station who had been there at the time.

The flight from Bandits to the Sørsdal Glacier would take about thirty minutes and, as we chatted through the headsets, the conversation was soon directed at me.

'So how did you get here?' asked Kiwi, the lead pilot for the season, who was returning for yet another summer at Davis.

'The dream started a few years ago,' I replied, 'when I did a trip with some mates down to the Antarctic Peninsula on a small yacht out of South America to go mountaineering. But I ended up falling in love with the wilderness, so then found a way to get back here professionally. It wasn't too big of a leap from what I was doing at embassies around the world, just colder.' We flew over the glacial cliffs that towered some 200 feet above the rocky surface. 'The glacier looks like a pavlova, don't you think?' I said to Kiwi.

'You mean like the famous cake from New Zealand?' he said, quick to trigger the age-old debate about the famous dessert's origins.

'Regardless of where it's from, it still looks like a pavlova.'

'What you're seeing is the crevassing formed as the ice moves across the rocks below and the pressure moves outwards and finds space to expand as it approaches the coast,' Mitch said, jumping in with a more scientific explanation for the pavlova effect, and reminding me that field training officers are not known for their sense of humour.

Mitch was the senior field training officer. My boss back in

Kingston had told me, 'If we could clone Mitch, we would.' As a new station leader, I was surrounded by accomplished expeditioners like Mitch in the core leadership team to offset my lack of experience.

Mitch was next-level, though, revered by his peers, but humble about his own experiences. There was almost nowhere in the Davis operations area he hadn't been. Mitch had seen the best and worst of what Antarctica can throw at you; for him, this was just another summer at Davis and another new station leader to keep an eye on. Expeditioners like Mitch take a lifetime to develop and the value of their experience cannot be overstated. On the flipside, they can be a pain in the arse to work with if you want to do something slightly differently from the way it was done last time! But Mitch and I soon developed a good working relationship and found we had a similar approach to crisis and emergency management.

Arriving back at Bandits after the flight, I expected a bit of grief from the team I'd left there.

'How was the flight, Mr Rock Star?' someone teased as the noise of the helicopter faded into the distance.

'Ten out of ten. Would recommend that flight if you get a chance,' I said, knowing that, unfortunately, deep field and glacial work was generally reserved for a select group of scientists.

I noted the late hour on my fancy Garmin watch, which also displayed dashed lines in lieu of the sunrise and sunset times. 'Bedtime?' I asked, looking at Jarrod.

'Nope, more lessons,' he said, killing the mood. We continued with field lessons and planning for the next day, before we tucked ourselves into our giant sleeping bags and fell asleep in the surprisingly warm hut.

* * *

The next day we continued our journey around the frozen fjords and lakes as we learned about the area that would be our operating field for the year. The various states of sea ice are best experienced rather than taught. An area that is safe one day at low tide might be unsafe and flooded the next at high tide, as the pressure breaks through weak points. The area where the ice meets the land is known as a tide crack and, as the season progresses, a series of cracks remain like frozen waves approaching the shoreline.

These are dangerous and tricky places to navigate and, sure enough (possibly on purpose to create the training scenario), Jarrod got his bike bogged in a deep snow drift between two tide cracks. We had to set up the recovery gear and tow him out. One advantage of the quad bikes was that without a rider on them they were relatively light; with the five of us all being quite sturdy, well-fed gentlemen, we could just grab a rope and pull the bike out of its bog.

Our destination the second night was Platcha Hut, which was nestled right up against the Antarctic Plateau and on a rocky area between the ice cliffs and sea ice, giving it a feeling of remoteness. It was originally built as a meteorological station detached from Davis.

As we approached, I asked the obvious question. 'Why's it called Platcha Hut?'

'Well, I've heard two theories. One is that it's an abbreviation for "Plateau Chateau" and the second is that some bloke nicknamed "Platcha" came up with theory number one to get his name on a hut,' Lewis responded. The truth is probably somewhere in the middle.

Although Platcha was another comfortable hut, tonight

we'd be sleeping outside. (I'd have said under the stars, but in an Antarctic summer you could be waiting a long time for the sun to set.) This activity was a crucial part of our training. When out in the field, every expeditioner carried the contents of their survival bag in a more appropriate field pack with some additional items, most importantly an Antarctic 'bivvy bag'. These were affectionately known as 'chip packets' for their crunchy and noisy material, but a lightweight and simple system allowed you to engulf yourself inside within seconds, to be immediately out of the wind and safe. You wouldn't be comfortable, and you may not be all that warm, but you would survive until the weather abated or rescue arrived.

With twenty-four hours of daylight in the summertime in Antarctica and a beautiful evening sitting on the rocks overlooking the sea ice in front of us, no one was quick to get into their chip packets and we sat around sipping tea and getting to know each other. By design, we were all part of the winter team who would be at Davis for the whole year. For all of us besides Jarrod, this would be our first winter.

I studied the station doctor, who couldn't have looked less like a doctor if he tried. A giant lad, similar to my own stature at 191 centimetres (six foot three in the old money), and hovering around the 100-kilogram mark, I guessed, with a Santa Claus–length beard and thick head of hair, he could do a good impersonation of a Viking warlord if required.

'Doc, what's your story?' I asked.

'I've been working in remote medicine since university, out in the deserts of Central Australia and up the Top End of the Northern Territory out of Darwin,' explained Doc, glossing over his years of hard work in remote communities as the lone doctor responsible for curing anything and everything that came through his door.

'Why Antarctica, then? If all goes well, you'll be the most professionally bored member of the team. The average season has a few stiches, maybe a broken bone, gym-related strains, plus the isolation mental health battle,' I said.

'The history, and look at it! I love this place,' he said, pointing towards the towering ice cliffs and frozen fjord in front of us, with the evening's sunlight bouncing golden rays in every direction. It was written in his eyes as he spoke that Doc had a complete and utter drive for a 'true Antarctic experience'. He was a scholar of polar history intent on furthering his own knowledge of what the heroes of yesteryear (Scott, Shackleton, Mawson and Amundsen, to name a few) had endured, and he was keen to make the most of every opportunity Antarctica offered.

I woke up the next morning at 4am and I rolled out of my chip packet to a tranquil and still Antarctic morning. There was no wind and the silence was only broken by the occasional loud cracks and moans of the nearby glacial shelf and sea ice around us. We slowly boiled up some tea, had some brekky and started loading up the bikes to return home. On the way home we spotted some emperor penguins. I figured this must be normal, so I didn't get 'the good camera'[7] out of my bag and just watched them waddle around.

---

[7]   I often get asked if I took a good camera so here's what I had: a Canon 7D MkII, a Canon 7D MkI, a Canon 100D, a GoPro 7 Black, a GoPro 5 session and an iPhone. My favourite lens was the Canon 70–200L and my 'full stalker' 600mm Tamron was good but heavy. Most of the time, the iPhone was the easiest for point-and-shoot. The Canons could take a beating and would often freeze overnight but recover perfectly; the GoPros were good in the summertime but had trouble once the temperature fell below minus 10. There is also one still out there somewhere near Long Fjord after it fell off a bike, never to be seen again.

It would be months until I saw another emperor!

This was my first overnight trip off station and it felt like I was returning home when we rounded the final islands and Davis came back into view. I'd thoroughly enjoyed this break from station life and, although I was still the station leader, I had briefly felt like just another lad on the trip, which I'd appreciated. I would seek this feeling out on future fieldtrips to take a mental break from being the leader and enjoy the field for what it is – breathtaking.

Chapter 2

The Case of the Dropped Burrito

Day 53: 16 December 2019
Temperature: -2.3°C to 1.0°C
Station population: 83

With everyone through the honeymoon phase, it was time to get the summer routine bedded down. Aware that my early focus had been on the field operations and science, I made an effort to catch up with the multitude of other roles on the station. The biggest team per capita was the trades. The trades were led in the summertime by two engineers, and featured a very experienced and seasoned team of tradespeople from across Australia.

The biggest project this summer was to construct a new 600,000-litre freshwater tank next to the two existing tanks of the same design: cylindrical steel tanks with a cone roof. The team had partially built the tank in Australia before leaving, as part of their training, and now set to work quickly. The other trade projects included digging new culverts for draining snowmelt away from building foundations, annual inspections and servicing of the diesel generators in the two powerhouses, and checking and repairing the array of pipes connecting all the buildings. With the annual temperatures at Davis ranging from minus 30 up to 5 degrees

Celsius, and metres of snowfall and accumulation burying much of the station's infrastructure, it was an annual battle to repair everything in the summer, when temperatures were reasonable for outdoor work. This process went on and on every year – just existing in Antarctica was a constant battle.

My approach from the start was to trust the trades team as a whole, and from what I'd seen there was no reason not to. That changed when we had three relatively serious industrial accidents – 'near misses' – and I was looking for answers.

With only one doctor on station and limited medical capability, the smallest injuries can have serious consequences for the individual and the team. Not all roles had redundancy, so whereas back home you can find someone to fill in temporarily if you break your arm, in Antarctica there was no one to cover your shift. That's just the minor injuries. If there was a serious accident, we'd have to stop everything and focus solely on supporting the doctor and patient until we could evacuate them, which often took weeks to coordinate, so it was vital we ran a safe workplace. If there was one thing you didn't want to do during your season, it was an emergency medical evacuation, otherwise known as a medevac.

The two engineers would only be on station during the summertime, overseeing the industrial side of work, split between maintenance and projects. But the powerhouse of the trades team was the building services supervisor, Gaz, a no-nonsense builder who had worked all across Australia, as well as a gap year in Canada working at ski fields and framing houses. Gaz would be staying for the winter and would lead the trades team with another supervisor who would fly in late in the season to lead the winter trade projects.

I could feel the disappointment in Gaz's voice as we spoke about the incidents. Gaz prided himself on the safety record of the team and balanced his role well between being in a leadership position and also part of the crew. With my bosses in Kingston looking for answers, I had to find out if we had a systemic safety issue on station or if the accidents were just an unfortunate coincidence.

As Gaz and I walked around the station and talked through each of the scenarios, it became clearer what the issue was. The first incident was a near miss of a heavy overhead crane component falling between two tradies repairing it. No one was injured, but it could have done some serious damage if it had hit either of them. Everything had been done correctly – the scaffold was in place, the plan was briefed well – but in the loud environment they were working in, along with earmuffs and frustration, miscommunication between team members had led to the mistake. This wasn't great, but there was no immediate evidence of systemic unsafe practices.

The second incident was a little more alarming. The individual involved was one of the more diligent and hardworking expeditioners, so it seemed strange that he had made such a rookie error. While decommissioning a high-pressure water pipe, he'd been sprayed with water, having not fully discharged the pipes. Thankfully, they were not at full pressure and the result was simply a warm shower, but if he'd waited a few more minutes there would have been no issue.

The third incident worried me. Working late in the day and up against the clock to make it to dinner, a team fixing a water pump rushed ahead without checking and narrowly avoided an electric shock. Even more concerning was the fact that they had called for an electrician but proceeded with the work before he arrived. Not good.

There didn't appear to be major safety problems, but we were not getting it right. People were now in their routines and momentary lapses in judgement or concentration had been a factor in each incident. We'd been on station for a month now and it was during this time that incidents usually started to happen.

A mountain of paperwork and phone calls to supervisors back home ensued, but I was keen to speak directly to those involved – not to interrogate them, but to check on them. I did not blame the individuals, or their supervisors. Right from the start, my mantra was to always seek the reasons behind mistakes and learn from them. This was as relevant to battlefield success as industrial safety. Throwing blame and raising my voice would achieve nothing. Understanding the 'why' and applying the lessons learned would promote growth and development of the team and encourage others to approach failure as a learning opportunity.

With over a decade of working in high-pressure and high-risk environments, I'd seen more examples of bad leadership than good ones. In moments like this, I recalled the way I'd seen incidents and near misses handled and knew that responding appropriately would be vital to the rest of the summer, and would set the tone for the year ahead. In conflict zones and dynamic environments, I had seen leaders cast blame on those around them and scold individuals for making mistakes, which only led to a culture of fear and non-reporting. I was determined to build a culture of transparency and growth. Today had also been a cold reminder of the dangers around the station being just as hazardous as the environmental dangers of frostbite and other cold injuries.

Entering the workshop the next morning to address the daily pre-start meeting, I looked around the room for a moment, before delivering my message, at the dozens of hi-vis shirts, beanies with logos of other Antarctic seasons, racks of power tools and chargers, half-finished projects and a thin layer of sawdust on everything.

'Everyone's hard work and dedication will be undone if we don't get this right and all go home safely,' I told the group. 'Slow down and consider each day and task carefully – there is no rush, nothing is life or death, everything can wait and, above all, report mistakes and learn from them.'

It was simple and to the point – people were rushing and had to slow down. These were some of Australia's best tradies but many of them had never worked in Antarctica before and were still learning the ropes. Egos, attitudes and opinions were strong throughout the group, and Gaz had his work cut out managing the team that would stay on for the winter.

I later spoke one on one with the engineers and adjusted our communications model to include more mentoring and advice to develop their own leadership skills and maximise their professional development. One thing I was adamant we should not do was to micromanage the teams and create an environment of greater stress.

The reality of managing such a large and complex industrial site was that we couldn't achieve a perfect safety record. What was more important was to develop a culture of reporting and growth, making sure every member of the team was constructive with their approach to understanding what had gone wrong and what they could learn. There was, however, another unsolved community incident that was brewing.

* * *

The first major party of the summer was organised by the social committee, which was anchored by a number of the team who returned to Davis almost every summer, and it had become a tradition at Davis to hold an 'Alphabet party' where you come dressed as something beginning with the first letter of your name. Events where you donned a ridiculous costume and often a new persona were vital for mixing it up a bit when you're with the same crowd for months on end.

Antarctica has a long history of dress-up parties dating back to the heroic age of early Antarctic explorers, but there is a fine line between 'hilarious' and 'inappropriate', and at times you might be confronted with an image you can't unsee. As I talked to an expeditioner dressed as the Little Mermaid in a coconut-shell bikini, it was important to maintain eye contact, although I gently reminded him that he probably should have manscaped a bit more before selecting the revealing costume.

With nearly ninety expeditioners on station in the summer months, we had better gender diversity than I'd expected – around sixty–forty – but this didn't stop a few of the lads cross-dressing to continue a time-honoured tradition at fancy-dress parties in Antarctica. This tradition dated back to when Antarctic stations were male only; I briefly toyed with the idea of wearing a ball gown I'd found in the dress-up cupboard but went for something a bit more low-key.

I was never going to win any awards but my costume included a clever play on the almost-daily 'seal survey' teams, who would fly around and count seal populations as part of ongoing environmental studies. Dressed as a 'seal surveyor', I wrote a survey that asked much deeper questions about the seals' thoughts on being surveyed so frequently and if they identified as either a Weddell, elephant or refrigerator seal.

It was a breath of fresh air to have a bit of fun. I awarded the best dressed for the night (the Little Mermaid) and then socialised while fielding work questions and eliciting rumours from the group. It wasn't my place to be the last man standing, so I retired early and got a good night's sleep for a change. The aftermath of such a night was always the bigger worry and, sure enough, it was the party that led to our first community incident.

* * *

'Can I talk to you for a minute?' said the on-duty chef as I was grabbing breakfast the next morning. He approached me just as I was ladling porridge from the big pot into a small bowl before adding just enough honey to make it sweet, but not too sweet.

'Sure, if you don't mind me eating while we chat,' I said, and we moved to the chef's office at the back of the kitchen and closed the door. I was still half-asleep and so wasn't really sure what was going on, but it seemed serious.

'When I came in this morning there was an absolute pigsty all over the floor. I shouldn't have to clean up after someone who doesn't know how to use a mop and bucket,' said the chef.

'What was it exactly?' I asked.

'Burrito, everywhere. It exploded in the microwave first and then they dropped it onto the floor and decided that instead of cleaning it up they'd cover it with a tea towel and flee. Utterly unacceptable.'

I finished my porridge and got to work solving the case of the dropped burrito. But the rumour of the incident was already out on the streets. As my team and I sat in the operations room waiting for the daily briefing to commence, Kiwi asked, 'Did you hear about the burrito bandit?'

'I'll get onto it after this. We need to keep the chefs happy,' I replied.

Since there are no formal police officers in Antarctica, as part of my role I'd been appointed as a special constable of the Australian Federal Police for emergency purposes. Deciding this did not quite meet the criteria of an emergency, I decided to have a wander around the station and chat to a few of the team.

As I approached the construction site of the new 600,000-litre tank I ran into Johnny, one of the more social butterflies of the team and, thinking that he might know something, I stopped to talk to him.

'Did you see who the last man standing was?' I asked.

'You asking me to snitch, boss?' He smiled.

'It's like that, is it – prison rules down here?' I smiled back. As a rookie leader I was still learning the traditions and culture of Antarctic life, and so was expecting this. Social indiscretions and non-serious matters were outside my jurisdiction. I would need a different approach.

At the next station meeting, the audience had all been speculating who the burrito bandit was, and I could feel their eyes assessing me as they waited for my response to the incident.

'I want to talk about community. Everyone is doing an amazing job and we're kicking goals operationally and scientifically, but we are also a community and this means the common areas and social events need to be an environment of trust and equality. Above all, this means cleaning up after yourself when you make a mess! So, Señor Burrito, I ask not that you identify yourself to the masses, but that you apologise to the chef who had to clean up your mess at 4am instead of making more of the delicious meals we all enjoy each day.'

I finished lecturing and studied the expressions on the faces in the crowd – curious smirks and eyerolls from those who had heard the same spiel every year from the station leader whenever something like this invariably happened.

That evening, as the kitchen was being cleaned and prepped for the next day, I stood over the sink, helping wash dishes with a few others, when the chef tapped me on the shoulder and informed me, 'Confession received, very apologetic, offered to do extra chores next time I need someone.' Case closed.

I was glad this approach worked. If only I could work out a way to make sure people sorted their rubbish correctly, I thought as I scraped the burnt crusts from that evening's lasagne into the food waste bin and saw the plastic wrapper of a chocolate bar sitting on top of an apple core. I looked at the large laminated sign above the bin that said 'Food Scraps Only' and sighed.

* * *

When it came to fieldtrips, I approved all off-station travel but relied on people like Mitch to sign off on the field aspects of any trip, relying on his knowledge of the Vestfold Hills around Davis and across Antarctica. As recreational trips became more and more creative over the summer, a request came in for a journey involving a team to be dropped out near the Antarctic Plateau and left to walk the long way back to the station over a few days. Blisters would be guaranteed in the rocky and icy terrain, and once they were dropped off they'd need to be self-sufficient for the trip. This meant around 15 kilograms of gear and food was required for each hiker.

I've always had an approach of 'find a way to say yes' to such requests but the conditions were unknown in this region, with thawing lakes and melting snow impacting the safety of certain crossing points. To better understand the risks, Mitch, Kiwi and I would take a quick flight out to have a look and assess the proposed route. It was the second time it was good to be the boss.

I felt relieved to be off station and away from the constant questions and workload and, looking across at Mitch, I could tell he felt the same. The two of us were very different but we shared the same burden of responsibility for overall field safety, which breeds a constant mental alertness and, if not managed correctly, can lead to burnout and bad decisions.

As we flew over the melting rivers and fjords it was hard to tell exactly how deep the water was at the crossings, and Kiwi found a suitable area to land nearby so we could get out. Stepping off the helicopter and walking over to the stream, I realised this was the first time I'd heard running water in a while, as the temperatures were now hovering above zero more often.

As I looked at the stream through the nearly frozen water, it seemed to move differently. These pure glacial streams had a darkness that appeared almost black as they flowed out from a gorge along the small river, making their way to the ocean as part of the annual melt that occurs each summer. Here at the end of the Earth, this was a scene unchanged for thousands of years, as each year, without fail, the fjords and lakes freeze in the winter and melt in the summer. With the area relatively untouched by people and with nothing but ice, rock and water around us, you wouldn't believe the planet was inhabited if you crash-landed here in a spaceship.

Breathtaking scenery aside, we were here to assess the field safety. It wasn't that complicated – you can either walk across a river or you can't. As we rock-hopped along the riverbank and across the river, taking photos along the way, we decided it was safe for the walking route to be approved.

Further upstream, the river ran under a huge snow bridge that looked inviting to walk over but could collapse at any moment (or never). Here, we simply sat and listened to the water melting its way through the frozen snowbanks at the bridge. For a rare moment, Mitch, the most vigilant and alert man I'd ever met outside the military, looked relaxed.

* * *

Day 57: 20 December 2019
Temperature: -1.4°C to 3.0°C

The weeks before Christmas in Australia are always busy as everyone tries to finish things off and enjoy their holidays at Byron Bay, Phillip Island or some other suitably Australian beach location. While we were still working during this period, it was also an important halfway point in the summer season and an opportunity to relax a bit before the new year.

There was also a natural changeover during this time, as we farewelled a number of expeditioners who'd sailed down but would depart via our air link to Casey station and the Wilkins Aerodrome that enabled intercontinental flights back to Australia during the summer season.

Enter Brian. Brian was the operations coordinator for the summer season and was the powerhouse of operations, providing the tempo for the season. A towering man with a great laugh and a can-do attitude, he'd been working with the Antarctic program for many years in multiple roles, from having to wrestle juvenile elephant seals on Macquarie Island for scientists to tag, to working as a plant operator building runways at the Wilkins Aerodrome near Casey. With that experience and his brilliance with spreadsheets and digital calendars, Brian was a perfect fit for the role.

Brian and I had worked closely from day one, turning the season's field projects and expectations into a workable and deliverable plan. Right from the start I felt that his approach would require minimal supervision and that I could trust him. The relationship between us – the station leader and the operations coordinator – felt professionally familiar. Also, from my military experience, it was identical to the way in which the commanding officer and the operations officer would operate in a task group HQ – the corporate equivalents of general manager and operations manager.

It was a relief in an otherwise unfamiliar workplace to have such a familiar system humming along around me. Antarctic stations had been run in many different ways over the years, and it had previously been up to the station leaders to decide exactly how to structure the station's leadership group and operational planning systems. But this year, the AAD had implemented a new operations framework that would align the operations and planning for all Australian Antarctic stations and voyages. Back in Hobart before we left for Antarctica, we were briefed on this new system the AAD would implement.

Pleased by the change, I turned to my boss, Rick, an ex-SAS officer and former station leader. 'So the new AAD system is pretty much the NATO military system but friendlier and for science?'

'Yep.'

We both laughed. It was reassuring to know that my boss and I had a similar way of thinking and planning. The military system for planning, briefing and operating isn't perfect, but when done right it's the best methodical and logical planning process I've ever used and the gold standard for anyone trying to run complex and dynamic operations. It came naturally to me and others who were products of military academies around the world, so it was fascinating to see civilians like Brian and Mitch seamlessly adopt the same processes without the years of marching up and down the square.

Rounding out my senior leadership team in the summertime was the senior aviation ground safety officer, Sam. These officers, known as AGSOs and part of AAD aviation, are a team within the team, defined by their stylish aviation-branded clothing. Their role is to manage all aspects of aviation at Davis.

To enable operations deep into the Antarctic wilderness, we had two fixed-wing aircraft based at Davis for the summertime. In early summer, when the sea ice was solid, we used a runway known as the Ski Landing Area (SLA), which was right out the front of the station. As the summer temperatures rose and the sea ice melted away, we had to move the airfield to a location 40 kilometres away, perched up on the Antarctic Plateau, aptly named Whoop Whoop.

Sam kept her team on track and busy the whole summer. Even when there were no flights, she'd have them crushing old 44-gallon drums for return to Australia or offering to help around the station. A veteran of many Antarctic seasons, Sam had a calming nature when she spoke and was never caught up in the pressure or stress of everything we were working to achieve. She simply got on with the job at hand and worked tirelessly to ensure success. She was a pure dynamite addition to the team.

'You're a bit young to be a station leader, aren't you?' said Sam as she wandered into my office, noting a beard trim that had revealed my baby face.

'Makes it easier to manage the kids running around here when I can relate to them better,' I joked. In fact, the average age on the station was early thirties, with a good mixture of experience and youth across the board. 'What can I do for you?' I asked, as there were seldom visitors to my office who simply wanted to chat.

'It's time to take the snow groomers from here and up the hill to Whoop Whoop,' she explained.

To keep the icy runways smooth for landing we had two snow groomers that would be driven up and down for hours or days before each flight, depending on how much snow had accumulated. While we were still operating the sea-ice runway out front, the groomers, which were currently on station, would need to be driven to Whoop

Whoop over the sea ice to do the job up there before it decayed and broke out.

'Agreed,' I said. Operating from the sea-ice runway was much easier than the rigmarole involved in operating from Whoop Whoop, but it was time to shift.

The remote runway camp at Whoop Whoop was basic – just a few shipping containers on sleds for accommodation – and it was equipped with a weather station, generator, workshop and a cache of fuel drums. For the AGSO team, it was their home away from home and they'd often spend the better part of the week up there preparing and servicing the runway. Once the sea ice was closed, we could only access Whoop Whoop with the helicopters, a thirty-minute flight each way.

The other problem was that, once we drove the groomers up to Whoop Whoop and the ice eventually broke out in early January, we'd have to leave the two snow groomers and one of the Hägglunds up at Whoop Whoop, to be recovered later in the year once the sea ice regrew around mid-year. But there was no way around it.

For the changeover to Whoop Whoop, Sam would lead a convoy to move the two snow groomers in preparation for the next round of flights. From now on, it would become a daily task for the helicopters to ferry the AGSOs, pilots and travellers back and forth between Davis station and Whoop Whoop.

'What happens if you get stuck up there?' I asked Sam.

'Technically you could walk home, but it would take over a week and you'd have to navigate around the crevassing and ice cliffs near Platcha Hut to get back to the rocks – bugger that!' She laughed at the impossible scenario, knowing that, due to the risks, we'd only ever operate Whoop Whoop when we had our own helicopters or sea-ice access.

'Alright, get me the fieldtrip paperwork for the groomer move and I'll confirm with Brian that we're moving to Whoop Whoop flight operations from here on out.'

* * *

Aviation has a long history in Antarctica, dating right back to Mawson and the heroic age, as they sought to reach remote regions of the continent and avoid the hazardous and gruelling conditions of travelling overland. The backbone of resupplying the stations with food and fuel would always be icebreaking ships, but in recent years the aviation link back to Australia was the main method of moving expeditioners back and forth throughout the summertime.

Despite weather delays and the basic facilities, Antarctic aviation was surprisingly reliable, though in remote regions it still carried additional risks. With limited or no alternative runways if you have a problem, you need to be extremely cautious. To manage these risks, we relied on good forecasting and pilots experienced in polar aviation.

Throughout the summertime we had two aircraft based at Davis, a BT-67 Basler and a Twin Otter[8] operated by Canadian

---

[8] The BT-67 Baslers are rebuilt DC-3s with modern avionics and turboprops, although they retain the classic DC-3 or C-47 look, which I always enjoyed watching as they took off and landed. One of the world's most versatile aircraft and renowned for its short take-off and landing capability, I'd flown on Twin Otters before when trekking around Papua New Guinea and skydiving around the world, so had fond memories of this classic plane. Sadly, I didn't get a chance to fly on one this time around.

contractors from Ken Borek Air (KBA). The Canadian aircrews were great value and brought a good international flavour to the station and social life. KBA was also contracted by the American and Chinese programs, which meant from time to time we cooperated with the Chinese and American stations to transfer passengers around Antarctica. This international cooperation and established contractor relationship ensured that our safety procedures and standards were in line with broader Australian aviation standards.[9]

In the summertime, the aviation link between Antarctica and Australia is via the Wilkins Aerodrome, 1400 kilometres away from Davis. I'd flown to Wilkins on a familiarisation trip in February 2019. It was a scaled-up version of Whoop Whoop, capable of landing intercontinental aircraft such as the C-17, C-130 and the A319 ('Snowbird 1') Australia used as its dedicated aircraft for passenger transfers to Antarctica. Wilkins was the only 'international airport' in the Australian Antarctic Territory and a vital link back to Australia for our stations.

Wilkins was first opened in 2006, and at 3.5 kilometres long and 150 metres wide it's easy to spot from the air on a clear day on the otherwise barren Antarctic Plateau. With limited fuel storage and no hangars or workshops, Wilkins was at the maximum range of aircraft flying from Australia to Antarctica. There was no way of flying directly from Australia to Davis and we relied on ferrying passengers to and from Wilkins with the smaller aircraft.

---

[9]   All aviation, maritime and industrial activities are conducted to Australian standards. In years gone by, and certainly in the heroic age, there was a rogue mentality of just 'getting it done no matter what', but in the modern age this was not acceptable. As a government program it was essential for us to maintain a high standard and manage the risks appropriately, even if this meant having to say no more often than I would have liked to.

The other problem with an ice runway is that if it gets too warm it starts to melt. In mid-December, as we were preparing to send a number of scientists home to Australia via the airlink from Wilkins, we received some bad news. When Brian walked into my office, I could sense the concern in his body language. He laid out the facts.

'Wilkins is warming up earlier than predicted – we have to bring the next flights forward and get anyone leaving to Wilkins as soon as possible or they'll be stuck here into next year.'

'Bugger,' I replied. There were about a dozen scientists due to leave in the next week who were already behind, and now we'd have to tell them to stop what they were doing and fly home. Some teams don't mind getting stuck in Antarctica a bit longer, but with the station at near capacity in the summer I couldn't risk it being overcrowded, with the strain that would put on the infrastructure and consumption of fresh water and food. I felt like a hotel manager.

Our priority now was to get the team of outgoing scientists to Casey/Wilkins[10] so they could meet their international flight home. If the scientists were stuck at Casey with nothing to do, they would have to wait until Wilkins reopened when the temperatures dropped again in February, or find berths on the *Aurora Australis* when it arrived at Casey for resupply around Christmas. It was time to chat to Ali, the station leader over at Casey, and one of the most experienced in the program.

'What are you doing to me?' she laughed down the phone as I went through the list of passengers and cargo we'd need to transfer across. Ali and her operations coordinator could read the

---

[10]   Although they are separate locations, Casey Station and the Wilkins Aerodrome operate as one operational location, although it is a very dull four-hour drive across barren Antarctic ice between them.

manifests and passenger lists, but what we had to discuss was the human factor. It was important she knew the full picture of what was happening.

'Hopefully nothing to worry about,' I said, 'but if the team we're sending gets stuck there you can expect the frustration to grow and lead to backlash.' They'd already had their field activities cut short, and if they had to wait at Casey station with nothing to do they would certainly be asking, 'Why didn't we just stay at Davis?' If there was one thing every Antarctic station leader needed on their desk, it was a crystal ball to predict the future.

Sitting down in my office to debrief the outgoing scientists ahead of their flight to Casey, I noticed they were upbeat about their project's success, even with the impact of the changed flights. Brian entered my office and, reading the room, got straight to the point. I could tell he knew that what he was about to say was important to all of us.

'Wilkins is not looking good,' said Brian.

'Define "not looking good",' I replied.

'From this morning's temperatures it's right on the limit, and with the warming trend of this weather system it's going to overheat in the next twenty-four hours, so they need to get out of here asap or they're staying,' said Brian. 'Get the Weather Magician over here.'

The 'Weather Magician' was our lead forecaster, an experienced expeditioner who led the Bureau of Meteorology (BoM) team during the summertime and was responsible for the twice-daily forecasts at Davis. She'd spent time at Casey in previous years and understood Antarctic weather better than anyone I'd ever met. Ordinarily we held our daily operations meetings at 0800 each day, but time was against us as we gathered the pilots, ops team, myself and the

Weather Magician for an unscheduled afternoon ops briefing to look at ways to get the flights to happen.

The weather dictates everything you do in Antarctica. While back home you can make do on a rainy day or deal with the heat or cold, if Antarctica says you're not doing anything today, you listen. Naturally, these conditions gave the honour of opening each ops meeting to the Weather Magician or one of her team.

'The good news is that it's clear at Davis and Whoop Whoop, but if we look at Wilkins or Casey it's cloudy with possible snow showers,' said the Weather Magician, knowing this would limit visibility for the international flight from Hobart to Wilkins.

'What's the latest on the ground from the Wilkins team?' I asked Brian.

'Temperature is still stable but the runway probably only has about forty-eight hours until it's too warm to land. The cloud is probably helping prevent it overheating while blocking the direct sunlight but visibility is poor.'

The pilots themselves would ultimately make their own decisions to fly or not, and Brian and I would then sign off on the flight plan.

'Can we see the runway sites in the satellite picture again?' the pilots asked.

'As you can see, the satellite shows broken cloud around Wilkins, and the alternative landing area near Casey station has a clearing trend with predicted good visibility around the time of arrival,' said the Weather Magician.

'The chance of successfully landing at Wilkins and meeting the A319 there for a direct transfer back to Australia is low, but that's not our decision,' Brian said.

'So, we send the group across and hope they get the A319 from Hobart to Wilkins in the next twenty-four to forty-eight hours and take them home?' I asked.

'Confirm, but that increases the risk of them getting stuck at Casey,' he reminded me.

'I know. I'll chat to Ali and Rick, but it's the better option to get them home as planned, although they have nothing to do at Casey,' I mused. I loudly exhaled as I pondered the fifty-fifty decision with no way of knowing exactly what the weather and the temperature at an ice runway 1400 kilometres away would do. 'Get everything ready to send them to Casey, and I'll speak to Ali and Rick to make sure they are on board,' I said.

Brian would round up the outgoing expeditioners, Sam would get her team ready to fly to Whoop Whoop with the pilots, and the helicopter team, as usual, was ready to fly everyone up and back as needed.

I messaged Rick and Ali and quickly set up a teleconference between the stations. Brian sat in my office as we went through it all again. Rick and Ali both understood our thoughts on the plan and concurred: this was the best option.

This was the first occasion we'd had to exercise dynamic operational judgement with a range of unknowns. Refreshingly, the conversation between Rick, Ali and me was open and honest, with each of us laying out the facts without bias or influence and respecting each other's point of view. This level of operational maturity and trust in those on the ground at each location was well honed within Australia's Antarctic operations.

In previous theatres of operations, I had all too often seen the balance of decision-making deferred too high and too far away from the realities on the ground. On this occasion, common sense would prevail and we would take the risk of having the team of scientists stuck at Casey with nothing to do over being stuck at Davis indefinitely. It was time to say goodbye.

As everything came together quickly after the briefing, I was soon standing at the helipads farewelling the group of scientists on their way to Whoop Whoop and then Casey. Many of them routinely visited Antarctica. This was just another field season wrapping up, with the real science to begin back home when they could study their samples and data. At the other end of the spectrum were the first-time expeditioners and visitors who knew this might be the last time they would see Antarctica.

Wandering back towards the main living quarters along the now-muddy road – the snowbanks around the station had melted away in the afternoon heat – I ran into a straggler who was standing on the balcony looking seaward towards the horizon of icebergs and rocky islands.

'Mate, aren't you on this flight?' I asked.

'Just taking it all in one last time,' he said as he gazed steely-eyed into the distance at the incredible postcard-like view in front of him. 'I never thought I'd get here and doubt I will again.'

He changed his tune as the faint sound of the helicopters returning to station echoed in the distance, signalling it was now indeed time to get himself to the helipads or he'd miss his flight. 'Thanks for having us!' he shouted back at me as he ran off.

His was a tale of great opportunity and luck. His employer back in Australia undertook routine maintenance and inspections of various plant and equipment used at the Antarctic stations to ensure they were still safe and operable. Back home, you simply take your crane or forklift to the service centre and pick it up later that day but, in Antarctica, sometimes it was easier to fly the inspector down to Antarctica rather than ship heavy equipment home. So the next time your boss asks if you have a warm jacket and are free next week, say yes.

Everything went to plan: the outgoing team made it to Casey and were on a flight back to Australia the next morning. With Wilkins now closed until it refroze again in February, we had a good window without any new arrivals or departures via this route.

One group would arrive in early January, though, including the director of the Australian Antarctic Program, Kim Ellis, who was leading an Antarctic Treaty inspection team around the Australian territory. He was at that point in New Zealand awaiting a flight into the US station at McMurdo from where he'd make his way across to Davis.

Until then, we needed to focus on getting as much done as possible in the clearer weather of peak summer, and also enjoy a white Christmas.

* * *

After dinner, as I sat looking out across the now broken and decaying sea ice to the iceberg horizon, I debriefed a couple of scientists who'd just returned from a week in the field at a penguin rookery. They'd been studying the birds during their breeding season, when they return to the land, plump and ready to mate.

As I looked around the room, the mood was similar all round: Jarrod and Lewis from the wintering team intensely playing chess, aircrew and mechanics throwing darts and cheering away, a group playing Xbox in the cinema and a few others reading quietly in the corners, the perfect balance of peace and quiet … or so I thought.

As I relaxed into the couch and the penguin conversation and took a sip of wine, a noise broke the otherwise tranquil setting – *Pa-donk, pa-donk, pa-donk* – as the two expeditioners I'd recently started calling Ping and Pong fired up for their nightly routine of table tennis right in the middle of the lounge. Whose idea was it to put the ping-pong table in the middle of the lounge?

I canvassed the room. The chess players were now looking from Ping to Pong with each move, the readers were pulling beanies over their ears to muffle the sound and the darts players didn't care.

'Who's winning?' I asked as I moved past the table, feigning the need to check the cinema booking board.

'Oh, we're not playing a game, just hitting,' replied Pong.

'Wouldn't it be more fun to play a game? Bit of competition never hurt,' I offered. At least that would give the noisy game a logical conclusion.

'Yeah, maybe, we'll see,' replied Ping as I walked back to my seat and returned to my conversation with the scientists.

I could have told them to stop playing, but when everything on station is regulated by standard operating procedures, bookings, rosters, shifts and routines, I was reluctant to dictate social rules. I'd also recently met severe backlash when enforcing a 'no singlets in the mess' rule following complaints that, with shoulder-to-shoulder seating, it was inappropriate. Thus, dictating a 'no ping-pong after dinner' rule was not something I was willing to do.

So we continued our wine and penguins discussion to the peaceful sound of *pa-donk, pa-donk, pa-donk.*

* * *

As December raced by, it was time to dig out the Christmas decorations. The main warehouse where we stored all our food, equipment and spare parts was known as the greenstore. It also housed a gym on the mezzanine level and, much like a household attic, a storage area was wedged above the gym with all sorts of special-occasion items: for Christmas, the mid-winter swim, the Melbourne Cup carnival and so on.

For Australians living in Antarctica, December on Davis was a rare opportunity for a white Christmas, and on a designated Saturday morning we went full steam ahead to 'deck the halls'. After a day's work, we had the whole lounge area decorated in Christmas cheer.

There were two other great Antarctic traditions that would help create some atmosphere for Christmas while we were separated from family and friends. The first was setting up a 'Secret Santa' system before we left, so everyone had a pre-purchased random gift to hand out. For the more creative types, it was also the chance to create something special out of scrap timber and metal in the station's hobby hut.

The second tradition was to have expeditioners' families secretly send presents down on the ship, which I'd kept under wraps in my office until a week before Christmas, when I placed them under the tree, to be opened on Christmas Day.

It was still a workplace, though, and what we needed was an end-of-year Christmas party to set the scene. To recreate the festive vibes of an office party back home, the team from Helicopter Resources[11] and the chefs joined forces to create a pizza party up in the heli-hangar. The main attraction was the two shiny red helicopters, with aircrew on hand to talk about them, much like firefighters talking about fire engines at a community barbeque back home. Even though the pizzas and the crowd were the same as at any other night in the mess, the change in location and vibe made the event feel new and exciting.

To finish the night, we all stood outside in the chilly evening breeze as snowflakes drifted down from above and posed in front of the helicopters for the Christmas photo. This photo now represents the last moments of a world before COVID-19. In the coming days, everything would change, but, for now, we celebrated a merry Christmas and wished one another a happy 2020!

---

[11] The AAD's long-running contractor for rotary-wing operations.

Chapter 3

What's COVID Got to Do with It?

Day 75: 7 January 2020
Temperature: -2.3° to 2.1°C

I'd enjoyed Christmas, felt I'd found my rhythm as the station leader and looked forward to what lay ahead. The team was relaxing too and I shared a good laugh with them at my own expense as Jimbo did a cheeky impression of me while we waited for the weekly meeting to begin. 'Urrgh, excuse me, I'm the station leader,' said Jimbo in a high-pitched teenage voice.

With the snow around the station melting away to expose the rocky ground and late-summer heat, this was the prime time to send teams out to deep field, far away from the station, and I was keen to get involved where possible. This was often easier said than done, as the helicopters filled with essential scientists and equipment, leaving little room for the station leader to squeeze in.

What I could do, though, was help facilitate a truly unique international science symposium at the nearby Indian station of Bharati. This is what happens when you send a diplomat to the furthest corner of the Earth and the role requires 'keeping up foreign relations'.

The Larsemann Hills was another rocky oasis similar to the

Vestfold Hills around Davis and was about 100 kilometres away, or an hour by helicopter. I'd first gone to the international stations there in December as part of an annual tradition for the new leader to visit those at Bharati, the Chinese at Zhongshan station and the Russians at Progress station. They were all close together and shared an ice runway up on the plateau behind the hills, much like Whoop Whoop but with better access via the rocks rather than sea ice.

While chatting with the Indian station leader about our projects and activities, we agreed it would be great to get all the scientists from Davis and the international stations at Larsemann Hill together for a conference. This had never been done in Antarctica and I agreed to support the concept.

The Indian team went all-out coordinating and planning the event, so I started working with the scientists at Davis to put together the Australian contribution. Our main aim was to run through the different fields of research at Davis that season, with representatives from the AAD, Geoscience Australia, the BoM and others representing Australian universities and institutes.

Getting a chance to visit foreign Antarctic stations was a real privilege – seeing how other stations manage the same problems in their own way would give us a new perspective on the difficulties of Antarctic life. On the tour of Bharati station, I was immensely jealous of their recycled waste-water system and ability to run year-round reverse osmosis (desalination) of sea water to create safe drinking water; Davis had perennially struggled with access to fresh drinking water.

Bharati's drinking water capability was also due to the station being much newer than Davis and with a completely different layout.

Bharati was a single building with everything inside, which meant you rarely had to brave the outdoors in the depths of winter. Davis, along with Zhongshan and most other stations, were decentralised buildings spread over a large footprint so that if any building was damaged by fire or weather, you could manage. Neither way is perfect, but it was fascinating to see the alternative design up close.

People assume that everyone in Antarctica is a scientist, but in reality, only 50 per cent of those at Davis in the summertime were, and this number dropped to 20 per cent in winter. But everyone who goes to Antarctica has an interest in science. I'm certainly not a scientist, but it was an honour to have a front-row seat for the presentations, pinching myself that it was part of my job to be involved in some of the groundbreaking science that goes on in Antarctica across the various nations.

It was a presentation from one of our own scientists that blew me away, though. Seeing definitive proof of climate change in Antarctica is hard to come by in the short term; you know it's happening but it's hard to see unless you know where to look. Australian scientists had been collecting samples of the various lichens and mosses that grow in the barren rocky regions of Antarctica, where little can survive in the bitter cold and desolate environment. But life finds a way, and if you know where to look you can find the subtle and unglamorous signs of nature's simplest plants.

Moss studies probably isn't the most exciting scientific field but it's the simplicity of moss and its ability to adapt to the climate in Antarctica that, for me, was a smoking gun in the climate change debate. We were shown three separate photos from the same location: the first from the early 1990s – a barren wasteland of rock with perhaps a small patch of green – then a mid-range picture from the early 2000s, and finally a recent picture capturing the ever-expanding green covering the rocks of a continent where for thousands of years nothing had been able to grow.

If I'd ever needed convincing the Earth was warming and Antarctica's ecosystem was adapting to higher temperatures, then this was it. Moss is taking over from ice. These time-lapse photos of the most remote region of Earth evolving due to the slow but steady impact we've had on the planet were heartbreaking.

* * *

'They're on their way now,' said Brian one morning as he wandered into my office with a cup of tea for our daily catch-up.

'Fun times ahead having the director and an inspection team hanging around on station,' I replied.

It was an important part of Kim's role to visit Antarctica each summer. We'd spent time together at Casey station in 2019, and even done survival training together, but having the AAD director on station would create a few unique challenges for Brian and me as we managed the team's expectations.

They'd be based at Davis for a few weeks to conduct a number of inspections of international stations as part of the complex Antarctic Treaty system, which ensured good environmental management of human impacts on Antarctica. The good news was they were relatively self-sufficient and had a dedicated aircraft for most of their trip, so they wouldn't be an impost. The bad news was that the good news wasn't accurate.

Their ambitious inspection program required extensive field planning and, with constant weather delays, they were anxious to succeed. My job managing expectations was easier when the team didn't include the boss. 'Managing upwards' wasn't a new concept to me: I'd been involved in numerous high-level visits to Pakistan when I was working at the Australian High Commission, and every politician and high-ranking general arrived with an ambitious program to meet everyone from the president to the chair of the Pakistan Cricket Board in the forty-eight hours they were on the ground. I also had to famously upstage the Governor of Punjab province at an Australia Day function when his speech ran well past the five minutes allocated and towards the one-hour mark. My boss at the time turned to me and said, 'Well, MC, time to earn your keep.' The solution? Walk confidently towards the lectern, start clapping and get the crowd on your side, smile and say, 'Thank you very much, Your Excellency, for those magnificent words.'

Brian and I finished our catch-up abruptly as a call came through the radio and Brian left my office. Left alone at my desk (which I'd recently discovered was a modern sit or stand set-up), with my back to the door, I gazed out the window towards the horizon of icebergs and the station's wharf and sea-ice access. I was half-daydreaming as I watched the Australian flag outside my window waving in the icy-cold Antarctic breeze.

The Antarctic program has quite a casual and relaxed vibe on station when it comes to formality and leadership, with most of my team simply calling me Dave, David or Knoffey. It certainly wasn't uncommon for people to wander into my office for a chat or to ask a quick question, but when I heard someone confidently walk in behind me and take a seat in one of the 'comfy chairs', my sixth sense told me it was Kim.

'Dave, we're very keen to make this Molodyozhnaya trip happen,' said Kim as a follow-up to an earlier meeting where we'd discussed the week's priorities and upcoming tasks – including the treaty team's ambitious trip to the remote Russian station of Molodyozhnaya, far beyond the stations we regularly visited and about as far away as feasible at around 2000 kilometres from Davis.

'I know. I'm doing what I can to make it happen but it's getting towards the business end of the season and, as you know, there are a lot of competing priorities,' I replied, knowing this wasn't what my boss wanted to hear.

'It's our highest priority destination and this might be the only chance we get to conduct an inspection there for some years,' added Kim.

It wasn't as if Kim had a crystal ball telling him the world was about to shut down, but even without the pandemic, organising the inspection team, coordinating it with the other nations and then flying the team around Antarctica was an ambitious and complex challenge the AAD only attempted every few years.

'I hear you. Looking at this morning's report on their ice runway and the support they can provide for the aircraft, we're good to go, but the issue is how long you might get stuck there. Then we need that plane to have enough time to complete a few more Davis–Casey–Davis flights at the end of the season to get our final winterers, and at the end of the season to get out of Antarctica via the South Pole and back to Canada for the northern summer,' I said.

The director already knew this, but I wanted to make sure we were on the same page.

I approached anyone who came into my office the same way; it was important to make sure that everyone understood that there were dozens of other projects and operations going on around them, not just their own. What I did respect, though, was that despite Kim's authority as director – which meant he could prioritise his trip ahead of others – he understood the situation and let us make the decisions we needed to make.

Antarctic operations are incredibly complex, and every day I had to both understand and embrace risk. Opportunities to achieve success were fleeting and it was always difficult to predict how the days and weeks would play out, with weather and operational factors constantly changing. Luckily for Kim and his team, the weather stayed fair for their departure, with a stopover at Mawson along the way, and acceptable risks and wiggle room for them to be delayed or stuck. All going well, they'd be there and back in about seventy-two hours. *Bon voyage, Kim!*

With Kim gone, I could focus again on station operations and I realised how removed I felt from life back home. I'd hardly spoken to anyone since Christmas and I assumed they were all just relaxing and enjoying summer. I made a plan to reach out tomorrow. As I walked into dinner and noticed the array of chicken parmigianas and chips in the bain-marie, I remembered something.

'Happy birthday,' whispered Rhonda from behind the counter as my eyes lit up at my favourite dish – it would become a tradition to be able to select the meal prepared on your birthday and elect for either a public or private acknowledgement.

'Thanks – I'd almost forgotten,' I said as a few expeditioners overheard the exchange and leaked the secret for why we were having 'Friday-night food' on a school night.

I enjoyed dinner and had a beer or two as I called home. My sister and mum had been in Hobart to see me off in October, and besides a few messages here and there since arriving I hadn't spoken to them, so I set up a group chat to find out what was going on back home.

'Nothing much, usual summer holidays back here, a few bushfires, and the prime minister is in Hawaii instead of Canberra, but that's about it,' my sister said.

'Waffle says hello,' my brother-in-law chimed in as the camera panned to my sister's fashionable mini-groodle puppy, named for his waffle-coloured coat.

'Your dog looks like a mop' I replied, realising how much I missed dogs.

'It's not as hot as the same day thirty-six years ago,' said Mum, reminding me for the thirty-sixth time that it was hot the day I was born.

'Yes, Mum,' I said, sighing. 'How's Melbourne life?'

'Nothing much happening, getting ready for the Australian Open tennis to start soon, and I might fly up to Queensland to see the other side of the family but they're all busy with new grandkids this year,' said Mum. Everything was pretty standard for our family's summer holiday routine.

It was good to chat, but I was beginning to feel the effects of the continuous pace of summer, and soon I made my way back to my room, rolled down the blackout shutters needed to keep out the sunlight, and went to sleep.

* * *

Day 77: 9 January 2020
Global pandemics: 1
Temperature: -2.0°C to 6.8°C

On a normal day at Davis, I'd wake up each morning about 0630, roll out of bed, punch out a few push-ups and do a few stretches to get the blood flowing. I'd then shuffle to the bathroom and either hop in for a quick shower or return to my room if my neighbour had beaten me to it.[12] I'd get dressed in my King Gee workpants and decide between my favourite Arc'teryx or icebreaker T-shirt and head down to the mess for breakfast.

I liked to start each day with a short slide across the floorboards in my socks towards the porridge as I greeted the chefs and looked at the live weather monitor above the noticeboard. I enjoyed this slightly goofy start to the morning, channelling Tom Cruise in *Risky Business*, and by the end of my time at Davis I'd only slipped over once.

In early January, the Australian news can be slow, with workplaces still recovering from holidays and stories about cricket dominating, but today was different. I opened one of the iPads on the table and the lead story in my news feed was about a virus from a place I'd never heard of and needed a map to find: Wuhan, China. That story would define 2020.

---

[12] Wintering expeditioners all have their own room with a king single bed, desk, cupboards and good amount of storage for all their gear. Everyone shares a bathroom with at least one other, and sometimes two or three others. There were no perfect rooms; each had its downside of location or layout, and proximity to banging doors or loud snorers.

I didn't think much of these early stories, and we felt safe being well and truly isolated from the rest of the world, but, having worked at the Department of Foreign Affairs and Trade and Australian embassies around the world, I had a good grasp of international relations. The degree of seriousness from organisations such as the United Nations and the World Health Organization worried me.

As those early days of January rolled on and we learned more about the virus, everyone's fear started to grow about what impact it might have on international travel. With expeditioners due to start flying back into Wilkins from Australia in a few weeks, there were some frantic moves back in Kingston to make sure they didn't unleash this new virus onto an Antarctic station.

The AAD has its own team of medical practitioners who monitor and manage the health of expeditioners on station, as well as the overall medical capabilities and strategies for the program. The Polar Medicine Unit has a long history and established links to organisations such as NASA to monitor and understand the effects of long-term isolation. The unit was now front and centre of the AAD's pivot to understand what this virus would mean for the Antarctic program.

Every Thursday, all four stations and key stakeholders back in Australia had a teleconference focused on shipping and flight schedules between the stations – but not today.

'We're instigating a formal Crisis Management and Recovery team to manage the response to the emerging virus in China and what it might mean for us,' said Rick, back in Kingston.

'Ack,' we said succinctly, acknowledging that Kingston was now in crisis-management mode, something ordinarily reserved for responding to a plane crash or medical evacuation. It also meant that all stations would reduce activity in order to be prepared to support the incident response. It seemed like overkill for a flu outbreak in China.

'Are we on a go-slow?' said Ali, dialling in from Casey. She needed to clarify whether we should keep activity to essential operations, which would reduce the likelihood of a secondary incident.

'No need for a go-slow, but be prepared for an update to the season plan,' Rick responded.

Brian and I looked at each other quizzically as the meeting ended, neither of us knowing what to say. I felt they were overdoing it by going to a full crisis response, even as we didn't need to actually change anything. There was clearly a lot we didn't know.

'Probably just means no Chinese interactions,' said Brian, knowing that two Chinese icebreakers, the *Xue Long* and *Xue Long II*, often used Hobart and Fremantle as stepping stones to Antarctica. We also sometimes flew Chinese expeditioners in and out of Antarctica on our flights to Wilkins.

'That's not going to impact us at Davis, so let's get on with it,' I said to Brian as we went back to work.

With Kim back from his trip to Molodyozhnaya, he and his team became increasingly anxious to get home as the season was winding down and the pandemic response ramping up. The AAD was in crisis mode and the director was currently stuck at Davis desperately trying to get back to Australia to lead the division's response to the global pandemic along with the rest of the Australian Government.

There was also another once-in-a-generation event that was about to be thrown into chaos by the pandemic. The AAD was preparing to receive its new icebreaker, the RSV *Nuyina*, in 2020, but it was still being built in Romania. A seamless transition from the soon-to-be-retired *Aurora Australis* to the *Nuyina* was now looking unlikely, and without an icebreaker the Australian Antarctic Program would grind to a halt.

For thirty years, the *Aurora* had been the backbone of the Australian Antarctic Program. The first and only icebreaker built in Australia, she was almost unchanged from the day she launched in 1989, and had brought the last huskies back from Antarctica in 1993. An icon of the program, she'd famously survived engine fires and a grounding at Mawson to prove her worth as the always dependable 'Orange Roughy'. Now, after thirty years of Antarctic operations, this would be her final season, and so everyone was relying on the RSV *Nuyina* being finished in 2020 to begin a new era in Australia's Antarctic operations.

As I read the news and listened to the updates from the AAD about what the pandemic response might involve, I started to get a sense that 2020 might not go to plan.

The *Aurora*'s final voyage to Antarctica would be to resupply Mawson station in late summer, once the sea ice surrounding Antarctica had broken up, and then pick up the summer team from Davis and take them home. Access through the sea ice to Mawson was notoriously difficult: there was just a brief window between the beginning of February and the end of March when ships could access the station. This final voyage of the 2019–20 summer season would see the ship depart Hobart and visit Davis briefly on its way to Mawson station, then it would complete the Mawson resupply and return to Davis to collect anyone not staying for winter.

As the *Aurora* got ready to leave Hobart, I started to grasp the seriousness of the pandemic. Chatting to the voyage leader over the phone before they sailed to Davis, I found his plan confusing.

'We'll aim to arrive at Davis after twelve days of sailing and drop off the cargo, but will not allow any passengers ashore until we have been at sea for a total of fourteen days. So you can expect us to "stooge" off the coast for a day or two. How copy, over?' said the voyage leader, known as 'Chunky', in his jovial British accent, maintaining radio comms protocols even on a mobile phone.

'Yep, copy all of that,' I replied, still processing what had just been said. I ran it through my head once more. Despite the *Aurora* expecting to arrive in twelve days and being capable of completing all cargo and passenger transfers in one day, Australia's one and only icebreaker, which would ordinarily seek to complete each voyage as efficiently and quickly as possible, would sit off the coast of Davis, burning fuel, until it had spent fourteen days at sea before discharging some short-stay scientists to Davis and heading to Mawson. This was serious.

I had no idea what was going on, but I needed to get my head around how the station would manage an outbreak. As far as I knew, Antarctic stations were not equipped to handle the outbreak of a severe respiratory illness.

I called Doc. 'You free? I'm coming around,' I said.

'Agree, we need to chat about this. It's getting bigger,' replied Doc.

I threw on my jacket, stuffed my feet into my boots in the cold porch and wandered over to the medical suite, about 50 metres away on the ground floor of the medical quarters. Being in the accommodation building gave Doc the privilege of not technically needing to go outside to get to work. Because of this, he was often dressed in board shorts. Today, however, he looked serious.

Apart from the snow outside the window, the medical office was identical to a typical doctor's office back home in Australia: bookshelves with volumes of medical references (many of them polar focused), models of knee joints, stress balls with medical brands on them and posters of human skeletal and muscle groups.

Closing the two sets of doors to increase our privacy, I sat down and got straight to the point. 'What do we actually know about this virus?'

'Not much. It's not Ebola or plague but it's highly contagious. Essentially, once you've got one case you've got thousands, so if it gets to a station we're all getting it,' explained Doc.

'Grim,' I replied. 'What can we handle here and what can we do about it if it happens?' I shifted focus from understanding our situation to brainstorming a plan of attack.

'I'll show you.' Doc stood up as we walked out of the office and into the medical suite. I'd been here before when we'd talked through all the capabilities of the operating theatre, the two-bed ward, the pathology area, drug storage and first-aid kits, but the scenarios we had trained for and focused on were things like hypothermia, crush injuries, frostbite, ice axes through leg bones, or some other Antarctic-related injury. Never once did we worry about a pandemic on station.

'So, as you can see,' he explained, 'we've only got two beds in the ward plus the operating table. I've got one ventilator but, essentially, we can deal with one critical patient and maybe two serious cases, and then we're full. Oh, and we'd need round-the-clock assistants on a roster system to keep things going. We can set up the telehealth video link to Kingston to get other doctors helping remotely but we'd be overwhelmed pretty quick.'

I tried to comprehend what Doc had just explained. He was the only doctor; when the ship arrived and dropped off the short-stay, end-of-summer teams, we'd have ninety-three people on station again until the *Aurora* returned from Mawson. If what he was telling me was true, and one of the new arrivals brought COVID-19 to Davis, soon enough we'd have most people infected with what could be a severe respiratory illness.

'Well, we can't change what we've got here anytime soon. Keep me posted on anything you need and I'll make sure we meet the quarantine rules and restrictions for new arrivals,' I said as we walked out of the ward. I realised the meeting had been quite intense and, although we were both busy, I figured we had time for a more casual chat. I turned back to Doc and asked, 'Coffee?'

'Roger,' replied Doc. We made our way to the lounge area.

It wasn't uncommon on station to have a professional conversation with someone, even a disagreement, and then ten minutes later you'd both drop your professional personas for some upbeat, social time together. Arriving at the mess, we made a couple of lattes with powdered milk and a commercial-grade machine, complete with a 'flicky-flicky' grinder and the 'bang-bang' style bin that reminded me of every hipster coffee joint in Melbourne.

'What are all your doctor mates back home saying?'

'Preparing for the worst but no one really knows. They have to shave their beards, apparently for better mask seals, so I'm lucky I get to keep mine.'

'Family?'

'Yeah, fine, not in the big cities. Just getting on with it and glued to the news each day. Yours?'

'Mostly in Melbourne and Queensland. A bit confused about it all but none of them are in overly high-risk categories so it should be fine.' My family was healthy, unlike those with pre-existing health issues and elderly people, who were at a much greater risk of becoming seriously ill should they catch COVID-19. 'Hopefully it's overkill and just another SARS or bird flu situation. Shouldn't impact us too much.'

'Yeah, probably. I'll let you know when I know more. Have a good one,' said Doc as we walked off in separate directions and went back to work.

Running through our limited capabilities, I was worried. The only thing working in our favour was that the rigorous selection criteria for Antarctic expeditioners meant that no one on station had pre-existing conditions that would increase their risk of serious illness if they caught COVID-19.

* * *

Day 97: 29 January 2020
Temperature: 0.4°C to 5.2°C

As the summer drew to a close, many expeditioners would depart and leave only the small winter team, but just how many would stay for the winter was changing daily. The Wilkins Aerodrome had reopened and we were waiting on the last of our winter expeditioners to fly south from Hobart into Wilkins and across to Davis. This included the winter field science leader. More importantly, we needed the other building services supervisor, Rocky, who was summering at Casey, to make it to Davis and take the weight off Gaz to manage the trades team. Fearing the worst, we started canvassing the summer team to see if anyone could stay and fill in these roles if the last flights were cancelled.

'Knock knock,' said the Weather Magician as she crept into my office for a chat. 'I'm thinking of applying for winter field scientist leader – would you mind being a referee? What do you think my chances are?' she asked.

'Happy to referee, but it's up to HR and the powers back in Kingston. I just run the station; they do all the hiring and firing. Could be the best chance you get at a winter,' I said optimistically, knowing a number of people were interested and scrambling to pad out their résumés with any scientific qualifications they could find to meet the criteria.

* * *

Every time I spoke to Kingston, it was more bad news, with COVID-19 now wreaking havoc across the globe. It went from bad to worse as I walked into Brian's office, knowing he was on the phone to Casey desperately trying to coordinate the last flights.

'No more flights. Northbound passengers only,' said Brian as he hung up the phone. The bad news kept coming. There would be no new arrivals via the airlink as COVID-19 had made its way to Australia and the AAD couldn't risk exposing the stations. This meant the A319 would fly south empty and retrieve the summer team from Casey, but we wouldn't get our winter field science leader.

'Please tell me we can get Rocky across from Casey. We need him for the winter trade projects,' I said.

'Nope, the Basler can only do a one-way trip from here to Casey and then it'll head to McMurdo, South Pole, Rothera on the peninsula and back home to Canada.' Rocky would be flying back to Australia, which meant an increased workload for Gaz to manage both maintenance and infrastructure projects in the winter. Promoting one of the tradies on station to replace Rocky wasn't really an option; we needed Rocky for his experience at Davis. This worried me as we headed into winter.

There was some good news, though: the Weather Magician would stay on for the winter as the field science leader, and so would be responsible for seal surveys and numerous other ad hoc requirements around the Vestfold Hills. This was one of the best roles on station if you liked getting outdoors in the freezing cold. When the music finally stopped and the ship arrived to collect the summerers, just twenty-four of us would remain for the winter.

* * *

Day 122: 23 February 2020
Temperature: -6.6°C to 1.4°C

As the *Aurora Australis* returned to collect the summer team and say farewell to Davis, a sense of uncertainty about what lay ahead pervaded the air. Standing on the wharf as the last barge was preparing to depart, I worried about what 2020 had in store for those of us staying here over winter.

'Good luck, you've got a good team and I'll see you in November,' said Mitch as he threw his waterproof bag onto the barge.

'Thanks for everything. Good luck back there with everything that's unfolding, and see you next summer,' I said as we shook hands.

And that was it: the last interaction I'd have with anyone outside the winter team until we went home in November. Everyone had their chance to put their hand up and leave but we were committed. No turning back now. As the ship's horn echoed across the bay, we lit flares on the shoreline and stood silently on the rocky shore, watching as the 'Orange Roughy' sailed into the distance.

All the while, at a far-off dockyard in Romania, the engineers working on the *Nuyina* were being told to wear face masks, critical engineers were having to isolate if sick and the frantic pace required to have the ship ready to make its maiden voyage to Antarctica and collect us in nine months' time was quietly slipping away.

Part II

WINTER

Chapter 4

The Sound of Silence

Day 123: 24 February 2020
Station population: 24
Temperature: -6.9°C to -3.9°C

With the *Aurora Australis* sailing north and the dust of summer settling, Mother Nature flicked the switch to winter mode. As I walked across to my office I looked out across the sea and saw dark clouds and a strong breeze whipping up white-capped waves and the first slicks of what is known as 'grease ice', for its resemblance to an oil slick on the water – the first phase of sea-ice growth. There were also telling signs of frozen sea water around the wharf, where the high tide had left a crusty white line on the rocks. Winter was coming.

I slipped over on the icy road between the living quarters and the operations building and landed on my arse. This would now become a weekly occurrence for most of us, as we misjudged our footing and faceplanted or arseplanted into the snow.

The plan for the first few days of the winter was simple: ease into our winter routines and set ourselves up for the darker months ahead. By now, everyone was in tune with their work and knew what was ahead of them – powering down and sealing buildings we no longer needed for accommodation, taking batteries out of plant and equipment only used during summer and parking them in places they wouldn't get buried in snow. It was important we recalibrated the community side of things as well: after averaging around eighty to ninety expeditioners on station during summer, there were now only two dozen of us.

So, sitting in the comfortable couches and leather chairs of the now quiet upstairs lounge, armed with cups of tea and snacks from morning smoko, we held an open forum for everyone to voice their ideas and suggestions. The lounge had the same feeling of calm that passes over a household after hosting Christmas lunch when all the guests leave. You breathe out, sit down and look forward to some peace.

'This is it,' I said, 'just the twenty-four of us to get through the winter. We can now make a few adjustments to the routine and the station tempo based on what we learned through the summer. As long as it goes to achieving everything we need, then I'm open to any ideas.'

The kitchen is the heart of the whole operation, and Rhonda followed my lead. 'I'm happy to do whatever works for special occasions, casual dinners, DIY meals and so on, and let me know if any of you want to cook or do barbeques and I'll set you up.' During summer, with the three chefs and a frantic pace, it wasn't possible for the expeditioners to get too involved with the cooking, but with the smaller group the catering arrangements could be a bit more of a family affair.

Next up was Gaz, who laid out the major works for the months ahead, when everyone would be asked to help out. 'We'll get on with winterising the buildings, then we'll get into the smaller maintenance things. The big one, about October, just before the planes get here, we'll refill the station's tarn.[13] This will take a couple of weeks and everyone will be involved. It's relatively straightforward, simply pumping sea water up the hill and into the tarn so the next team has plenty of water to desalinate next summer.' Gaz was blunt and to the point, as would become his custom at future station meetings.

I looked around at everyone nodding their heads and listening intently as we went around the room and each of the team leaders and individuals added their bit.

'We need to finish some field training, and then everyone will need to do Hägglunds blizzard training to learn how to navigate blind, but we have to wait for the sea ice to regrow,' added Jarrod, providing a natural transition for the lead mechanic, Lewis, to jump in.

'Häggs are probably the most expensive vehicle you'll ever drive, so be careful.[14] We've only got so many spares and just three mechanics. Once the sea ice is strong enough, we'll head up to Whoop Whoop to bring back the Blue Hägg and then the two snow groomers we left up there. Then, around September–October, we'll build the runway on the sea ice,' he explained calmly.

The trio from the BoM went through their slightly different working arrangements, which saw them working different days from the rest of us. Once again everyone nodded along, but I wanted to emphasise a point.

'Some teams and expeditioners will do different hours and have very different roles, so don't get caught up judging why so-and-so is reading a book at 11am on a Tuesday while you're at work,' I added.

---

[13] The tarn is a glacial-formed reservoir at the back of the station and the sole water source.

[14] About $250,000 each.

This was once again met with collective nodding and grumbles at being told the same thing for the tenth time. Those who'd been south before knew this eventually became a problem every winter. Would we be any different?

While there was a lot of work to be done, the AAD had well-established routines for the season. Over *Aurora Australis*'s thirty years of operation, the shipping schedules had been lined up with the sea-ice growth and decay patterns to ensure access to the stations during the voyage windows. Supplementing the shipping schedule, since the opening of the Wilkins Aerodrome in 2006, the main focus of each winter season was working towards the first flights into Antarctica in October, to commence the next summer. This left us just seven months of true isolation before we'd greet the first aircraft back at Davis. Everything was mapped backwards from there to complete a detailed winter maintenance schedule on all the equipment, recover the groomers and Hägg left up at Whoop Whoop and then use them to build the sea-ice runway. The one extra responsibility we had this year was refilling the station tarn, which is only completed every five to six years. It sounded easy enough.

* * *

Day 157: 29 March 2020
Temperature: -20.5°C to -13.5°C
Maximum wind speed: 93 kilometres per hour

Early in the winter, it's a waiting game for the sea ice to regrow, with each day bringing a glimmer of hope as I looked out across the bay at slicks of grease ice and the various stages of growth. After grease ice, as the sea starts to form more solid layers, it's call 'frazzle' and has the consistency of a slurpee. After that, the ice clumps together in circular patterns and is known as 'pancake ice', which often includes chunks of old icebergs, or 'bergy bits', to use the technical term.

Each morning as I got my hopes up, the pancake ice would melt away during the day as the sunlight hit it and the prevailing offshore winds blew it out to sea. Finally, after weeks of restrained optimism, the sea ice locked in around the wharf and coastline stretching out from the station to the nearby islands. It was time to test the ice!

In years gone by, sea ice was tested by roping up a team of three to four expeditioners with harnesses and a climbing rope, spacing them out and walking onto the ice to see who broke through first. There was an old-timey photo in the accommodation block of this brave and/or foolish activity to remind us of yesteryear. In 2020, it was a bit more sophisticated but the same basic theory.

Jarrod ran us through the procedure, which included watching a 1990s safety video for the patented 'rescue alive' platform we would use to increase safety over the thin ice. The system was simple – if you connected your grandma's walking frame to two canoes you'd get the 'rescue alive' platform. Jarrod would lead the way for the test, but about half the station was there to participate and learn about the rescue system. The platform meant that if the ice broke through as you walked across it, you could support yourself with the buoyant pontoons. It also had a paddle so it could be used as a canoe, and it was connected to land or an area of safer sea ice with a long rope.

'Alright, safety line connected?' asked Jarrod.

'Confirm, good to go!' the reply came back from Jimbo, his designated assistant from the SAR team.

I watched Jarrod move quickly out on the ice with the rope trailing behind him. About 20 metres offshore, he stopped, drilled a hole, checked it was at least 20 centimetres thick and jumped up and down a few times before declaring, 'Looks good!' I laughed at the simplicity of the moment. Like I said, sea ice is both dangerous and simple; it is either strong enough or it's not. If you can jump up and down, it's good.

Jarrod had a bit more experience with sea ice than most of us and had wintered at Casey station previously. When it came to canoes and the ocean – well, he is the only man to have successfully kayaked around Australia solo, including Tasmania, so we tended to trust him on the water.

With the initial test done, one by one we all practised using the rescue platform to save someone stranded on thin ice or in the water. I enjoyed the training – it was actually quite fun. Towards the end of the activity, though, as my gloves were now wet from working on sea ice and holding onto metal ice axes, for the first time since arriving in Antarctica I really felt cold.

I could feel the loss of dexterity and speed in my hands as I tried to grip onto things, and as I looked around I realised I wasn't the only one. Everyone had their hands inside jacket pockets and were subtly shielding themselves behind vehicles to block the biting wind. It was time to pack up and head back up the hill to the station.

While we were out there, we'd also done some more official drilling of the ice to check its depth and test the quality. It was only 30 centimetres thick, which was fine for walking but not quite enough to safely deploy the quad bikes in the event of a search-and-rescue situation, so we would wait another week or two until it reached 40 centimetres before declaring the sea ice officially open.

To keep us occupied while we waited, the Davis band had been rehearsing and put on an evening of music and entertainment after dinner. At one point, there were more in the band than in the audience, as we picked up triangles and added layers to everything from Van Halen to KC and the Sunshine Band's greatest hits.

To show that station leaders aren't all bad, I'd been secretly working on a few songs as the opening act for the night, to break the mood and settle anyone's nerves about performing. Complete with an outrageous American accent, I sang a rendition of the song made famous in the Netflix series *Tiger King* – 'I Saw a Tiger' by Joe Exotic – and received a good laugh.

I went to bed that night with the unofficial anthem of our year stuck in my head. It was first played during the summer open-mic night and carried on through the winter at every event. I lay there and stared at the ceiling, my ears still ringing with Darius Rucker's 'Wagon Wheel'.

Just as each song has many layers, I was slowly discovering there were many subtle layers to the team, and as the year went on these talents and hobbies would grow and develop in the unique isolation of the station community.

* * *

They say in Chinese the word for 'crisis' and 'opportunity' is the same. Not speaking Mandarin, I cannot verify this fact but I like the theory.

One evening, a discussion about the impact COVID-19 was starting to have on global share markets invited some curious comments from those who'd never dabbled in investing before. This gave me an idea that worked well with my plans for the recently launched 'Davis community college'. Once a week we would run a seminar or workshop for professional or personal development. To help get things started, I teamed up with another investment enthusiast and we delivered Stock Market 101 to an eager crowd of expeditioners.

I opened the session: 'First of all, I am not an expert at this, but I can talk about what I've done and where to find more info about it so you can make your own decisions. You are all in the best possible situation to get started. Everything back home is uncertain and that's why the market has plummeted. For us, we'll keep getting paid as long as we're here in our comfortably isolated station, so you've all probably got a good amount of cash sitting around to play with.'

My own goal was to grow the amount of cash I had available to finish renovating my house. In February 2019 I'd had one of the busiest weeks of my life when I'd moved into my new 'renovator's delight' in Melbourne to discover it needed new gas lines, new water, a new roof, a new kitchen, water damage repairs, new stumps, new floorboards and many other general repairs. In the same week, I flew up to Sydney for my sister's wedding, and then capped it off by flying to Casey for a two-week familiarisation visit before joining the Antarctic program.

The problem was, I'd only half-finished the list of projects for the house before I was down in Hobart getting ready to head south, so I was constantly trying to manage repairs remotely through the two mates I had living in the house while I was away. 'It's leaking again' was a pretty common message to see on my phone until we found a roofer, which proved nearly impossible in the middle of the lockdowns and restrictions. So the more cash I could make out of the share market while I was away, the better my backyard and new bathrooms would look. Being surrounded by plumbers, chippies, sparkies and builders on station was also quite handy for daydreaming and planning over a Friday-afternoon brew.

Most of the group had a basic understanding of how shares worked but had been hesitant or unsure how to get going, so we talked through the apps, websites and risk strategies as optimism spread like wildfire. To finish the night, we watched *The Wolf of Wall Street* in the cinema, and thus the 'Davis stock market club' was born.

What would an ex-army officer and diplomat know about the stock market? Well, I had my dad to thank for that. When my brother and I were kids he'd once set up a stock market game where we both chose ten different shares out of the newspaper listings and then 'bought' $1000 worth. Each day, once Dad had finished with the financial section of the paper and I'd read the sport, I'd check my shares and see how they were going. I was amazed: you can make money by doing nothing other than owning a thing?

Until then, to earn money I'd been mowing lawns, working at Dad's warehouse during the school holidays and installing computers for my mate's dad's company, and I'd also been watching my brother work his paper route each morning. But this concept of investing seemed like the way to go. It took a few years to get going properly, but as soon as I was making enough cash to set some aside and buy shares, I did.

Some of us at Davis would develop some nice little side hustles over the year; others, myself included, expected Virgin Australia

Airlines to survive the year. I guess I should have bought more bitcoins!

The stock market club and community college were just the beginning of how we kept ourselves stimulated and busy throughout the evenings and outside of work. In years gone by, building a community at the station was the only way to get through when teams of Antarctic expeditioners were isolated from all other forms of social and community life. Alas, in more modern times, with wi-fi,[15] everyone had either a laptop or a TV in their room, which meant there were those who finished work, ate and disappeared for the evening.

There is no right or wrong way to endure the isolation and struggles of a small remote community, and I'm not a psychologist, but in the long run I felt those members of the team who took it upon themselves to drive community events and be 'active citizens' fared better overall and were able to turn the negative aspects of our year into an overall positive experience.

* * *

Day 174: 15 April 2020
Temperature: -19.7°C to -8.9°C

One day in every twenty-three, on a complex and ever-evolving roster system, each of us helped Rhonda in the kitchen for a day

---

[15] The internet connection on station via satellite was temperamental and inconsistent. Some days it was as good as a bad connection back home, and good enough to buffer Netflix in the station cinema if we all turned our phones off. On other days, nothing.

and did the domestic cleaning around the common areas. This role on the Aussie stations was known as 'Slushy'.

You had to get up bloody early to beat Rhonda, so by the time you reported for duty at 0800 (or earlier to get a head start, as most of us would learn to do), there would already be a mountain of dishes next to the sink and lists of odd jobs for you to do on top of the mandated list of essential daily, weekly and monthly tasks. All going well, you'd work hard until about 1500, get a break in the afternoon and report back about 1700 to prepare for dinner.

Depending on your role on station, it was often a good break in routine to spend a day outside your team, doing mindful and simple tasks on a list. I always enjoyed it, and it gave me a good chance to spend the day chatting to Rhonda about anything and everything going on back home and on station. As I washed dishes, I pondered what my brother had just told me over the phone about a new 'work from home' model, which had curtailed his daily bike riding routine to the office. It meant trying to supervise my two young nieces, who were also at home more often as schools and childcare were continually opening and closing based on outbreaks and cases.

On station, though, there was some serious business to talk about. The collective mind of the community had been alert to events back home and what impact they would have on us.

Australia was closed. For the first time in our lifetimes, the international borders were slammed shut, even to Australians trying to return home. States were plunged into lockdowns, mass gatherings were cancelled, and weddings and funerals were limited to small groups. What would this mean for us?

'What are they saying about the new ship?' asked Rhonda after

I'd made a good start on the dishes and was ready to be distracted.

'Officially it's still on track to be delivered to Hobart later in the year, and at least make it to Davis in early 2021; less officially, they're securing a second vessel to come and get us. It might just be the *Aurora Australis* under a new contract or a different ship altogether,' I replied.

'Can the *Aurora* be rehired?' asked Rhonda.

'It's an antique – it needs to be upgraded to the new international Polar Code requirements before it can be approved for polar operations. With port facilities closing around the world, and travel restrictions, I doubt they can simply rehire it.[16] This means finding another, newer icebreaker, but there just aren't that many icebreakers lying around waiting to be hired,' I said.

'But they can still get us with planes, right?' asked Rhonda, already one step ahead.

'Yeah, that's shaping up as the way we'll be going home. Might mean a few people staying on if they choose, but most of the team will fly out in November via Wilkins. Would you stay if you could?' I asked

'For sure. You?' replied Rhonda.

'If they'll let me; my other job won't be too happy, though,' I said. It was good to know that we were on the same page. I pondered the conversation I'd have to have with my other employer, who had

---

[16]   There were multiple hurdles to rehiring the *Aurora* besides the new Polar Code requirements. It was also 'out of survey', which meant a thorough and detailed engineering inspection in dry dock to recertify it as seaworthy, a process that would take months. Additionally, the *Aurora* was owned by international shipping company P&O and the exclusive contract to the AAD had expired, meaning the Australian Government had no influence on its availability. International shipping is a complicated business model.

agreed to twelve months' leave without pay but would be reluctant to extend the arrangement.

'Can you explain all this to everyone?' asked Rhonda.

'I'm waiting until there's a more solid plan rather than just feeding rumours, but I'll update everyone at the next meeting,' I said, staring back at the still-accumulating pile of dishes.

It was always a tough situation to be in when I didn't have any firm news to pass on to the team, but I knew they needed something. With daily contact between each sub-team and their technical leaders back in Kingston, and the AAD itself being a relatively small satellite of the bigger Department of Agriculture, Water and the Environment, based in Canberra, rumours would often travel fast between Kingston and the stations.

The more experienced expeditioners knew that season operations often changed and were never concrete until the day you actually stepped onto the ship or the aircraft. There were always rumours and fears, but every year for the previous thirty years, the trusty old 'Orange Roughy' would somehow save the day. The short money was on an eleventh-hour deal to rehire the *Aurora*, tear through the red tape and send her south for one last glorious voyage!

This romantic dream died a grim death when the AAD hired an interim ship, the MPV *Everest*, for the 2020–21 season. As I jumped on a computer to google the ship and find out more information, I was struck by its odd-looking design, with the helipad perched above the bridge rather than at the rear, like on most polar vessels. It didn't matter, though – there was a ship and it would arrive in Hobart around November 2020 to start resupplying the stations.

We learned more about the ship as the days went on. While not technically an 'icebreaker' – it was a polar-class ice-strengthened vessel – it would be more than capable of making its way to Davis and Casey. We questioned how a non-icebreaking ship would get through the thicker and more persistent sea ice around Mawson station, but that wasn't our problem. I was just glad there was a plan and I could brief the team that we'd be going home on schedule in November.

At that Friday's station meeting, I laid out the plan.

'The *Nuyina* won't be ready in time to collect us in November. Once the planes get down to Antarctica from the Northern Hemisphere, we can change out the station team by ferrying people to Casey and then back to Australia via Wilkins and the A319. They won't do the Davis resupply voyage until early 2021 with the MPV *Everest*, so we can take that off the list of jobs we'll have to do before we go home and leave it for next summer's team.'

No one was overly surprised, and I fielded questions and rumours over snacks at the bar that afternoon. The team understood and it didn't really change too much for us, other than the fact we would now fly home rather than sail. A few of the more astute returning expeditioners saw the chance to stay on for a second summer and volunteered themselves if needed. But at the other end of the spectrum was Fred.

'Why can't they just use the *Aurora* to get us in November?' asked Fred, even though I had explained this in great detail at the station meeting.

'As I said, mate, it needs a massive upgrade to be certified for polar voyages – it's old and this new vessel looks fine.'

'Pretty poor planning to not have the new ship ready,' complained Fred, determined to maintain the topic.

'This wasn't exactly the plan. *Nuyina* was already delayed before COVID-19 but it had half a chance of being ready and now that chance is zero,' I explained, as we headed down the rabbit hole.

'Yeah, well, they should have kept the *Aurora* certified then,' retorted Fred, clearly not looking for an actual solution to his complaint.

'Well, I can't do much about that, can I?' I ended the conversation and got up for another beer. I offered to 'buy' another round for the table, reaching into the fridge to harvest our ever-improving Antarctic home-brew.

People needed to vent, and whenever I was at the bar, I tried to walk a line of not taking sides but explaining what I knew and why things were the way they were, as if I was just a knowledgeable bloke at the bar rather than the station leader. Most of the team got this, but a few didn't, and it grated on me that I couldn't relax for fear of slipping up and revealing my personal opinion.

Case in point: I loved riding the quad bikes on a nice sunny day and would often talk about this fact. It didn't mean I'd approve non-operational fieldtrips using the bikes, though, and it baffled me that there were some who tried to push the boundaries and quoted my love of bikes as some sort of rationale.

* * *

It was hard to get a sense of what was happening in the outside world as we sat around station worrying about how we'd get home. It wasn't until the decision was announced that there would be no mass gatherings for Anzac Day dawn services on 25 April that it really hit home. There would also be no service held on the Western Front in France or the shores of Gallipoli in Turkey. So, for possibly the first time since the commemorations of Anzac Day began, the services held on the Antarctic stations would be the only ceremonies with 'crowds', such as we were.

Each year on Anzac Day, Aussies and Kiwis gather at dawn to commemorate the fateful events of the First World War's failed attempts to capture the Dardanelles. On 25 April 1915, the Australian and New Zealand Army Corp (Anzac) units went ashore at Gallipoli.

In my family, though, that day has always been special for a different reason. Long before I served overseas alongside Kiwis in modern-day Anzac battlegroups and learned the traditions and history of Australia's military past, on 25 April 1919, in the wake of the First World War in the newly independent Latvian capital of Riga, my grandmother was born.

As we prepared for the dawn service at the civilised time of 1000 hours, thanks to the ever-shorter Antarctic days, I reflected on the turn of events in the history of my family that saw me standing here on the shores of Davis delivering the 'Ode of Remembrance' across a silent Antarctic landscape to a small team completely cut off from the world back home.

Both of my parents were avid travellers. Mum was a flight attendant for Ansett Airlines in the 1960s heyday of international jet setting. She had sailed over to London after finishing school and had worked at Harrods for a time. A highly independent woman, she'd grown up in a single-parent household after the unexpected death of her mother at a young age, leaving my grandfather to raise three kids.

They included my uncle, one of the last Australian kids to be struck down with polio just shy of the polio vaccine's introduction to Australia. Stories of how Mum and my aunty had to stand in a field waving to him in a hospital window seemed like fiction, until in 2020 similar scenes played out around the world. It was only then that I fully understood what my uncle and family had been through growing up with polio. If I'd ever needed proof that vaccines work, my family's experience was more than enough.

My father was equally well travelled. Born during the closing stages of the Second World War in what is now Poland, he'd emigrated to Australia with my grandparents and siblings and, in famous family history, broken his arm on the ship as they sailed into Fremantle. After completing school, he headed back to Europe and lived in Switzerland and even in Istanbul for a year, chasing a girl. This was a fact I would only learn when, after copy-catting it in 2015, my grandmother told me the cautionary tale – surprising both Mum and me.

As a young kid I shared a love of motorsport and computers with my father. He'd take my brother and me to Sandown Raceway on weekends to watch the touring cars and I spent many a Sunday night up past my bedtime watching Formula 1 on TV. When they announced a race in Melbourne, Dad even took me out of school for the Friday to see the cars hit the track.

Dedicated to his business, if Dad wasn't spending time with his kids, he was at work and would often combine the two by having the three of us work in his warehouse or answer phones on weekends and school holidays. These are some of my fondest family memories and, although I only ever recall being paid in McDonald's Happy Meals, it cemented a good work ethic and focus in me.

As a young boy, your father is everything and you never imagine life without him, but on Monday 23 February 1998, when I was just thirteen years old, after dropping my older brother, younger sister and me at the train station and driving to work, Dad sat down at his cluttered desk and had a heart attack. Despite the best efforts of those around him, nothing could be done, and the world as I knew it was over.

Growing up in a single-parent household left me no time for rebellion. Instead, my siblings and I developed a strong sense of independence and a determination to succeed as we did what we could to work together as a family. This meant Mum could continue to run the business she and my father had started, as well as raise three kids.

Now long retired, Mum often likes to say that to end up with 'two lawyers and a diplomat, I must have done something right'. Without knowing it at the time, her example of pure determination and resilience within our household set my brother, sister and me up for success in the real world.

After my father's death, it was our grandmother, Mutti, as she was known across the wider family, who brought us all together. Proudly of Latvian heritage but having lived all across Europe as it evolved, first fleeing Soviet expansion and relocating to Germany before eventually emigrating to Australia, she would outlive two of her children and experience many of twentieth-century Europe's darkest days firsthand. Right until the end, her memory was sharp as a knife as she retold stories of visiting her half-brother imprisoned in a Soviet gulag for reasons unknown.

Perpetually thankful for having survived the escape from Europe, Grandma was happy and grateful for the life she had created in Australia, and as I grew up and became first an officer in the Australian Army and then a diplomat representing her adopted country, we developed a bond that went beyond a typical grandson–grandmother relationship. It somehow added another layer to the family story.

Having missed countless birthdays and celebrations while abroad for many years, 2019 was one year I was sure to be in Melbourne as we counted down to her one-hundredth birthday. I'd never been to a hundredth birthday before but, as the years ticked by, we knew she'd make it. When the day rolled around on 25 April 2019, at a small family gathering in Melbourne we celebrated the life of an incredible woman. At one hundred, most of your friends aren't around to celebrate so it's a collection of grandkids and great-grandkids that fill the crowd. As Grandma looked through the photos of her life, reminding her of everything she'd done, we sat down for a moment to talk about my next adventure.

'Ah, David, what are you going to do now? Will you stay in Melbourne?' she asked in her joyfully strong Latvian accent.

'Not yet. I'm going to Antarctica for a year, then I'll come back to Melbourne and settle down,' I said, having just days before received the news that I would be taking over as station leader at Davis in the latter part of 2019.

'Another adventure for you, David! Always travelling, like your father.' She smiled, as she knew how unlikely I was to stay in one place very long.

Usually for Grandma, in her later years, a good couple of hours was all she could manage before being dropped home. But that day, a once-in-one-hundred-years celebration, she was in fine form and was intent on spending time with her youngest great-grandkids, my two favourite penguins/nieces, and watching them play well into the afternoon.

Within a week of her party, Mum called to tell me that, after catching a cold and then pneumonia, Grandma had died peacefully in her sleep. What a way to go, partying too hard at your hundredth birthday party – a fitting end to an incredible life. I often wondered how she would have handled 2020.

As I stood in front of the team at Davis that Anzac Day morning and we remembered those who'd died in all wars and the pursuit of peace across the globe, I also remembered my grandma, who would have been 101 that day. If she could endure the tragedies of life and still face the world with a smile, then we could get through this year. Lest we forget.

* * *

In an ordinary year, people back home get on with their lives and forget about what's happening during winter in Antarctica. But 2020 was different, as my home town of Melbourne plunged into a lockdown that was supposed to last two weeks (or so they said) and things went from bad to worse. Businesses and schools were closed and everyone adapted to working from home and being cooped up with their families or flatmates, or isolating alone.

A conversation with my brother about how he was adapting led to an interesting series of talks and then news stories, as those I spoke to shared the stories I'd told around their workplaces and homes about just how 'the experts' on an Antarctic station managed isolation and cramped working conditions.

There were also a few of the usual requests from Australian newspapers to the AAD about how we lived down there and what we did to keep busy, so we explained the traditions of band nights, social events, fieldtrips and cooking lessons. This year, though, it was beyond the regular level of interest, and we were glad to help out those back home who'd been forced into a situation similar to ours. In a strange way, our isolation in Antarctica had brought us closer to everyone isolating back home.

Friends and family all over the country were sending photos of articles we'd written from Antarctica that were distributed right across Australia. One request, though, I initially thought was an April fool's joke: I was asked to be interviewed for the *New York Times* and featured alongside an astronaut as experts on isolation. I was chuffed. Ironically, during pre-departure interviews with the team, I'd learned that almost half the group had wanted to be astronauts growing up but, due to Australia not having a space program (and other reasons), we'd all joined the Antarctic program as the next best thing here on Earth.

The other highlight from this period of media attention was being on Triple M's *Hot Breakfast* radio show. Doing a breakfast radio show when your time zone is four hours behind isn't ideal. But *Hot Breakfast* was recorded right near where I lived in South Melbourne and I'd listened to it for years. I felt right at home talking about all things COVID-19, football and Antarctica, including reminding one of the hosts that, in fact, Antarctica did not have polar bears. He didn't seem to appreciate my reminder, but Eddie McGuire and the rest of the team got a good laugh out of it!

What I loved most about this, though, was how connected it

made me feel, despite the isolation and distance. I was live across my home-town radio and, as the hosts sat in the studio just near my house, I had a strange feeling as if, for just a moment, I was right there with them.

The intent of these engagements was to try to provide a unique perspective on what was unfolding around the world. At the time, Antarctica remained the only continent on Earth with no COVID-19 infections, and media outlets seemed to love this.

* * *

Working closely with the AAD's media team, I gathered the team on station together one Saturday morning for some 'organised fun'. Instead of station training or work, we'd split into teams and film sketches to be compiled into a short film. This would also be a dress rehearsal for later in the year, when we'd film our contribution to the annual Antarctic forty-eight-hour film festival.

The brief was simple and most of the team enjoyed the morning as the inaugural 'COV-AID' film festival began. The result? A hilarious video featuring some classic tongue-in-cheek Aussie humour. This short film, titled 'Isolate like an Antarctican', would go on to become one of the most downloaded and watched videos the AAD had ever released, surpassing a video of a penguin stealing a GoPro and another of a penguin jumping into an inflatable boat and squawking about.

We also filmed a few more serious interviews about what COVID-19 on station might mean and the impact it would have on an isolated community, which would later air on *Weekend Sunrise* and the nightly news.

Of course, expeditioners like Fred were too cool to participate and scoffed at the idea. This sort of attitude just confused me. There was nothing else to do on a Saturday morning and everyone on station, no matter how busy and important, came together for events like this. But there would always be a few who didn't want to join in. It weighed on me and drained my energy to keep morale up.

My approach to our predicament was simple: 'Make the most of what we've been dealt and create opportunity.' But I was starting to feel that some of the team favoured the 'sit around and do nothing' approach. It felt like high school, with the 'cool kids' sitting around poking fun at those who were getting involved and being proactive in community events.

I was surprised by this. In the army, extracurricular activities were often highlights, and attendance (although more militaristically compulsory) was enthusiastic and part of unit life. I'd expected the same on an Antarctic station, so I was frustrated when attendance was less than 100 per cent. But I made my peace with this difference in attitude and reminded myself that it was about creating opportunity and freedom for everyone to be involved or elect not to.

At times when attendance at 'organised fun' was low, I'd calmly remind myself, 'If it was worth it for one member of the team, it was worth it.'

* * *

With the months since summer flicking by, everything was in a nice rhythm. If this continued through the winter we'd be laughing all the way till the end. There was a long way to go: we'd just clocked over the halfway point of our expected duration in Antarctica.

By May, we were gearing up towards mid-winter and anticipating the six weeks of near-total darkness Davis would experience. The night-time aurora australis (the southern lights, not the ship) was a regular event and many of us would set up time-lapse cameras and brave the cold at night to catch a glimpse of one of Earth's most unique phenomena. I lay there one night in the snow looking up at the night sky, as the most stunning array of stars and the aurora danced across the sky, with satellites and meteors lighting up as they passed.

In this moment, I thought about the experience of astronaut Michael Collins, the command module pilot for *Apollo 11*'s mission to the moon. Everyone remembers the astronauts who first walked on the surface of the moon but, as they were down on the surface of the moon with TV cameras and flags, the lonely command module pilot orbited around them. Collins was the only human on the dark side of the moon, isolated from the rest of humanity as he looked at stars brighter than those back on Earth could ever imagine.

As I was lying near enough to a building, I still had wi-fi so it wasn't quite the same, but I certainly felt I was as far away from the world as I could be while still on Earth. I also wondered why, in the movies, aliens always go to New York. If I was a tour guide for aliens visiting Earth, I'd take them to lie in the Antarctic snow and look at the aurora and the Milky Way over the Statue of Liberty any day. No offence to Lady Liberty.

Chapter 5

Woah, We're Halfway There?

Day 236: 16 June 2020
Temperature: -27.4°C to -21.3°C
Maximum wind speed: 74 kilometres per hour

With the sea ice now regrown and strong enough to drive a Hägglunds across, it was time to get busy. We were racing the sunset as the days became shorter and the temperatures plummeted to nearly 30 degrees below zero.

Every time you stepped outside you could feel the snap of the frozen air hit you, your runny nose would freeze into a 'snotsicle' and beards were prone to freezing with the exhaled condensation and residual moisture, creating a rugged Antarctic look. I learned the hard way to leave time for your neck Buff to defrost before removing it when, one day, upon heading inside after my morning station walk around in the cold, I promptly ripped my Buff off over my head, tearing out a good amount of neck hair and beard along with it – ouch.

Crucially, we needed to get the Blue Hägg back from Whoop Whoop. Jarrod and Lewis would head up there with a few helpers for the first time since summer to fire up the Hägg and bring it back. This would be the first in a series of trips to the remote runway to recover equipment, and it was vital to ongoing operations to have all vehicles back on station.

On a good day, the trip to Whoop Whoop would take two to three hours, and with clear visibility you could sit back with your headphones on and just enjoy the drive up the coast along the sea ice before heading inland through fjords and up the moraine line,[17] where the Antarctic Plateau meets the rocks. From the moraine line up, it was a barren, white nothingness for nearly 2000 kilometres to the South Pole. The only thing near us was Whoop Whoop. This is a tried and tested route, and all vehicle GPS units had a series of waypoints and tracks loaded into them to make sure you stayed on the known path of safety.

After they made it to Whoop Whoop, the team would dig out the Hägg's tracks, put the battery back in and fire her up. The secondary task was to make sure everything at Whoop Whoop was still there and well placed to survive the dark and cold winter. The most important pieces of equipment we had at our disposal were the two snow groomers we used to build the ice runways that had been left up there at the end of summer. Without them there would be no way of preparing a smooth landing strip at either Whoop Whoop or on the sea ice near station.

Later in the season, once winter had passed and the sea ice reached one metre thick, we'd head up and drive them back to station as the first real step towards receiving planes and starting the next summer season. But, for now, Jarrod would lead a team to get the Hägg, spend a night at Bandits Hut for good measure and return to station.

---

[17] The moraine line is the deposit of rocks left by a glacier. This region of boulders and gravel marks the transition from the Vestfold Hills to the Antarctic Plateau.

At the same time, the Weather Magician led a seal survey team out on the quad bikes to look for early evidence of Weddell seals in the fjords and along the coast. This had become a routine and sometimes mundane task for us to keep up during the cold months before the seals returned in good numbers. We'd often head out for a seal survey knowing the chances of spotting a seal were extremely low – but there was a saying that 'a zero count is still a count', and for the scientists back home it was valuable data to gauge seal populations. It was simple 'citizen science' – drive along a series of marked routes that hugged the coastline and likely seal locations and, if you saw a seal, count it and mark the location on the GPS. When you got back to station, the data was sent home to the scientists who had been tracking seal populations and locations for years.

Closer to station but vitally important for some of the long-running science, multiple sensors needed to be installed within the sea ice itself that could measure the different stresses and seismic elements of the ice. Sea ice may appear stable, but it is constantly floating and moving under enormous stresses and pressure from all directions. As the ice moves, it creates 'pressure ridges' rising metres above the sea ice and creating spectacular formations and ice sculptures. It reminded me of the movement of tectonic plates under the Earth's crust, but on a smaller scale and with more immediate signs of movement. After a blizzard, it wasn't uncommon for large cracks, or 'leads', to open up between areas of sea ice; these were wide enough to swallow a vehicle if you weren't careful.

With all these activities, it was one of our busiest days since summer and the station was a ghost town. As a bare minimum, we always maintained a core team of six people, plus either me or

Rhonda, on station so we could respond to any incident there, such as a fire or power outage.

With everything going on back home and the uncertainty around just how we would be returning on everyone's mind, being busy was a welcome distraction. I learned there was a direct correlation between petty disputes and work tempo, and daydreamed about how much easier running the station during the frantic pace of summer was compared with the long, slow grind of winter.

Just as Simon had foretold during the station handover, things were getting weird. I'd recently had to mediate a dispute over a doorstop and whether a particular door should remain propped open throughout the day or not. As everyone adjusted to sharing their surroundings and found their own routines, small disputes over things like noisy gym users and cutlery arrangements in the kitchen became more frequent. We needed something to break it up.

* * *

Since 2006, there has been one annual tradition like no other across Antarctica. Each year around mid-winter, about two dozen Antarctic and sub-Antarctic stations shoot a five-minute video over a forty-eight-hour period. Each station has to include a number of set items, phrases and other things to steer their theme – the more creative the better. It's a humorous novelty for the dark winter months, and the distraction we all needed.

At Davis, we had an ace up our sleeve. 'Cometh the hour, cometh the man,' they say, and Dan was that man. Dan's main role on station was as our electronics engineer, which involved overseeing a range of scientific instruments and arrays littered around the station and the Vestfold Hills. Some instruments were low-tech, and I'd often enjoy a day out with Dan to swap out memory cards in remote cameras or replace solar panels and batteries that hadn't survived the harsh Antarctic winters. But, behind the scenes, Dan's role involved ensuring the continuous delivery of data from the instruments, with many hours spent staring at multiple screens and problem-solving on behalf of scientists back home as he tried to figure out why they were 'not getting any data'.

A tall, incredibly intelligent classical musician, Dan was naturally a bit shy but passionate and hardworking. When the shoot for the forty-eight-hour film festival arrived, Dan waited to see if any others were keen to take the lead. When there were no takers, he grabbed the camera and ran with it.

From the start, Dan had a plan. More than half the station was keen to get involved in some way, coming up with complicated scenes and special effects as the weekend evolved and the creative juices flowed. Dan even handed out call sheets for the day and roles such as 'gaffer' and 'key grip' were snapped up, even though none of us really knew what they entailed.

So where did we start? Like any good project, we needed a plan. We broke into groups to develop plot options and themes for the film, reconvening to debate the merits of each and decide as a collective. The weather was against us, with blizzard winds up to 172 kilometres per hour blowing outside, so it would be an indoor shoot.

We asked ourselves some key questions. What spaces did we have indoors where we could shoot and develop a story? The kitchen. And what did everyone love these days? Reality TV. And so the mockumentary TV show *Totally Cooked* was born, with elements of all the world's major cooking shows combined with ridiculous costumes, bad accents and overacting. We were on a winner for sure.

Fittingly for 2020, the awards ceremony was held online, with the world's first international Antarctic station Zoom call, complete with 'you're on mute' moments and 'can you hear me now?' every time someone tried to talk. The Australian stations, along with the French, British and a few others, had good enough internet for a jerky, low-resolution call and good audio. At the other end of the spectrum were stations that dialled in via satellite phone.

As we sat in the cinema and listened to the French MC's jokes and acknowledgements, the moment came to announce the winner of the overall best picture in the prestigious five-minute short-film category.

'And the winner is … Davis station for *Totally Cooked*!'

We jumped for joy, hugged, high-fived, spilled wine on the carpet and cheered – what a weekend! The hosts promised to send the trophy to Davis from their station at Concordia, via the French station at Dumont d'Urville and then, on their icebreaker, to Hobart, and after fourteen days of quarantine, finally to us on the next voyage to Davis. A journey of some 5000 kilometres for a trophy made of scrap plywood and spray-paint. As far as I know, it still hasn't arrived yet, but we were over the moon to have won!

* * *

Day 238: 18 June 2020
Temperature: -26.8°C to -16.9°C

On a beautiful day in mid-June, with the temperature hovering around minus 20 degrees, we decided that the chilly but windless conditions were ideal for the annual mid-winter swim. Technically the swim was not an official tradition of the Australian Antarctic Program, but for most expeditioners it was absolutely part of the winter tradition. From our team, all but three would take the plunge – which ensured we had a few dry members of the team to be safety officers and helpers.

Setting up for the swim was a process in itself. Along with a few others, I identified a patch of ice just off the station's wharf area. The wharf was now surrounded by sea ice nearly a metre thick, and you could walk out over the tide cracks and onto the frozen sea. Picking a spot close enough to the wharf but deep enough for a swim meant scouting a location about 50 metres from the shore.

We marked the place and set up the lights and paraphernalia around the site. This made it a bit more of an event and also made it easier to identify the spot again after it refroze overnight. If left unmarked and it got covered in a thin layer of snow and ice overnight, it would become a booby trap.

With everything set up, we convened in the cinema for a safety briefing from Doc on the risks associated with cold shock. The main rule – 'don't put your head straight under' – precluded entering the water via a cannonball or swan dive, but otherwise it would be a straightforward in-and-out dip.

Following the formal briefing, we were all keen to discuss the popular 'Wim Hof' benefits of cold-water immersion, and I felt a buzz of excitement around the room as we watched videos of hardcore adventurists Bear Grylls and Wim Hof in preparation.

With no drinking allowed before the event, it came down to sheer will to get yourself into the icy water. I was brimming with anticipation and excitement. We'd set up the RMIT van (an old sled-mounted caravan developed by the Royal Melbourne Institute of Technology University for polar traversing) next to the hole and cranked the heater to maximum so we'd have a 'warm' change room, heated to about 10 degrees. Inside the van felt like a sauna, though, when compared with the minus 20 degrees outside. It would also serve as a first-aid option if anyone suffered cold injuries before we could drive them back up to the station.

I wanted to be first into the water and, as no one objected to my plan, it was agreed I'd have the honour, followed by a quick-fire rotation of everyone else, finishing with Doc.

Time to go for a swim. I stepped into the RMIT van to strip down and get ready. As a giant human in a small caravan with full winter gear on, I felt cramped and awkward, and I banged my head on the low bunk a number of times as I tried to get my heavy boots and socks off. Finally, I was down to just running shorts and a pair of trainers and gloves. (We left our gloves and shoes on so our skin wouldn't stick to the metal ladder.) Over the top I added a rock-climbing harness, which was to be attached to the safety line before I went in. I exhaled, wiggled my head like a boxer before entering the ring and opened the door of the RMIT van.

Smack! The icy-cold air stole every ounce of heat my body had harnessed inside the van as my skin tightened and I saw a tell-tale cloud of fog leave my mouth with each breath. My excitement won the battle as I stepped down towards Jarrod, who would affix the safety line. I knew Jarrod could tie a figure-eight climbing knot blindfolded, but waiting for him to tie the safety line to my harness while I stood there almost naked in minus 20 degrees was probably the longest and most excruciating ten-second wait of the year.

'Good to go!' declared Jarrod as I stepped towards the ladder, which was partially submerged in the water and illuminated with underwater lights. Staring down into the water, I could see the surface trying to refreeze and krill swimming around the lights. I hoped there were no seals down there.

I remembered the warning from the briefing: no jumping. But, as every kid knows, getting into a cold swimming pool via the stairs is the worst, and an icy-cold metal ladder was no different. I didn't feel my feet entering the water as I moved down the ladder one step at a time, psyching myself up for the moment I'd slide backwards into the cold.

As soon as I was about knee-deep I let go of the ladder and slid back, feeling my whole body freeze instantly and my alertness and senses skyrocket with the sudden shock of the bitter cold. After a few seconds, I dunked my head under, surfaced and headed back to the ladder. All in all, I was in the water for twenty seconds at best and, without doubt, it was the coldest I would ever be in my life – or so I thought.

Just like getting out of a pool, it felt colder climbing out. Metres from the warmth of the RMIT van, I watched Jarrod undo the now soaking-wet rope. I laughed at myself for my earlier assertion that 'knots are safer than carabiners' for the safety line, a decision that was now costing me seconds in the cold air. But soon enough I was back inside the van and high-fiving the next swimmer on the way to their icy bath. What a rush!

With the time pressure to get through everyone quickly, I couldn't hang around in the van too long, so I got rugged up into my dry clothes and full-weight jacket and pants to stand around and watch the others. Standing still is your worst enemy when you're this cold, so I quickly took over the job of 'chief stirrer', which involved keeping the water in the hole moving so it wouldn't refreeze and fishing out the ice crust and chunks of ice that were floating around. I started to realise just how cold my fingers and toes were; I danced around and wiggled them as hard as I could, but to no avail. It would be hours until they returned to full function.

With time for a quick team photo at the end, which even included a life-size cut-out of Rocky, who should have been there for the winter, we packed up the swimming hole and headed back up to the station.

They say the best way to treat cold injuries such as frostbite is to heat up the area in warm (not hot) water for about thirty minutes, so naturally the most popular place on station right now was the hot tub[18] in the gym. By the time I got there, it had quietened down a bit and I was able to squeeze in and crack an ice-cold can of beer to celebrate the mid-winter swim's completion in style. Cheers!

* * *

Day 239: 19 June 2020
Temperature: -24.1°C to -12.1°C

---

[18] It sounds luxurious to have a hot tub on station but it was the best method for re-warming extremities after hours outside in the freezing cold.

In the days before the mid-winter dinner, we had a particularly disruptive night, with the fire alarm going off in the middle of the night in the main powerhouse. The fire alarms on station are hypersensitive and there is nowhere more important to the running of the station than the powerhouse.

I was lying in bed dreaming of a warm tropical island and clear blue skies – and then the next minute … *Briiiiiiiiiiing!* It took me a moment to adjust as I shook off my dream and realised where I was and what had woken me. The building was dark and the emergency lights were on.

'The power is out, let's go,' I said out loud to myself. In the cold of winter, we had about thirty minutes to get the power restored or manually fire up the emergency powerhouse before all the pipes across station froze, expanded and cracked beyond repair, but first we mustered.

My job was to ensure everyone was accounted for and we understood where the problem was, so I couldn't waste any time getting to the muster station in the mess.

Pulling on my clothes, I heard the heavy fire doors opening and closing as the team made their way sleepily across the linkway and down to the mess. I arrived, grabbed the muster list, glanced at the board and started ticking names off the list. 'All on station,' I told myself as I watched the fire team help each other put on heavy breathing apparatus and masks over their firefighting overalls and jackets.

The on-call sparkie stared at the fire alarm panel and confirmed: it was the main powerhouse. Lewis overheard and added himself to the first response as we needed to get the power back up asap. In an emergency, it's important to focus on your job and not get in the way of others doing theirs – micromanagement can be disastrous – so I quickly ran through the basics with the fire chief as he headed up the hill to the powerhouse.

'All accounted for on station. Let me know what you see when you're up there but obviously getting power back up is key,' I said, having completed the muster as everyone else sat down in the mess or radioed in as they arrived at other locations around the station.

One of our Hägglunds was a firefighting vehicle, the bright-red Fire Hägg, always on standby and specially equipped with hoses, spare breathing apparatus, air tanks and extinguishers, as well as maps and schematics of the buildings. As part of the drill, the designated Fire Hägg driver and one other would muster at the vehicle shed to start the Fire Hägg and meet them on the scene. I directed the driver over the radio to meet the fire chief at the powerhouse.

I stayed at the communications desk with the rest of the team as the fire crew moved the 70 metres up the hill past the unoccupied summer accommodation buildings to the powerhouse. The fire chief reported back: 'No flames and no smoke, engines are all shutdown, permission to enter? Over.' This all but confirmed it was a false alarm.

'Copy that, head on in, let me know what the mechanics say about firing it up,' I replied, knowing it was now critical to get the system back online. The fire chief explained that the sprinkler hadn't triggered, so it looked like it was an auto shutdown. The smoke detection system had triggered and caused the shutdown but didn't reach the threshold to fire the high-pressure sprinkler systems, which was good news and meant they'd have it back up and running shortly. This wasn't uncommon around the station, and the system was extremely sensitive for good reason, but looking at my watch and noting it was now 0300, I wasn't exactly singing the praises of the hypersensitive system.

'False alarm, back to bed and see you all in the morning,' I said to the crowd in the mess, some of whom were contemplating heading to the gym or starting work early as they were wide awake. I had a quick chat with Rhonda while making a cup of tea – later, we would get started on planning the extravagant mid-winter feast we'd be enjoying in the coming days. I then headed out the door towards the main powerhouse.

There was a gaggle of expeditioners dressed in fire gear standing outside around the intake vents as I approached, and even in the darkness and blowing snow I could tell from their body language and figures that they were Gaz and Lewis pointing and theorising.

'What's the cause?' I said, sneaking up behind them in the darkness.

'Watch the snow coming down from above and the small bits of soot,' said Gaz, and I craned my neck towards the roof of the powerhouse and the exhaust cowls. I could see the snow and flecks of soot swirling back down and being sucked into the air intakes of the powerhouse.

This was one of those moments where Mother Nature had simply outsmarted us. In the summertime, with ample clearance between the buildings and the ground, this had never occurred, but, over winter, snow had accumulated between the building and below the air intakes, which, combined with the strong wind, was pushing the exhaust downward and into the air intake. This may or may not have been the cause, but we had to rule it out and get shovelling.

Inside, the electricians and mechanics were searching for other explanations or causes. At the same time they had already fired up the powerhouse so we wouldn't freeze. I had a quick chat to the sparkie, but as it was creeping towards 0330 he was keen to get all systems online and call it a night. I agreed. These false alarms were often tricky to pin down to an exact cause, as opposed to more obvious faults such as powerboards or heating elements shorting out.

I wandered back down with the last remnants of the fire team as we left Lewis and a sparkie to monitor things a little longer. As we sat down for a cup of tea, the mood was flat and exhausted. Everyone responds differently to alarms. Some can simply switch off and head back to sleep, others remain hypervigilant for hours afterwards and need to debrief and talk through the events. We'd had plenty of false alarms by now; in fact, with an average of one a month, we rarely ran fire drills and could focus our monthly fire training on practical or technical elements of the response.

At around 0400, I headed back to bed. Lewis and the sparkie were back too, and would try for a few hours' rest before returning to work. Ideally, they'd take a late start and get a good rest, but this was where theory and practice often disagreed. With limited trades on station to manage the complex systems, taking a day off really just meant you'd have to work twice as hard the next day. Knowing that we had mid-winter's day coming up and a low-tempo couple of days off after that, it was better to find the exact cause of the alarm now and enjoy mid-winter without the fear of another alarm waking us all up the next night.

We were becoming so used to emergency procedures and drills

that they were second nature. Each time the alarm rang, the team handled the emergency response calmly and methodically, often adjusting on the fly. If one team member was late to muster, another would step up and take over. It was reassuring that we were good in an emergency.

Weeks later, we found the cause and rectified it: an exhaust pipe in the powerhouse had been spontaneously opening a valve and sending a small puff of exhaust inside the building, which was just enough to set off the alarm. After that, we never had another powerhouse fire alarm.

* * *

Day 241: 21 June 2020 (Mid-winter's day)
Temperature: -19.7°C to -5.1°C

Mathematically, we were well past the halfway point of our season but, psychologically, mid-winter's day marks the turning point. The winter solstice in Antarctica is a unique experience that few get the privilege to enjoy. Steeped in tradition and a welcome distraction from the darkness and bitter cold, it was the most formal dinner of the year. I hadn't seen the kitchen this busy since summertime, with Rhonda dictating how to plate up the hors d'oeuvres and arrange the shrimp cocktails or watching the slushy work frantically to keep ahead of the pile of dishes.

We'd decided to move the dining room upstairs for the occasion, so a team of helpers was decorating the tables with the finest silverware we could find and ironing tablecloths and laying out menus. To add a level of elegance never before seen at Davis, Bob had carved two ornate ice penguins to be the centrepiece of the table. Having never worked with ice sculpture before, Bob had done an incredible job and it really completed the Antarctic vibe of the table.

Rhonda had also prepared an array of cakes and desserts that would be set up secretly in the cinema, for a big reveal later that night. This would feature caricature miniature penguins of each of us standing around the Davis street sign to recreate our station photo. Each penguin had a telltale identifier, from our favourite beanies to my radio, along with miniature Häggs and station paraphernalia.

Another tradition was for everyone to receive a winter memento, which was ordinarily a replica vintage ice axe. Wanting to make sure people were happy with this choice, I'd cast a ballot for ideas. I soon learned how the United Kingdom's new icebreaker, the *Sir David Attenborough*, had originally been named *Boaty McBoatface* by the public.

'What's a kazoo?' I asked the leader of the 'Kazoos not ice axes' campaign.

'One of those little buzzing things – you blow into it like a pipe and it makes a bzzzzzzzz noise,' replied Mr Kazoo.

'That's what you want to commemorate your Antarctic winter? Instead of a replica ice axe engraved with Davis 2020?' I replied, still bemused.

'Well, you can't argue with democracy,' replied Mr Kazoo, knowing it had won a good number of votes in the ballot.

I was pretty sure that, down the track, a replica ice axe would better commemorate our Antarctic experience, so I needed a new plan.

I found Gaz and offered up my limited trade skills. 'Can you make enough ice axes and kazoos to keep everyone happy and end this saga?' I asked, expecting that he'd need to work overtime to produce them all.

'Leave it with me. Once we're set up I can make enough – they're pretty easy to do,' said Gaz. We were standing in the carpentry workshop surrounded by power tools and half-finished hobby projects. A handmade surfboard took pride of place among the usual picture frames and bottle openers we made using scrap timber.

'I love democracy,' I said as I walked off, regretting the decision to take votes.

* * *

With preparations done, we gathered for pre-dinner drinks at Nina's bar. The station bar was named Nina's after the last husky to leave Davis nearly thirty years before. Adorned with black-and-white portraits of Antarctic heroes of yesteryear and with an antique wooden sled hanging above the bar, it looked every bit how you'd expect an Antarctic bar to look. In the total darkness of mid-winter's day, time was irrelevant, so we gathered at 1600 in our finest attire to celebrate.

To add a bit of history to the day, we accepted an invitation from the ANARE Club to join them in a Zoom call they were having in lieu of their annual dinner. The ANARE Club was much like a 'returned services league' of Australian National Antarctic Research Expedition veterans, where expeditioners of yesteryear gathered to remember their time down south. It was a clear reminder of how lucky we were to be having a dinner with twenty-four people when many Australians and friends around the world were still banned from going to indoor gatherings and events like this.

Our tech guru had set up cameras and a screen in Nina's and we dialled in and saw the *Brady Bunch* Zoom windows of the ANARE Club members online. I opened with a spiel about Davis station and our winter projects, and explained briefly that we were still not sure how we'd be getting home but, all going well, we'd be back by Christmas 2020.

One of the old-timers was quick off the mark to respond.

'We never knew how we'd get home in 1987 at Macquarie Island when the *Nella Dan* sank either!' he said, reminding us that being stuck in Antarctica was not unheard of.

Back in 1987, while resupplying the sub-Antarctic Macquarie Island, the ship *Nella Dan* had run aground. The passengers were all taken ashore to Macquarie and watched as their ship sank into the depths of the Southern Ocean. The island is a few days' sail from Tasmania, so they were stuck until they could be rescued.

We heard a few more anecdotes from the Antarctic veterans, then moved on. This link back home and to the history of Antarctica broke up the evening with some new faces, broadening our network beyond the same crowd we had dinner with each night. We played messages from Governor-General David Hurley, Minister for the Environment Sussan Ley and the AAD's director, Kim Ellis, but there was one surprise that made us all miss home just a little more than we expected.

In the lead-up to mid-winter, families, friends and random

celebrities were invited to send written or video messages to the wintering teams. Standing around Nina's we all watched as the videos played, showing families gathered at home surrounded by dogs and children and green grass. The bar was silent. When one of the lads broke the silence saying, 'I'm not crying, you're crying,' we laughed, but he was right.

Resetting the mood, a surprise celebrity message played from Australia's most famous equine songster, Daryl Braithwaite, who'd taken the time to send us a message wishing us a happy mid-winter. 'Thanks, Daryl. Play "Horses"!' we all chanted, and soon his hit song was played on repeat.

I'd also taken time to print out messages from families and others who'd written to us celebrating mid-winter and wishing us a safe return home in a few months. The prime ministers of Australia and New Zealand, Scott Morrison, or 'Scomo' as he's known, and Jacinda Ardern, had taken the time to reply to my invitation to dinner but were both too busy dealing with the pandemic to attend. Her Majesty the Queen only accepts written invitations and, without any means of outgoing mail until the next flight in October, she never received her invite and didn't attend either.

Rhonda prepared a special menu, including prime cuts of beef, rack of lamb, oysters, lobster salad and pork belly. Why would you go out when you could dine like this in Antarctica? For one night of the year, every option was available and, similar to how you feel on Christmas Day, the struggle became finding room for seconds and thirds. With our bellies full, it was time for the formalities of the evening.

'As always, thanks, Rhonda, and those who helped prepare the feast and set up the room for tonight,' I opened and led a round of applause to everyone, as there had been no idle hands preparing such an extravagant event.

'Tonight, we join the long history of those who have had the honour of wintering in Antarctica. As a team of strangers 241 days ago, we sailed south into the unknown, and as we've endured the year of challenges and uncertainty we can now look forward to the beginning of the end. In a few weeks we'll head up and collect the snow groomers from Whoop Whoop and start building the runway ahead of the first flights in October. We are past the halfway point and the darkest days are behind us. Each day the sun will shine for longer and the weather will improve as the summer returns. It's my honour to lead the station, and I thank each of you for your hard work and dedication. To Davis station! Cheers!'

We raised a toast and then I introduced the surprise act of the evening. 'Now, to recite an original poetic verse, ladies and gentlemen, the Doc.'

The scandalous content of the poem he regaled us with about the story of our journey and the realities of life on an Antarctic station shall not be repeated, save for those who were there to witness the reading, but here is how it ended:

> But from this day forth the sun will rise
> Each day gone by be brighter
> May your yearnings for home, your family and friends
> Become a little lighter
> Breathe the air, face the breeze
> Observe the snow that patters

For Antarctica will watch us go
So be conscious of what matters
Look after one another
Be joyous, gentle and kind
Let's make the type of memories
That will never leave our mind
Out of the dark, mid-winter gone
We shall look on in adoration
And be proud of what we have done
To have wintered at Davis station

—Doc, 21 June 2020, Davis station, Antarctica

As I went to bed that night, I was happy. Everything so far had gone to plan and we were more than halfway done. Ahead of us was the downhill stretch, preparing the station for the upcoming summer season. Collectively, we all felt the hardest part was over. We could see the light at the end of the tunnel, with the first flights in just a few months' time that would signal the beginning of the end and our ticket home.

But that was all about to change.

Chapter 6

The Bombshell

Day 243: 23 June 2020
Temperature: -16.6°C to -7.3°C
Days until expected return: 131

With mid-winter fresh in our minds, we returned to work after a well-deserved day off. Scrolling through the usual overnight emails, I saw a meeting request for 1000 hours with Rick back in Kingston – nothing out of the ordinary, as we spoke most days in one way or another and had recently transitioned from quite a formal message tone to including the odd emoji.

One positive from the pandemic's impact was that our meetings were now via video, as the AAD was forced to flexible work-from-home arrangements. This often meant that, instead of sitting in the AAD's operations room, Rick was in his spare bedroom, and would occasionally drop out or freeze as his kids hogged the wi-fi while homeschooling.

The meeting started pleasantly, discussing the joys of swimming in minus-20-degree temperatures and the accompanying hot tub or sauna afterwards, but soon moved to the more serious issues at hand. Over the last few months, Rick and I had talked through contingencies and operational options for the season ahead, and now the writing was on the wall. It was becoming increasingly unlikely there would be a safe way of getting my team out of Davis in 2020 and we'd face the challenge of remaining for a second summer season, well beyond the twelve months we'd signed up for. So I asked the million-dollar question: 'Are we going home in November?'

Out of options, having searched far and wide for an icebreaker and found nothing, the only way we could go home in November was via our aircraft, which were based in Canada and needed to make their way to Antarctica.

With COVID-19 spreading rapidly across the globe, particularly in the USA and South America, the planes and their crews would be forced into fourteen-day quarantine stops in between each country, which made the ordinarily routine flight path from the Northern Hemisphere a nightmare. There were limited options to access Antarctica from South America and make the jump across the Drake Passage to the British airstrip at Rothera station on the Antarctic Peninsula, and they were carefully managing the number of flights they would allow to ensure their station remained COVID-free. Even if the planes could get to Rothera, they then needed to fly via the US station at the South Pole to Australian territory, and the US were being equally strict about access to the South Pole for the same reason.

Rick inhaled slowly before delivering the news with a hint of trepidation in his voice. 'Sorry, mate, no flights in November, and the *Everest* will have to do a Casey resupply before they can come to Davis in early 2021 or Casey will run out of fuel.'

Rick was a former station leader and one of the few people who understood the gravity of the situation we faced. Enduring an Antarctic winter is hard enough without it being extended or watching the world grapple with a global pandemic.

'An extra six months? This is going to devastate the team – we were so close to going home,' I replied flatly, still contemplating the reality of the situation.

This would be far longer than any team had remained isolated in modern Antarctic history, but then, as we all knew, 2020 was a year for the unprecedented. All the permanent Antarctic stations were established after the Second World War, so there had never been a global pandemic in the modern age of Antarctic operations.

'How are you for food and fuel?' asked Rick, knowing the stations were oversupplied for contingencies such as this. Casey was the exception: the largest of the Aussie stations, it required refuelling every season but its closer proximity to Australia and easily navigable approach made this an acceptable risk.

'I'll double-check the figures, but in terms of food, fuel and fresh water we can survive into 2021 without serious rationing. Beyond that, we'd have to look at abandoning buildings and reducing power usage. It's the human factor that will be the issue,' I replied. Being fed and warm was one thing; missing a second Christmas away from families back home, especially as they were dealing with a global pandemic, was another.

We discussed the best way to break it to the team and ultimately decided it would be me who delivered the news. This would be followed by formal communication from the director shortly after.

'We will be okay but, I won't lie, some are really going to struggle with this. We were counting the days until that first flight,' I said to Rick. After saying goodbye, we closed the video and I was left standing there alone in my office.

I stared out the window towards the icebergs and across the ocean, remembering what it looked like when the *Aurora Australis* was parked in the ice during resupply and when the planes had been taking off and landing right out front. It would be a long time until either of those scenes was possible again. The now tattered Australian flag was waving in the dim winter's light, an ominous reminder of the effects of spending your days being battered by Antarctica's harsh conditions.

Rick was just the messenger for a collective decision involving the AAD weighing up the risks and options, and, really, there was no other decision to be made. We were forced into the decision by the circumstances: the unavailability of icebreakers and the inability of our aircraft to fly via North, Central and South America during the now-raging pandemic. There were no aircraft in Australia or New Zealand capable of making direct flights to Davis and, with each international Antarctic program focused on their own stations, we were out of options. I resigned myself to the news and started thinking about the road ahead.

I walked into the kitchen just after smoko and could still smell the hot dogs and other comfortingly warm food served daily from 1000. Smoko was everyone's favourite meal. Rhonda had a sixth sense and even the best poker player on station couldn't get past her. I was no exception; she read me like a book and knew what I was about to say.

'We're staying a second summer,' I said.

'Bugger, what did they say?' replied Rhonda. I could see her mind already calculating how to start rationing our supplies until the end.

I went through the conversation with Rick and the different options they'd looked at, with ultimately the best option being to leave us here. There was some good news. Kingston seemed to understand the situation and the impact it would have on the team, and from then on Rhonda and I started thinking about how we might change the station community to get us through the season ahead.

Staring silently at each other for a moment – we were lost for words – we then hugged, as we often did at the lowest points of the year. There was no hiding my emotions: my tone was flat, my shoulders drooped and my eyes stared off into space. I was preoccupied with what was to come. Starved for physical contact on station, often the simplest of physical gestures like a good old hug reminded me that, although we all worked together, we were becoming a family.

Contemplating the worst-case scenarios ahead, I walked over to the noticeboard and wrote, 'Station meeting after dinner – cinema'. Calling a meeting sooner wouldn't change much. Holding the meeting after dinner meant there were no competing events and gave me a chance to let the word out beforehand to a few of the team who would be worst affected. Some would have to reschedule their weddings, and others were now desperate to support family members grieving and experiencing the realities of life back home. By the time the meeting came around that night, I felt ready to rip off the bandaid and get on with it.

For the first time in a long time, everyone was on time and sat nervously in the cinema's leather swivel chairs. Some had a glass of wine, some had tea. Some chit-chatted while others looked at their phones, distracted and distant from the room itself.

'I'll just get straight to the point – there are no flights this season. We'll be staying for summer and heading home via ship in early 2021,' I said, laying the facts out cold.

The words hung in the air as everyone digested the news. I wasn't sure how the team would react and watched their facial expressions and heard sighs. As thoughts gave way to words, responses ranged from 'knew it' to 'the world is going crazy anyway' – but the most commonplace response was stunned silence. There was nothing we could do about it, and the mood quickly turned to more practical questions.

The meeting was over quickly, and the majority of us sat around afterwards for a frank but constructive discussion about what the second summer might look like. I noticed a few disappear to their rooms to jump straight on the phone to their loved ones. This was the hardest part about news like this. Before we ventured south, we'd all thought we'd be home by the end of 2020, but, through no fault of our own, that plan had now become a promise to wives, husbands, children, girlfriends, boyfriends, dogs, cats and families that we simply couldn't keep.

That night, after the meeting, we watched *The Martian*, starring Matt Damon in yet another role where governments spend millions of dollars and efforts to rescue him, this time from Mars. As the movie unfolded, he was left stranded on the red planet while NASA worked out how to get him.

During a scene where scientists and administrators debated the various rockets and options available before he ran out of food or went crazy, one of the lads joked, 'The AAD right now trying to work out how to get us!' We all laughed but, with the AAD trying to manage resupplying the Antarctic stations, keep them all COVID-free and getting the RSV *Nuyina* online, it wasn't far from the truth. I didn't envy their position.

* * *

It took a few days for everyone to come to terms with the news. Like the stages of grief, each expeditioner's response was human and understandable. But what about my own thoughts? I was in the privileged position of knowing the intricate details and the sheer lack of options, but was this what I'd signed up for? I'd been happy to stay on for a second summer if they could only do a limited changeout, but I didn't want to lead a team of people who didn't want to be here.

I did a lot of soul searching and contemplating as I considered the situation I was faced with. I'd expected a challenge, but recent developments had taken it far beyond anything I'd considered. Watching the world unravel back home wasn't helping the lack of certainty. If we extended for another summer, what if the world got even worse? Would it turn into a second winter?

I wasn't getting any younger either, and had told myself this would be my last big overseas gig for a while before settling down in Melbourne and reconnecting with my family after nearly a decade overseas, and now that would be even further delayed. On the plus side, from what I could tell of life back home with lockdowns and international borders being closed, I probably wasn't missing much. If I tried to look on the bright side, being stuck in Antarctica wasn't a bad option.

The next morning, I headed out for a walk around the station and along Dingle Road, one of the few routes you can wander alone. As I meandered along the rocky and frozen road, I resigned myself to the realities of what lay ahead. Metaphorically, wandering alone along Dingle Road captured the essence of how I was feeling inside, but I knew I didn't have an option beyond facing the situation head on. Fate had dealt me a leadership challenge unheard of in modern Antarctic history, and I decided then and there that I would rise to that challenge and seek out the positive experiences to be had on even the hardest days. This was my only option.

My newfound positive outlook didn't always rub off on the team, though, and things were about to go downhill fast as those who were desperate to go home turned their anger towards me.

Later in the day I headed to the gym to let off some steam with a simple but fast-paced circuit I'd developed with the space and weights available. Entering the gym a little later than I'd planned, I found a few regulars there already, getting a workout in during the golden hour before dinner. I could feel their eyes on me and almost hear the questions in their minds as we all silently worked out in our own zones and tried to escape in our heads.

Although some days I felt like just another gym user, today was not one of those days, and moments like this reminded me just how cramped our living arrangements really were. Everyone was trying to find a method to deal with the longer stay, but in such close quarters it was impossible to get space from each other.

* * *

A few days later, once the dust had seemingly settled a bit, we had our weekly station meeting. These were ordinarily pretty dry affairs and I disliked them as much as the next person as I waffled on about the upcoming week and everyone else added their ten cents. Often the most entertaining moments came when someone aired a hilarious grievance. Recently someone raised a complaint about an unknown nail clipper who had been cutting their toenails in the music lounge and leaving the cuttings on the floor. But a few meetings were more memorable than that.

The air was thick with anger. As we went around the room for questions there was a tense silence until finally someone said what was on many people's minds: 'Why are we hearing this from you? What are they doing about this? They can't just extend us without asking. We signed up for twelve months and this is ridiculous!'

'I don't like it any more than you do,' I said, trying to unify our predicament. The blame game was about to begin.

'Why have they just left you to tell us this news? Where's the sorry? What are they doing to acknowledge this?' continued the crowd. The planned follow-up video call had been delayed, and I sat there facing a barrage of questions about a decision I hadn't made.

Their anger was understandable. I felt similarly but it wasn't my position to vent and throw blame. The time lag between the bad news and the formal communication from the director and operations team was too long. This had been to ensure that the team on the ground heard the news first, so it didn't leak down through the backchannels of Kingston or administrative mistakes … but was there really a better way to deliver such heavy news? Would hearing it via a bad video link have been the solution? No amount of 'sorry' or video calls, or letters from politicians, would change the fact we were stuck here.

Why was I getting this grief? I hadn't made the decision. I wrapped up the meeting with a poignant statement that would go on to be my mantra around the extension: 'At the end of the day we're all in the same boat, and that boat gets here next year.'

I was sick of being the face of this. I pointed a few of the team towards the phone to call the director of the AAD and ask him why they changed the plan. This was the closest I'd ever felt to fronting an angry press conference about lockdowns or quarantine rules. It was important to not lose my cool.

Over the coming days I struggled to separate my own emotions and ego from the negative responses and blame game. People were right to be angry, and this was tough news to manage. Now more than ever, I felt all eyes directed at me to solve the problems ahead. It would be up to me to lead the team through this.

* * *

There was always a plan for the AAD director or Rick or someone on a video conference to answer everyone's questions. The problem was they were busy actually managing the AAD's response to the pandemic. By the time we got the video call set up between Kingston and the station, things had cooled down a bit and most of the crowd sat silently in the room and listened as the video feed cut in and out over the patchy internet connection.

There was one big win. Working Saturday mornings had long been begrudged by every expeditioner in the program but was set in stone with an ironclad rule for all stations. Finally, we were able to have this opened to discussion and removed as a requirement for the second summer, to enable a more sustained work tempo as fatigue and exhaustion wore us down.

What did I learn from all this? Delivering bad news to people who don't want to accept it will never go well, no matter how you do it. Those who had taken their frustration out on me sat silently when given the opportunity to speak to the people who had actually made the call. It was in these moments I had to detach myself from my position and realise that if venting their frustration at me got it out of their system and helped them move on, then I wouldn't take it personally.

By the next week, I was hell-bent on making the most of this situation and delivered the revised season outlook to the team via a town-hall session on ideas and options for the road ahead. Flexibility with work hours and pace was on the table, provided we didn't compromise capability, but the bigger win was the additional long weekends in November for everyone to get out and enjoy the best of the peak sea ice and better weather. All in all, the prevailing concept was that, since the situation had taken something from us, it was time to get something back – and we needed this win.

The other major win, which slipped by quietly and met strange resistance from a minority, was an agreement to allow people to undertake online or remote training, with the AAD footing the bill and their supervisors allowing reasonable study time during work hours. Almost half the station quickly signed up for remote courses, from building and electrical certificates to business units and the theoretical components of a marine coxswain's certificate.

These were welcome distractions and kept us busy as the time rolled on.

From here on, things were different; we were headed into overtime and I knew we would all be facing a challenge far beyond what we had signed up for.

Chapter 7

When the Novelty Wears Off

Day 331: 19 September 2020
Temperature: -15.8°C to-14.1°C

Although many were still grappling with the impact of the delay to their return to Australia, more pressing matters required our attention. The sun had returned and, as the days got longer, the clock was ticking on the sea-ice season.

Sea ice reaches its peak growth around October–November but it wasn't quite as thick as expected for mid-September, at 110 centimetres, along the coast to Bandits and Whoop Whoop. Historically it had been a bit thicker but it was time to retrieve the snow groomers from Whoop Whoop and bring them back to the station for servicing and what would usually be the preparation of the sea-ice runway. Once we had them back on station we'd get on with refilling the station tarn. But first, the groomers.

Abandoned each summer at Whoop Whoop after the sea ice has closed, the two snow groomers are the backbone of the capability to build runways. Without them, it would be almost impossible to prepare a safe ice runway on the sea ice or at Whoop Whoop. Some of the aircraft can land anywhere it's relatively flat, but the risks of hitting unseen obstacles is high. Antarctica has a long history of aviation incidents on unprepared airstrips causing damage to the aircraft's skis and undercarriage, which is not ideal when there are no workshops around. There's nothing particularly special about the groomers – they're exactly the same machines that drive up and down ski slopes to create a nice smooth surface.

The plan to retrieve the groomers was simple. A team of six would set off, with four of us headed to Whoop Whoop and two who'd stay at Bandits Hut as back-up.

Abandoning the groomers for the long Antarctic winter isn't altogether bad for the machinery. With the right preparation, the vehicles should fire up with a new battery and some mechanical know-how from the mechanics. The unknown was how much snow and ice had accumulated around the vehicle tracks and made its way inside every opening. I'd never realised how sneaky and persistent snow was until I'd seen just how much blizz can sneak through one tiny gap in a door seal or window and then, after weeks and months of blowing snow, fill the entire void with snow and ice.

Our best estimate of our workload was based on the last visit to Whoop Whoop back in June, when there was some accumulation but not too much, so we figured it would take about a day's work to clear. The plan was an early start from the station, drive to Whoop Whoop, dig out the groomers, get them going, stay the night there to consolidate a few things, then drive back at first light the second day. The days were still a bit shorter than normal so light was an issue and, as soon as darkness fell, working outside in minus 15 degrees would become difficult. We all agreed that a two-day operation was the best way to safely crack this egg.

Weather would play a major role and the Weather Magician

gave us a comprehensive briefing before we left. The forecast was alright but not amazing. There was a clear window of about seventy-two hours to complete a forty-eight-hour task, but there was a blizzard on the horizon. Even so, we all agreed it was safe to go.

I'd lead the trip, but Lewis and second mechanic were the key players in the whole operation. Much like the separation of church and state, I've always believed in separation of technical and operational leadership. Moments before heading out, though, I had an odd sense there was an alternative theory on the best way for this trip to be structured and was quietly informed from the sidelines. Expeditioners who were not even involved felt that the overall lead should reside with the mechanics and not me or Jarrod, the field training officer, who was also on the trip but would remain at Bandits.

This pissed me off no end. This was just another comment from sideline experts on everything from building design to project priorities, vehicle maintenance schedules, meal times and now field operations. After nearly a year away, everyone was now scrutinising those above, below and around them, looking for faults. It was downright exhausting, and I wasn't the only one feeling it.

As always, the last thing I did before we left was pop into the kitchen and confirm the handover arrangements with Rhonda and run her through our reporting schedule for the trip. She could sense my frustration as I entered the mess to turn the tags.

'What's up?' Rhonda asked, not even batting an eyelid as she read my body language.

'Just more sideline experts commenting on how we should be doing this job,' I replied.

'Happens every year about this time, once the novelty wears off,' offered Rhonda to help calm me down.

With her previous winter season experience and sixth sense for community sentiment, Rhonda was usually on the money. The two of us couldn't have been more opposite in many ways but our shared goal of getting this community through to the end was ironclad.

'It's pretty straightforward. If the weather holds, we'll see you tomorrow night,' I concluded and moved towards the fire tags, turned the convoy's tags to red, double-checked our estimated return information, then turned around and made my way through the two sets of doors between the warmth of the mess and the outside.

Making my way down the metal staircase and around the towering snowdrift we had to navigate to get to the road, I gave a thumbs-up to the second Hägg and jumped into the lead Hägg, grabbing the handset.

'VLZ Davis, VLZ Davis, this is the Whoop Whoop party of the Blue and Red Häggs leaving station, next call one hour or when off the sea ice.'

'Copy that, stay safe and speak to you in one hour. VLZ Davis standing by,' replied Rhonda from her radio in the kitchen. The comms would transfer to the comms tech later in the day as arranged. The comms tech's main role was to maintain the satellite link to Kingston and keep the wi-fi on, but they filled in as the comms operator as well from time to time.

We had driven to Bandits numerous times now throughout the year and it was becoming routine. Two weeks earlier, we had made the same run up the coast, taking LPG bottles to the huts ahead of the summer, to map out the safest route between the icebergs and store it in the GPS units of both Häggs so we knew exactly where we were going. Ordinarily it's easy enough to turn around if you can't find a path but, because we were towing sleds behind the Häggs and were going to need efficiency with the groomers on the return run, it was important to have a well-mapped route. This also meant that even if we lost visibility in a blizzard out on the sea ice, we'd slow down but would be able to keep going on the same route. If there is one place you do not want to be in a blizzard, it's on the sea ice.

The run to Bandits took about two hours and once we got there we checked the gear had survived being rattled around on the sled and in the back cabins before leaving Jarrod and buddy at Bandits to wait with the Red Hägg. The next day, they'd meet us where the sea ice met the rocks on the way to Whoop Whoop.

This was the figurative halfway point, one of a series of waypoints along the well-trodden route. The halfway point was also an alternative helipad in the summertime if the team at Whoop Whoop couldn't be reached due to blizzard conditions on the plateau. The closer to sea level you were, the better the weather often was. It wasn't uncommon to have blizzard conditions at Whoop Whoop but blue skies along the coast.

As we reached the last waypoint before arrival at Whoop Whoop, I could start to see the outlines of the buildings. At first it was just a glimpse of small shapes on the barren white horizon and then individual buildings and the vehicles. But as we got closer, I could see the colours of the containerised accommodation, workshop and rows of aviation fuel lined up in 44-gallon drums, all colour-coded for their year of production.

We arrived in good time and would have the better part of the afternoon's sun to get to work and be done by dinnertime. The bad news was there was a *lot* of snow and ice around the groomers.

Digging out a vehicle buried under fresh snow was a common requirement on station, and rarely difficult. What I wasn't expecting, though, was that up at Whoop Whoop, the sun beaming down on the black tracks of the groomers over months had melted the snow, which had then refrozen – the tracks were now trapped in ice.

Despite early progress to access the battery compartments and top of the tracks, we then hit layers of rock-solid ice, which had locked the groomers firmly in place. Thus began the painfully slow excavation using picks, ice axes and shovels, all the while making sure to not damage the groomers or accidently sever a hydraulic line. This was good old-fashioned hard work.

As Lewis focused on the technical side of things, Jimbo and I got digging. We rotated the roles where possible and found a balance between the backbreaking excavation and more nuanced and delicate jobs like digging your hand around inside the air intakes and fan blades to remove snow. Without air flowing into the engines and over the radiators, the groomers could still overheat, despite the cold, so it was important to make sure there were no clumps of ice blocking anything up. I soon learned that it was easier to take my gloves off and just get in there with a bare hand and feel around – this of course was followed by quickly putting my gloves back on and trying to get blood flowing again.

I had started to consider my body's blood as radiator fluid, and was always amazed by how quickly my extremities could reheat when my body's core temperature was high. If I stood around and worried about my cold hands, they would remain cold, but grabbing a shovel and working hard digging snow and ice in a thick jacket would raise my core temperature and I'd soon be sweating and removing layers from my core and – ta-dah! – warm hands.

By 1830 hours it was time to make the scheduled radio call (known as a sked) back to station with an update: 'VLZ Davis, VLZ Davis, this is the Whoop Whoop party. We've got one groomer almost free and they're both running but just frozen solid to the plateau. We'll be at it for a few more hours to get them both free, then move a few things around to prepare for tomorrow, over,' I told Rhonda.

'Copy all that – do you want to do another sked later tonight?'

Knowing she'd be keen to get to bed early and stick to her routine, I replied, 'Yes, but no need for a formal sked. You can knock off and just let us know who's manning the comms.'

'No worries. Bob will take over comms for the night and he'll chat to you later.'

'Cool, Whoop Whoop party out.'

The groomer job was important but so was managing people's routines and making sure we didn't keep more people awake than necessary.

The problem was making sure someone was listening if we had any trouble, but managing reception around station for VHF comms to Whoop Whoop was an art. There was a main comms console in the mess and another in the operations building, so raising someone during the day was easy. At night, though, someone had to sleep with their ears open on the right channel if we needed them.

Nine times out of then this was me, and there was a radio base station hardwired into my room for this reason. There was also a satellite phone system, so in an emergency we could call anyone on Earth for help, or an individual's room on station to raise the alarm, but nice clear VHF radio comms were the easiest for routine operations. Tonight, though, Bob would be our man.

We kept working under the running lights of the groomers as 2100 hours came and went, with pitch-darkness all around us. We were on the verge of exhaustion. There's nothing like completing a task for a dopamine hit, though, and the elation and relief we felt after nearly ten hours of digging and excavation was incredible. 'Finally!' We celebrated and danced around as we freed the second of the two groomers from its frozen bed on the Antarctic Plateau and moved it to a parking spot near the accommodation to be shut down overnight, ready for the return trip.

We crammed into one of the two accommodation sleds as a team of four to have a quick meeting and meal before hitting the sack. We were tired but had achieved everything we needed to.

I updated the team on the latest weather report that had been sent through earlier. 'The forecast was for the blizzard to reach the plateau late tomorrow afternoon, which still gives us plenty of time to get back down the hill to Bandits, meet the other Hägg and return to station as planned by dinnertime.'

There were no questions. It was late and we were knackered, so we finished our dehydrated meals and fell asleep.

* * *

The howling wind woke me before any alarm could have a chance as the shipping container accommodation sled created a full range of musical notes from growls to whistles as it rattled in the katabatic winds whipping downhill from the South Pole some 2000 kilometres further south and elevated at 2835m above sea level. I could faintly hear the sound of an engine in between gusts, which meant the mechanics were already warming up the groomers for the run home.

As I was getting ready to venture outside and see where things were at, Lewis burst into the hut, holding onto the door so the wind wouldn't rip it off.

'She's blowing already out there!' He laughed.

'Groomers running already, then?' I asked.

'One is; the other isn't playing ball. We're trying to set up a generator to warm the engine block but the generator is also frozen.'

'Grim. Let's do what we can to get packed up and ready then and hope the weather eases off a bit,' I said.

'Agree, let's get out of here.' He headed back out the door, holding on tight as it swung hard in the raging wind. An experienced mechanic who used profanity as punctuation, he knew more about snow groomers and Antarctic aviation than anyone on station so his motivation to get moving that morning told me he was worried.

It was 0600 hours and there was only a faint hint of light coming through the clouds and blowing snow obstructing our view, but we worked with head torches in the dim light as we prepared to leave. Everything in Antarctica takes longer than you expect and, with the weather not letting up, we battled cold hands and biting wind as we tried to keep our backs against it. Lashing down equipment to the sleds that would be towed behind the groomers took about an hour, and finally the two groomers and the Blue Hägg were ready.

I radioed back to station and the team at Bandits that we'd aim to meet them halfway to Bandits in about two hours and head back as a convoy from there. When I informed Rhonda that the weather was getting rapidly worse at Whoop Whoop, the message that 'it's glorious here at Davis' was a welcome ray of light in our cold and bleak surroundings.

With a blizzard howling behind us and the mechanics driving the groomers and heavy sleds cautiously over the bumpy terrain, we were barely making 10 kilometres per hour downhill. I was riding shotgun with Jimbo in the Blue Hägg out front, and we kept a continual flow of communications back and forth to ensure the spacing and course were right.

Conditions were now a complete whiteout, with visibility almost zero. I had to squint to make out the vehicles. The rear-vison mirrors of the Hägg were covered in snow and useless. The wiper blades couldn't keep up as the snow seemed to be coming from all directions. A few months earlier we'd trained for this situation by blocking the windscreen with a foam mat and driving blind with just a GPS screen and the dashboard to guide us. I had a strange sense of satisfaction that this odd training requirement we hoped never to need was, in fact, quite relevant to our current situation. In aviation terms, we were flying on instruments.

With no visibility and just the GPS and the gauges of the Hägg telling us where we were, it took incredible concentration and energy to keep the vehicle on the safe path, and that's when it went from bad to worse.

'We're losing power,' said Jimbo, as he calmly looked across at me with the bad news.

'Qué?' I replied, acknowledging what he said but seeking a bit more info.

'I've got it flat to the floor and we're slowing down while going downhill.' Jimbo started going through the obvious troubleshooting options while still driving. He switched the fuel tanks over – no change. Shifted through the gears manually on the automatic shifter – no change. Checked the park brake was off. We jumped on the radio to the mechanics behind us and did what anyone does when their car starts breaking down – called for assistance.

'Help, we're losing power,' I said.

'Copy. Coming alongside on your right, open up the centre engine cover and we'll have a look what's happening,' Lewis, driving the groomer behind us, replied, already troubleshooting the more common mechanical issues he'd seen with Häggs.

As the groomer pulled alongside us, I jumped out, barely holding onto the door as the tailwind was now close to 100 kilometres per hour. Losing a door now would mean a very cold ride home and I cursed myself for such a rookie mistake. As I jumped clear, Lewis took my place and quickly began looking over the engine, which was now exposed in the centre of the cabin. I jumped into the back seat to get out of the wind, holding on to the door more securely this time.

'She's idling okay and revs up alright but, as you're saying, it's got no power,' Lewis said. 'Belts and levels all look good, could be something in the intake but it looks pretty clear. I reckon it's safe to keep going downhill and hopefully we get below the weather.'

Lewis raced through both the mechanical and operational options in front of us and we agreed to keep going and see if we could get to the halfway point, where we'd meet the other Hägg and possibly drop below the weather. As we got rolling, I radioed ahead to Jarrod in the Red Hägg.

'We're having issues with the Blue Hägg and may need assistance. How copy, over?' I said, hoping he'd already heard what was going on.

'Copy that. We'll start heading up towards you and will meet you en route. Looking at your position and ours we'll probably cross paths about checkpoint 10 – sound good?'

I checked the map and found that Jarrod was spot on – checkpoint 10 was about halfway between where we were and the original designated halfway point.

'Copy. Good plan. We'll keep you updated and meet you there, out.'

I hoped for some luck to come our way. We could barely keep to 10 kilometres per hour, and each time there was a hint of incline or bump in the ice, we slowed down. We were just rolling down the plateau with the hurricane-strength tailwind pushing us home.

I started to go through the options if the Hägg couldn't be repaired quickly – and by quickly, in the raging blizzard, I meant immediately.

Option 1: Go for gold – we'd kept numbers down to six, to allow for the contingency of losing a vehicle. Theoretically, if we abandoned the Blue Hägg, we could put the two of us from the Blue Hägg into the Red Hägg and drive back to station as a convoy of the two groomers and one Hägg. The latest weather report on station was still sunshine and rainbows, but we knew there was a blizzard bearing down from the plateau that would soon reach the coast. If we were only halfway back to station out on the sea ice when it hit, we'd be in an unsafe and precarious situation of having to navigate the groomers blindly through the icebergs in a blizzard.

This was not something I wanted to do. Maybe the weather would hold. It's always worse on the plateau, I told myself, but again I came back to the worst case – this was not a risk worth taking.

Option 2: Pile into the Red Hägg – the Häggs can fit four people in the front cabin and about eight in the back, so we could all pile into one Hägg, leave the groomers halfway and make it back to station. But this created a major problem. Even though we could put two in the rear cabin of the Hägg, we never allowed passengers in the back cabin when travelling over sea ice, as there is no escape hatch from the rear. So if the Hägg broke through the ice and submerged, they'd drown. Additionally, the rear cabins were full of generators, gear and equipment, weighing them down. This wasn't looking great, but was slightly better than option 1 in that it would have everyone back on station that night.

Option 3: Safety first – leaving the groomers at the halfway point was fast becoming the best option, and the consensus within the team as I radioed back and forth to the mechanics, station and Jarrod in the Red Hägg. The question was now what to do with the humans. The vehicles would be safe but there was no refuge nearby and, although we had survival gear with us, it wouldn't be comfortable or ideal to stay and ride out the blizzard, which was expected to last a few days. We had to get to a field hut.

The Red Hägg had just driven the route from Bandits that morning and reported stable and good-quality ice in the fjords. And it was just thirty minutes away. Heading to Bandits was safer than trying to set up tents in the blizzard or driving across the more dangerous coastal sea ice.

* * *

Just as the terrain naturally flattened out before the rocky moraine and what would have been the downhill run to the halfway point, the Blue Hägg died, unable to muster enough power to crest the small rise. We would have to abandon it there, pile into the Red Hägg and get the groomers down to halfway asap.

The blizzard was now in full force, with visibility down to just metres and blowing snow that ripped at our clothing and any exposed skin. This was not a place to hang around. We managed to park the Blue Hägg into the prevailing wind, seal up the doors and double-check them, mark a specific grid reference on a GPS unit in case it became completely buried and make haste. The Red Hägg arrived on cue and we piled in for the ride down.

Once down off the moraine line, at the lower altitude, the weather slightly improved. As we looked back to the south, where we'd come from, we could see the storm clouds and blizzard in all directions – time was of the essence. The mechanics found suitable locations for the groomers, detached the sleds and sealed the doors and compartments as best they could in the short time.

I grabbed Jarrod to run through the plan from a field safety point of view, to make sure we didn't miss anything.

'We get the six of us into the Red Hägg and to Bandits. We'll be safe enough as a group to ride out the blizzard. If the weather looks okay we can draw straws and leave two there and send the Hägg home, cool?' I said, knowing that, although it was my call, I needed Jarrod to be on board from a field safety perspective, given it was outside standard procedures.

'So we need to put two in the back of the Hägg over the sea ice?' Jarrod asked. We'd be driving over frozen fjords, which was less dangerous than coastal ice.

'Given the distance,' I replied, 'I don't think we have any other choice.'

Technically, we needed to call Rick for the approval to break standard operating procedures. But as we stood in the middle of a blizzard yelling in each other's ears over the raging of the wind, all we could do was act.

'This is our best option and we're out of time. Safest thing we can do is get everyone to Bandit's asap and reassess when we're there,' I concluded as we gathered the others, briefed them and crammed two volunteers into the back of the Red Hägg, which was loaded to the brim with gear. I wanted to get in the back myself but was slow off the mark as others jumped at the opportunity ahead of me and we headed off across the ice to Bandits.

Arriving at Bandits, we had two options. The weather down at sea level was good for the drive back to station but I did not want passengers sitting in the rear cabin along the less stable coastal sea ice between the icebergs. This meant two 'volunteers' would remain at Bandits while the Hägg did a run back to station, before returning later in the evening to pick up them up.

There was a third option of calling up the dedicated search and rescue Hägg (aka Pink Hägg) from the station to assist but we were confident the Red Hägg could make it back before the blizzard hit the coastline. Deploying the Pink Hägg would only create more problems if it too became stuck in the blizzard. The two volunteers would be safe indefinitely at Bandits Hut, which was well equipped for such situations with about a month's worth of food and fuel.

'Who's staying?' I asked the group, knowing before they responded how this was going to pan out. I volunteered myself and vaguely looked around at the group before Jarrod stepped forward.

'I've always wanted to get stranded at a field hut down here, so why not now?' said Jarrod, and the two of us became the 'Stranded Bandits' for however long it would take to come and rescue us.

With time against us and the blizzard bearing down from the plateau, there was no time to waste and the team of four driving back to the station were gone in an instant. Jarrod and I immediately began moving supplies up the steep, icy hill to the hut, which was perched above the rocks about 20 metres above sea level up an icy and breath-zapping slope.

The hut was well stocked. We did a quick inventory of fuel and food as well as checking the seals on the emergency food containers to ensure we had what we needed to survive. The emergency rations were clearly labelled 'Emergency Food – No Chocolate' to ensure that visitors didn't get snacky in the night and break the tubs open to pillage the high-calorie chocolate found in most survival kits. Sadly, these ones were full of dehydrated meals and tinned miscellaneous 'food'. Luckily for us, the shelves of the hut were stocked with a range of better options, including the popular Fray Bentos pies (a staple of all Aussie field huts, an institution), Maggi noodles, Continental 'Cup-a-Soup's and a giant bag of Deb potato. Who needs to go out when you can have this at home!

Just over an hour later the Red Hägg approached the station. The weather remained clear, so they geared up for a hot refuel to drive back to Bandits to collect us. As appealing as this sounded to us, back at Bandits we faced a harsh reality that would seal our fate as the Stranded Bandits for at least one night.

The blizzard was now raging around us. The hut was howling and shaking in the wind, which was now hitting 150 kilometres per hour. Looking out the hut window, we could barely see the rocks just metres away, and the view towards the helipad, which was only 30 metres away, was a wall of white. So, with a heavy heart, I knew there was only one safe option.

'Weather up here is full blizz. It's not worth risking the trip up in whiteout and we're safe here for the night. Over,' I said into the hut's VHF base station.

'Copy that. We'll speak at 1800 for the nightly sked and in the morning to see where it's at; otherwise, enjoy the night!'

I hung up and sat down at the small wooden table in the hut to ponder our situation. This was about as isolated as you can get. We were stuck in an Antarctic field hut, cut off from the station and without a vehicle, but everyone was safe and that was the main thing.

The next morning was the same. Overnight winds on station hit 178 kilometres per hour and the blizzard was in full rage. There was no hope of a rescue so Jarrod and I settled in for what we knew would be at least another day at the hut. The hut had a few books and old magazines lying around, but the pickings were slim. I grabbed a copy of *The Odessa File* by Frederick Forsyth off the shelf and got stuck into another book in my favourite genre of post–Second World War espionage thrillers.

I vaguely quipped to Jarrod, who appeared to have a Bluetooth speaker with him, 'Got any good tunes?' He nodded, synced his phone with the speaker and filled the small hut with the dulcet tones of Metallica, live from Madrid. One man's easy-listening background music is another man's heavy metal, I thought as the music filled the small hut.

I politely thanked Jarrod and suggested he turn it down 'just one notch maybe?'

* * *

As dinnertime approached, we created the best meal we could with the ingredients available. An entrée of tinned tuna on a stale biscuit followed by a main course of 'Shepherd's Bentos', a frozen pie with potato deb on top, which was surprisingly tasty.

As we looked for topics to discuss outside our immediate predicament, Jarrod, who had heard rumours over the years about the somewhat secretive selection process for prospective station leaders, asked me questions he'd clearly put a bit of thought into.

'Is it true they take you all out into the wilderness like *Survivor*?'

'It's not far from it. There are more discussions around workplace culture and diversity than about forming alliances and winning immunity, though,' I replied, as I cast my mind back to the hoops I'd jumped through and the journey I'd taken to be stuck here in a small hut in Antarctica with him. With time up our sleeves and no wi-fi, TV or much else to do, I gave Jarrod the full story.

* * *

It was in 2012, early in my first diplomatic posting at the Australian High Commission in Islamabad, Pakistan, that my Antarctic story began. Our work in Pakistan revolved around coordinating high-level ministerial visits by Australian politicians and top military brass, as well as trying to coordinate Australia's role in helping stabilise the region and manage the impacts of international terrorism.

It was a dynamic time and life was good on posting. We put in long hours, with 'work' often involving long lunches, late dinners, sneaky whisky and cigars in a hotel speakeasy to find out the 'real story' behind the latest political issue or development in nearby Afghanistan as the war dragged on. Australian diplomats flew under the radar, and the term 'cricket diplomacy' was often used as we talked all things cricket to break the ice with the sometimes-frosty government officials.

It was everything I'd wanted for my first diplomatic posting: a dynamic political landscape with enough danger thrown in to keep us on our toes. Bombings, riots, protests and general unrest were commonplace throughout Pakistan at the time, and at one point, while escorting an Australian member of parliament on a visit to Peshawar, I was quietly informed of a complex attack unfolding nearby ... 'Time to go, ma'am. I'll explain why in the car.'

Sitting in my office one day, surrounded by high fences covered in razor wire and patrolling armed guards, I had a conversation with the Australian High Commissioner, Peter Heyward, which first sowed the seed of the road to Antarctica.

'That's an interesting map – have you been south?' he asked as he entered my office to hand back a heavily red-penned cable I'd written, and noticed a map of Antarctica hanging on my wall.

'I'd love to go one day, but that map was hidden behind the safe when I rearranged the office. I thought it looked better on the wall.'

'You should apply to be a station leader down there one day. You'd be good,' he suggested. Having worked with the Australian Antarctic Program himself, he had strong links to the program and he spoke passionately about the voyage across the Southern Ocean and the unique environment at the end of the Earth.

I was intrigued. After he left my office, I googled the Australian Antarctic Program and what they were looking for in station leaders. Over the next few years, I'd gradually work my way professionally and personally to one day make the voyage south.

After my posting to Pakistan, I spent a year in Istanbul working freelance and travelling Europe with my girlfriend, who worked with the United Nations. Eventually I took a role at the Australian Embassy in Baghdad, embedded with Australian troops in Iraq, as we joined the coalition to push ISIS back from the gates of Baghdad.

By 2017, as my relationship ended due to too much time apart and our careers taking us in different directions, I decided it was time to get serious about Antarctica. I jumped through the initial hoops, with applications and screening interviews, until it was narrowed down to about two dozen station leader hopefuls. We then gathered at a Scout camp in the forests of Tasmania for a one-week selection and assessment process.

The week was a predictable mixture of practical and theoretical exercises designed to test every aspect of your character and suitability to lead an Antarctic expedition. Supervised by former station leaders and countless others, day and night we were pushed and tested and prodded and questioned until, on the final day, those of us who remained were interviewed back at the AAD's head office in Kingston, with hopes of being offered a position in the coming seasons.

There was no way to fake what they were looking for. In a strange way, I enjoyed the selection process and the way it gave us a sense of what Antarctic expeditions were all about. When given field problems, such as coordinating search and rescue plans or navigating through the bush, I was in my element. But the directing staff knew this and would offset success by giving you a mundane bureaucratic task or a common conflict you would face on an Antarctic station and expect you to perform equally well.

I had one thing against me – I was the youngest candidate there, at thirty-four. I was frequently made aware of this by both my peers and the directing staff themselves. Would this be my undoing? Would I have to fail now in order to return in a few years with more experience?

But what else could I do? My résumé was as jam-packed with experiences and stories as others twice my age. What did my age matter? I later found out there had been plenty of young station leaders, but at the end of the selection week I flew back to Melbourne unsure of whether I'd be heading south.

A few months later, I was on a plane to Wilkins for two weeks at Casey station for a familiarisation trip, and a few weeks after that, Rick called me up and offered me the job as Davis station leader for 2020.

'Now I'm here having dinner with you – what's your story?' I asked Jarrod.

'I love the outdoors. And Antarctica is the last true wilderness, so why not?'

A man of few words. As the only person to have paddled a sea kayak solo around Australia, battling months of setbacks, exposure, sharks, crocodiles trying to steal his kayak, and day after day of paddling in the open ocean alone, Jarrod was everything you'd expect from a rugged Antarctic field training officer. I never heard him complain once about the extension, the AAD, the people or the weather. He just got on with the job and kept paddling.

* * *

I'm often asked what makes a good Antarctic expeditioner or station leader. Besides qualifications and experience relevant to working or leading in remote environments and communities, for me it comes down to one thing: a fundamental sense of adventure within a person's own psyche.

We all had our reasons for being there, but those who sought adventure in every aspect of life, personal or professional, tended to do better. When pushed to the absolute limits of resilience or stress, it was those with this sense of adventure who could dig deep and find the extra energy to push through.

A close second is tolerance. You need to be tolerant. Because after four days in a hut with one other person, isolated and alone with nothing to do all day, you do start to annoy each other.

* * *

Day 335: 23 September 2020
Temperature: -8°C to -3.2°C
Maximum wind speed: 148 kilometres per hour
Rescues: 1

After four nights in the hut and the longest and most persistent blizzard of the winter, Jarrod and I were itching to get home, especially after a false start the day before. A Hägg had been despatched from the station, only to face atrocious conditions and complete whiteout on the approach to the hut; they were forced to turn around. It just wasn't worth damaging the vehicles or, even worse, breaking through a lead in the sea ice simply to pick us up when we were perfectly safe at the hut, no matter how bored or how sick of Fray Bentos pies we were.

Just as with storms back home, you get a sense when the worst of it is over. Slowly but surely the visibility was starting to lift: we could now see the tide crack below us, and at times across to the rocks of the shoreline nearly a kilometre away. Even more encouraging was seeing gaps in the cloud above revealing blue skies. We radioed this back to the station, and within an hour they were on their way to get us. We started packing the hut up for what we hoped was the end of our first forced lockdown.

Seeing the Red Hägg emerge through the clearing blizzard was glorious. With the weather still prone to changing its mind, we didn't waste time grabbing our packs and four days' worth of rubbish. As soon as the Hägg arrived, we opened the back cabin, threw in our packs and jumped in.

'Who was big spoon and who was little spoon?' asked Jimbo, who was driving the Hägg.

'Some things will remain a secret,' I laughed back as I crammed in. During the drive back, jokes were aplenty about a station coup, raiding of Jarrod's field store for all the shiny rock-climbing equipment and so on, but we still had a job to do.

The two snow groomers and the Blue Hägg, abandoned in the blizzard this whole time, were probably buried in snow. Over the headsets of the Hägg we talked through the forecast for the next few days and the team we'd need to assemble to manage the recovery.

The blizzard still had about forty-eight hours to run but the wind was now below 100 kilometres per hour, which meant it was easing. The weather would then clear in two days' time. If we started early and with the right team, we could get everyone and everything back to the station in one long day. We'd have to have a Plan B if there were delays, but in our favour was the closer location of the groomers at the halfway point, and the fact we knew they had been running and would only have a few days' snow accumulation, compared with what we'd faced at Whoop Whoop. It was a matter of about one hour's preparation and not an entire day, like the initial groomer-retrieval mission.

As the Hägg bounced over the sastrugi,[19] we discussed the next day's plan over the intercom headsets and, between us, worked out the plan that would finish what we'd started.

* * *

Day 338: 26 September 2020
Temperature: -14°C to -6.9°C
Maximum wind speed: 44 kilometres per hour

---

[19] Parallel wave-like ridges caused by winds on the surface of hard snow, common in the polar regions.

The day arrived: first light was 0700 hours and we set off from the station just as the sun was hitting the sea ice and lighting the way for us to the north. I often forgot how different things are at the polar regions; the old 'sun rises in the east and sets in the west' saying was obviously not written by a penguin. As we drove generally north-north-east, the morning sun was blindingly in our eyes most of the way – but this was better than a whiteout!

To increase our numbers and allow us to split into two teams, we took the trusty Red Hägg as well as the dedicated search and rescue Pink Hägg, each with four people. This was the same group of six from the original team plus a couple of extras. Once we arrived at the halfway point and saw that the groomers were not as deeply buried as we feared, there was good sense of relief among the team. All we needed now was to drop a team up at the Blue Hägg, dig it out and get it going.

The Blue Hägg was the cleanest and newest looking Hägg we had, with a fresh paint job from a few seasons earlier and sporting logos from the Tasmania-based 'Stay Chatty' mental health charity; it was often the vehicle of choice for fieldtrips.

Arriving where we'd abandoned it was incredible. From the angle we approached, through the rocky moraine line of boulders the size of cars, I was expecting to see the Blue Hägg easily among the brown rocks and white snow, but I could barely see the antennas and roof-mounted survival kits as we drove right up to the vehicle! Luckily, this was just a bad angle: the snow had accumulated on one side, leaving the other more exposed. After a few moments' contemplation, it was time to start digging.

We left the Pink Hägg team with shovels and they became their own separate field party as we drove back to the groomers. The priority for us was getting the groomers back to the station and we couldn't let anything slow us down a second time.

Having done the same job a few days earlier as a team, we barely talked while digging the groomers out, cleaning out the snow accumulation from the air intakes, repositioning the trailers and securing the loads in preparation to depart back to the station.

'Pink Hägg, this is Dave. We're pretty much ready to go here with the groomers and will start heading back to station via the coastal route as planned. How are you going up there? Over.'

'Copy that. We've got the Blue Hägg running but it is still a bit stuck in the snow so we'll have to dig for another half an hour or so and then we'll head off. Over,' replied Jarrod.

'Great. Let us know when you're on the move and we'll meet somewhere along the coastal route home, as you'll be a lot quicker than us. Over,' I replied, reiterating the plan we'd discussed earlier.

'Copy that. Drive safely!'

The groomers roared into position as we got ready to roll. We lined them up behind the Red Hägg and headed off down the final slope of the hills and onto the frozen lakes that soon joined the sea-ice fjords and the path out to the coastal sea ice. With blue skies and good spirits, it was a perfect day for the journey. Despite the slow pace of the convoy, we made good time to Bandits and soon turned south towards the station. The radio fired up from the Hägg recovery team, who were now on the move and catching up with us.

'Red Hägg, this is Ghost Rider requesting a flyby,' they said, cheekily paraphrasing the famous line from *Top Gun* as the Blue and Pink Häggs now approached the back of our convoy.

'Negative, Pink Hägg, the pattern is full. Join the back of our convoy and we'll drive home together,' I replied, smiling. Everything was coming together.

Out on the sea ice, each field party would usually check in with the station on the hour to state their position and intentions, along with a simple 'ops normal'. Call signs were usually the colour of your Hägg or purpose of the trip plus the word 'party', which often resulted in names such as 'Penguin Party' and 'Seal Party'. But this time, looking in the rear-vison mirrors and seeing the long convoy of vehicles behind me, I broke with convention as we approached the station and radioed ahead.

'VLZ Davis, VLZ Davis, this is the VLZ Convoy. Ops beautiful. Just about to round Anchorage Island and be back on station within the hour – put the kettle on. Over.'

'Copy that, VLZ Convoy. Request here from station for approval for a drone flight towards the convoy. Over,' replied Rhonda.

'Approved!' I replied, thankful for the initiative of our drone pilot. It was a stunning day and a rare photo opportunity to have the groomers and all three station Häggs out on the sea ice. I soon spotted the small quadcopter circling above us, glinting in the bright Antarctic sunshine.

As we navigated the tide crack and drove onto the shore, we parked the vehicles in a neat row, jumped out of the cabins and gathered for a team photo with the drone hovering in front of us. It had taken nine days to complete what, in theory, should have been a simple job, but weather and bad luck had been against us. I was grateful to have it finished and that everyone was safe. We could now turn our minds to the next job.

* * *

The high was short-lived. Within days of our return, the experts were everywhere with 'We should have done it this way' and 'I wouldn't have done that' remarks.

As the station leader, commonly everything bad tended to be my fault and anything good had nothing to do with me. But, on this occasion, it got to me. Yes, hypothetically, if we'd taken the 'go for gold' approach we could have had the groomers and everyone back on station a week earlier. But that would have meant risking getting stuck on the sea ice in a blizzard that had arrived a full day earlier than forecast. It also didn't account for the fact we had lost a Hägg through mechanical issues and would have had to risk passengers in the rear cabin over coastal sea ice. It was clear that those who wanted to blame me for the situation were selectively forgetting the considerable risks associated with worst-case scenarios.

How, I wondered, would I find peace with decisions that resulted in a safe and successful outcome but were now seen as overly risk-averse? I certainly didn't have the answer, but I knew who would, and I called Rick to talk through the whole series of events and decisions. At times like this, it was speaking to former station leaders that helped me move on.

'Somehow it was my fault the Hägg broke down and the weather closed in, despite the fact we now know it was ice accumulation in the air intake from the blizzard that killed the Hägg. And predicting Antarctic weather is as safe as crypto-currency markets,' I said to Rick over the video call.

'Classic!' Rick laughed, before giving me a bit more

encouragement. 'This happens, mate. At this point of the season, when everyone's looking for fault and problems, you're the easiest target on station. Don't worry about it. You made the right calls in the situation by the sounds of it, and if everyone is safe and all equipment recovered then it's a win.' Rick was telling me what I already knew, but I appreciated hearing it from him.

'Thanks. It just feels flat that, despite getting it done and the positives to come out of it, there are still those who just want to complain and find the negative in everything.'

'Don't dwell on it. If people want to complain and see it their way, then that's them, not you. Keep doing what you're doing. This is one of the tougher situations in recent years with the extension and everything else going on in the world, so just keep going and you'll make it.'

'Thanks. We just need a win. Chat again soon, no doubt,' I said, not wanting to take up too much time venting my frustrations. The AAD had enough going on back there, but sometimes all I needed was a good vent to get things off my chest.

As a team, we needed that win. I'd tried to turn the unfortunate events of this adventure into a positive and focus on the incredible efforts by the team along the way: our mammoth efforts on the shovels in truly Antarctic conditions, the impressive dedication of the mechanics to the tasks at hand, and problem-solving and forward thinking from everyone involved. So why were the negative opinions of a minority getting to me so much?

The reason was simple. I too was starting to feel the effects of our situation. I was exhausted, I faced constant criticism of the way our extension had been handled, and both individuals and teams alike were bickering over the smallest of issues and nitpicking over others' roles and habits. It was slowly wearing everyone down. We all needed a holiday, or at least a break from each other.

Unfortunately, what we had to do next was the total opposite. For the next month we'd work as a team to refill the station's water supply ahead of the summer. Another simple job in trying conditions, and an ordeal which would forever after be known as 'The Tarn'.

Handover complete from the outgoing station leader, Simon, in front of the *Aurora* during resupply, November 2019.

Sea-ice runway in the early summer. Note *Aurora* in the background.

Spectacular sunrise over station during a morning walk.

Adélie penguins on sea ice near Davis getting ready to head out to sea for the winter ahead.

Watch out for hop-ons! Penguins often mistook the inflatable rubber boats for icebergs and jumped on.

Davis Station at the end of winter. Note the sizeable snowdrift accumulation or 'blizz tails' on each building. The dark green building in the centre is the living quarters and my office was in the yellow operations building on the right.

Sunset iceberg cruise in late summer 20/21, taken at around midnight during the near-total sunlight of summer.

Farewell *Aurora*! The last visit of the historic ship to Antarctica in March 2020 just as the world began to change.

Anzac Day dawn service at 10am, 25 April 2020, one of the few 'public' services held during the pandemic.

Midwinter swim! Minus 20 degrees air temp, minus 2 degrees water temp. Getting out was colder than getting in!

The incredible aurora australis or southern lights.
Words cannot describe the spectacle.

Installing instruments into the sea ice to monitor stress and movement of the frozen ocean.

Juvenile elephant seal, penguins, icebergs and sea ice. The best of Antarctica in one photo!

Negotiating the tide cracks off the sea ice and onto land was always a challenge. Note the melt pools and areas the sea has flooded through.

Hägglunds adventure on the frozen lakes around the Vestfold Hills.

Watts Hut, one of many similar huts scattered around the Vestfold Hills and Australian station areas.

Tasting the kale in the station's hydroponics hut – a great daily task when on duty.

Digging the snow groomers out of the Antarctic Plateau in freezing conditions.

Returning to the Blue Hägg after abandoning it in the blizzard.

Groomer retrieval convoy back on station.

Packing up the tarn hose on a nice evening.

Overwater resupply from the MPV *Everest*, March 2021.

Navigating the pack ice on the approach to Mawson station onboard the MPV *Everest*.

The fire on board the MPV *Everest* as seen from the bridge.

Mullet hair and the faded 'good shirt' plus mask for arrival back into the fashion capital of Melbourne.

Chapter 8

Quitting Is Not an Option

Day 347: 5 October 2020
Temperature: -17.6°C to -4.5°C

The dictionary definition of 'tarn' is 'a small mountain lake in a hollow area surrounded by steep slopes and formed by a glacier'. See also: 'frustrating', 'never-ending', 'character building'.

Before we left Hobart back in 2019, we knew that one of the biggest tasks for the winter season would be to refill the station's tarn so the reverse osmosis desalination plant had a good source of readily available sea water during the next summer. My original questions to the engineers were, of course: why do we need to desalinate sea water when the Antarctic ice sheet holds 90 per cent of the world's freshwater ice? Isn't there snow everywhere and can't we melt that?

They are good questions, so I'll answer the easy one first. Melting snow isn't very efficient and you get very little water out of tonnes of snow, so it just wouldn't be enough. But the first question – about using the ice – is a bit more involved, so let's go back to the early days of Antarctic exploration …

In January 1957, an early Australian expedition led by Phillip Law was charged with establishing a station in the Vestfold Hills of east Antarctica. Law and his party set out to find the most suitable location for a station in the 400 square kilometres of rocks that are considered an 'Antarctic oasis'. There are four things that make a suitable long-term site for an Antarctic station: solid ground, a deep-water anchorage for resupply, access to fresh water, and wi-fi (a modern requirement).

Solid rock was everywhere in the Vestfold Hills, but the other criteria were proving challenging. Law and his party set off exploring the hills and sailing up and down the shoreline doing depth soundings and surveys – which they'd also done on previous expeditions in 1954 and 1955 – but again failed to find the perfect location. As with many decisions in Antarctic exploration, a compromise was made and Davis was founded in close proximity to a deep-sea anchorage to enable resupply and access. Law noted that fresh water would be hard to find.

In the early days, melting snow sufficed but, as the station grew and human sanitary requirements increased the need for showers and washing, Davis was never able to get ahead of the water supply issue.

To manage water consumption in modern times, we were limited to one minute of shower time per person per day. My routine was to have a thirty-second stone-cold shower in the morning to wake me up and reap the supposed benefits of cold-water showers, such as increased circulation and reduced muscle soreness. Then, following a workout or sauna, I'd savour another thirty seconds of cold goodness in the evening. Some of the team would save their shower time and build up for a long, hot shower on a weekend, but for those who sat next to them at dinner or could smell their shoes in the cold porch, it didn't seem a very community-minded approach.

So how do we make water? The small tarn located upwind from the station holds enough water for about five years of supply to be run though the desalination plant and stored in the station's water tanks, which hold about two years of fresh water at a time – to cover the population's use for one year as well as a reserve for a second year if needed. We drained the tanks equally so that if one burst, we'd have a similar amount in the remaining tank. (Everything on station was based on a two-year contingency so that in the event you get stuck, like we were, you'd have a whole extra year of fuel, food and water in reserve.)

The plant itself draws the salty water out of the tarn, does its magic and returns saline water back into the tarn while producing fresh water to top up the tanks. The flaw is that, over the years, this increases the overall salinity of the tarn to a point where the plant cannot process the hypersaline water and the whole thing needs to be refreshed. By 2020 the tarn level was the lowest it had been in decades, and was saltier than a jaded ex–prime minister, so we had to drain the hypersaline water out and refill it with sea water from the ocean.

You can only run the plant when the tarn isn't frozen, so that leaves about an eight-week window between January and March to run the plant and produce the next year's drinking water. During resupply in November, the *Aurora Australis* had been able to provide additional fresh water to the station for the summer season, but with no ship on the horizon until early 2021, refilling the tarn and getting the plant running were now more critical than ever.

So obviously you just fill it up in January when everything is melted and the weather is a lovely 5 degrees and sunny outside, right? Wrong. Mother Nature has a cruel way of reminding us that humans are just one small part of the planet, and as the sea ice melts in the summer and sunlight hits the ocean, the frozen ecosystem comes to life and produces an abundance of algae and krill that would clog filters, fill the tarn and then attract penguins, seals, killer whales and ecowarriors. So the best time of the year to pump sea water into the tarn is October, when it's still bitterly cold and you have good working conditions for about twelve hours before darkness returns and the temperature plummets.

If it had been an ordinary year, we would also have been preparing the runway and getting ready for the first flights to arrive in late October, signalling the end of our winter and the beginning of the journey home. But 2020 wasn't an ordinary year. We were three-hundred-odd days into our year and knew we would not be going home for another five months. This meant that morale was about as low as it could get on station, and patience and tolerance were wafer-thin, before we even started trying to refill the tarn.

If that wasn't enough, remember Rocky? He was the one last expeditioner who needed to fly across from Casey at the end of summer to complete our winter team and lead the infrastructure projects. He was an expert on tarn filling and was supposed to be here to lead the job, but he'd never made it. Instead, due to travel restrictions, he was back in Hobart.

* * *

The plan was simple. The station was divided into three core teams of five people, with everyone allocated a four-hour shift on the hose, which would be supervised by one of the three plumbers. Some of us, such as myself, Doc, Rhonda and the meteorology team, were not on the shift teams but would fill in gaps and be on call for either planned pack-up times or urgent emergency pack-ups in the event of a blowout or bad weather.

I was excited but apprehensive for the tarn refill. We'd briefed everyone and I'd always felt there was nothing like a shared objective and common task to build a group's cohesion. After so long away, though, we were far beyond the 'group bonding' stage and there were growing rifts and divisions. The weeks ahead would either make or break us as a team, and I was determined for that win.

With the forecast relatively good for the first few days, we intended to run the pump nonstop rather than having to set up and pack up each day. It could take over an hour to lay out the nearly 800 metres of hose, prime each length and get the flow rates stable, and then, when the job was done, we'd have to reverse this process to discharge each length of hose before it froze, before rolling up the hosing onto the purpose-built rack and putting it on the back of the Ute Hägg, which had a tray instead of a rear cabin. So, to save time and hassle, we planned to run the pump overnight. Time would tell if this plan would work.

The first morning went relatively well, although it was slow going to get everything set up for the hose, which was about double the size of a standard fire hose. To allow us to pump sea water into the tarn, we ran the hose from the pump down on the sea ice, through a hole to the sea water. The hose would then run up and over the rocky hill and snake its way towards the tarn. The hose was broken into shorter lengths of about 30 to 50 metres, which needed to be joined and then dismantled one by one at the start and end of the day if we had to pack up.

All that was required once it was set up was for the mechanic to supervise the pumphouse, about 100 metres out on the sea ice. The other members of the shift would walk up and down the line, checking for leaks or ice accumulation at the metal joints, which were insulated from the cold but still proved a weak point in the system. One person would always be sitting at the tarn end of the hose monitoring the flow and visually assessing if it had slowed or was in any way inhibited.

I wasn't on a shift the first day, but I periodically wandered down to see how it was going. By late afternoon, as the temperature started dropping, Gaz and I had a chat with the plumbers about whether it was feasible to run through the night as the air temperature dropped.

The decision was largely made for us as, despite the periodical tapping on the joints with a rubber mallet to dislodge the ice and the steady flow achieved throughout the day, ice was still accumulating at the joints and other spots along the hoses, and the outflow rate had gradually declined. The call went out for everyone available to assemble at 2000 hours, as the sun was setting, to pack up the hoses and call it a day.

* * *

There was a pack-up plan, but everyone had a different interpretation of that plan and, with temperatures plummeting, patience thin and the hour getting late, everyone became an expert.

Once again, it was simple in theory: disconnect each section of hose systematically, drain the water before it froze, lay it on the rack and then move on to the next length of hose until it's all packed up. Then, using the Häggs, we'd get everything off the sea ice and back into the warm storage to thaw out overnight. But this was the epitome of 'easier said than done', and right from the start, it just wasn't working.

'Where do you need us?' asked the expeditioners gathered around the Hägg, which was parked about 100 metres from the tarn end of the hose, at the meeting point for pack-up duty.

'Wait here until they drop the pressure and we can disconnect,' replied the nearest plumber, which satisfied the waiting gaggle.

Meanwhile, one or two people at the tarn end of the hose were radioing to those waiting at the pump some 800 metres away, well out of sight over the rocky hill in between the tarn and the sea ice.

'Drop the pressure and disconnect!' the radio barked back to the mechanic at the pump end.

'Copy that. Dropping the revs. Disconnect the first length,' came the reply.

The gaggle paused, knowing they needed to assist but hesitant to just start disconnecting hoses for fear of getting it wrong. As one of the figures from the tarn end hastened their approach to the group still standing near the Hägg, the goodwill of the pack-up team evaporated instantly.

'Why are you just standing around? Let's go!' someone barked at the group.

'What?' replied the gaggle as confusion reigned.

'*Go!*'

Realising there were not going to be clearer instructions or an allocation of tasks, the group dispersed to all sections of the hose and started 'helping' by lifting the hose off the ground to discharge the water before it froze. The problem was three separate groups were trying the same approach on different sections without coordinating their movements. It was ineffective and causing water to get trapped in the sections.

The logical question came from a willing helper and was lobbed at the nearest plumber. 'What if we started at one end rather than all at the same time?'

'Stop overthinking and just help,' the response came. This was not the time for suggestions, even good ones.

'I'm trying to help but this is all over the place,' one of the frustrated helpers muttered, turning towards the next length of hose and distancing himself from the group.

I glanced at Doc, Gaz and a few others who were observing the situation that was unfolding and, without saying a word to them, I got the sense we were on the same page.

The textbook solution was to stop, rebrief the plan, confirm which plumber was in charge, breathe out, acknowledge there was a better way and move forward. But at this point, with the wind picking up towards 30 to 40 kilometres per hour, the temperature plummeting fast towards minus 20 and darkness falling, the textbook would need to stay inside the library where it belonged and not out here in the frozen desolation of our remote predicament.

'Hose two, what's the plan this time?' I asked.

'Same again. Maybe we spread out before they disconnect,' the nearest plumber replied, stepping up to the task. He stipulated we should work from one end to the other using the slight gradient to our advantage. But it was too late. Two or three others had already wandered off, working to their own agendas.

The hose was disconnected and the gaggle of helpers raised the hose over their shoulders and worked as a team, but the two other teams at the opposing ends did the same thing and started working towards the middle, defeating the whole purpose of the activity.

'We're going from this end first! Downhill!' I yelled, as the opposing team silently dropped their end and trudged towards the Hägg.

'What's the plan now?' snarled Fred.

'The same. Just one end to the other so we don't accumulate water at the low points,' I said.

'I didn't know you were a plumber,' Fred's smart-arse reply came back.

'Don't need to be a plumber to know water flows downhill,' I replied, in no mood for his attitude. This was met with an eyeroll and further muttering in the now-howling wind.

'Maybe he should have listened to the plan instead of doing his own thing,' quipped those standing on the back of the Hägg trailer as we loaded the hose onto the rack.

'Teamwork makes the dream work!' joked Jimbo to break the tension, as we finished loading the second hose and the familiar call of 'Coupling!' echoed around, indicating the hose coupling was on the rack and we could proceed to the next length.

We muddled our way through that night and, despite the tension and frustrations, everything was packed up and back on station by 2200 hours after just over two hours of pack-up, for a total of eleven and a half hours of pumping and one tantrum.

* * *

The problem with shiftwork is that once it starts, everyone has their own cycle, with few windows to get everyone together and rebrief the plan without disturbing sleep routines and the other important station operations we were all squeezing in around shifts. Days before we started pumping, there had been a detailed briefing, with all on station nodding along, that the plumbers were in charge on each shift and everyone else's job was to be as helpful and supportive as possible. What I had seen that first night was not exactly in the spirit of teamwork and helpfulness. I needed a way to fix this without making a big deal of it.

I wasn't the only one who was keen to improve. Throughout the second day I spoke to each of the plumbers, along with Gaz, and refined the plan. We needed to make sure clear handovers were conducted and a clear briefing was given to anyone helping pack up so everyone was on the same page. This wasn't rocket science, and they'd identified the same factors, so after we talked all things Antarctic hoses and tarns, Gaz grabbed me for a chat on another worrying element of the previous evening.

'I don't think Fred will make it through this,' offered Gaz, knowing I too had copped his backchat and seen him generally huff about every instruction he received, no matter who it was from.

'Yeah, I saw it. I'll have a chat to him later when he's awake but we might need to tag him out of the shifts and use a floating reserve or something.' I was already working out the impact that would have on those who were not on shift and still working their usual jobs, now having to add a four-hour hose shift to their day.

'For the day shifts we can get by a man down for a while, but it's not ideal,' said Gaz, reminding me that we were struggling to deliver the original plan, which hinged on having three core teams of five people each.

'Thanks for the heads-up. See you tonight for pack-up.' I was dwelling on the fact we were on day two and the wheels were falling off already.

For a station of only twenty-four people, you'd think it would be easy to find someone when you're looking for them but at times you'd go the whole day without bumping into someone. If someone didn't want to be found, it could be even longer. Fred knew I wanted to see him and was successfully lying low, avoiding running into me, so I left a note with Rhonda to send him to my office when he next appeared for a meal. The kitchen was the one place everyone appeared at some point in the day.

'You wanted to see me?' said Fred as he quietly appeared at my office door.

'Come on in, sit down,' I said as I moved to close the door behind him. 'How's everything going?'

'Shithouse' replied Fred, flatly.

'Do you want to talk about it, then?' I sensed he was not interested in talking to me about anything.

'Nup,' replied Fred, giving me nothing to work with.

'Fred, everyone's struggling with this, but we need to work as a team or the next five months will be impossible.'

'I never wanted to be here this long. It's unfair, and I'm not here to be a plumber,' said Fred, finally engaging in the conversation.

'The tarn needs everyone on it and it's the priority right now.

If everyone just does their own thing, then that leaves the three plumbers all alone, which isn't practical. We all use water so we all have to help produce it.'

'Yeah, but it's disorganised.'

'Last night wasn't the smoothest operation but no one here has done this before and the methods we trained and briefed beforehand didn't quite work in the cold. We'll get better each day and fine-tune it as we go. This morning's set-up was already better,' I said.

'I told them beforehand it wouldn't work how they planned,' said Fred.

'Well, if they didn't listen to you, then that's on them.' I saw a segue out of what wasn't an overly constructive conversation and changed gears to try and get Fred back on track. 'Who's on your shift? Do you want to change teams?'

'It's not that. Can't I just work on my own?' He wanted out of the tarn and a return to his main job, where he was able to pick and choose independent jobs around station and work alone.

'Not on this one. Some jobs are independent but we need teams on the tarn.' It was clear he didn't want to play. 'When's your next shift?'

'Tomorrow afternoon,' replied Fred as he slapped the armrests and stood up, deciding the meeting was over.

After he was gone, I ran my hands through my now mullet-length hair and looked out the window to the darkening sky. This was draining me beyond anything I'd ever managed before. And it wasn't the first time a conversation with Fred had gone like this.

Over the previous few months, his visits to my office had become regular, and each time we'd agree on a way forward or a solution, he'd push the boundaries yet again and receive a further invitation to the station leader's office. Each time he'd arrive armed with excuses for why his actions were the fault of someone other than himself. He was wearing me down and disrupting the team around him.

I'd tried everything I could think of. Rhonda and I were out of options and I'd discussed it with almost anyone else on station who cared to try a different approach. Could someone else be doing a better job of this? I felt like the team was falling apart because of one bad egg.

* * *

Day 351: 9 October 2020
Temperature: -15.2°C to -12.3°C
Maximum wind speed: 56 kilometres per hour

After five days of solid pumping, we were getting into a rhythm. The set-up procedure was a slick operation and the evening pack-up was working like a well-oiled machine, with a refined method of draining the hose quickly and having everything done and dusted in under an hour. Spirits were higher than earlier in the week and, with some bad weather coming, we were likely to have the weekend off or be able to catch up on our regular jobs, but at a reduced pace. As always, I kept my radio attached to my hip and kept one ear on the radio traffic at all times.

'Um, can someone see what's happening about halfway up the hill? There's water going everywhere,' radioed the on-shift weather observer from the BoM office near the middle of the hose.

Luckily, he had been looking at the hose while doing the rounds of the weather instruments and gizmos scattered around the BoM building.

'Blowout, blowout! Can we get anyone available to the hose asap!' came the reply from Lewis down on the sea ice at the pump end.

'Confirm, massive drop in pressure at the tarn end – almost no flow,' replied Bob, watching the hose, as one by one people replied over the radio indicating they were either on their way or moving vehicles to help. It was the same drill we'd done each night to pack up, but this time the clock was ticking and the hoses were freezing.

The hoses below the blowout were fine to keep charged with water, so the plumbers gave the orders to keep the pump running and just drop the revs a bit. The problem now was the four to five sections – about 150 metres of hose – above the blowout, which would have a residual amount of water sitting in them as they lay on the freezing ground. The hoses weighed enough when empty and correctly laid on the rack system for transport, but if they froze while full of water they would become giant Zooper Dooper icy poles weighing hundreds of kilos, which we'd struggle to thaw out again without damaging them. We did have some spare hoses, but not enough to replace the entire length.

As each of us arrived on scene, we were directed by the plumber on the spot: 'You two, tarn hose, you two, second hose, disconnect them, drain them and get to it!' We were working together finally, a thousand times better than we'd all worked on day one.

As the crowd of helpers grew, we were able to get the hoses drained as best we could. We then called for the Hägg to come up so we could load the hoses onto the tray and pack everything up. Despite our best efforts and an overall victory, Mother Nature put up a good fight and at least one length of hose now had several metre-long frozen lumps inside. It was still able to be loaded on the trailer, though, and could be defrosted overnight inside the warm store.

Loitering around at the end of pack-up, I had a chat with the plumbers about what impact this would have.

'We can thaw them out – we'll need to replace a few couplings and shorten some lengths – but we'll probably have it done and be back tomorrow.'

'Alright, good work. We'll keep it all as planned but let me know if we need to change tomorrow. It's Friday, so it might be a good afternoon for an early knock-off,' I said tentatively. Everyone had been working hard this week and would welcome the chance to take an early mark and end the week with some bar snacks and beers, but it wouldn't be appropriate for the plumbers to be working late into the evening while everyone else relaxed.

I walked back to the station and found Rhonda working away in the kitchen. Having monitored the radio traffic, she knew where my head was at. 'Bar snacks and takeaway food tonight?' she asked. I noticed she was already working on this plan with the deep fryer full of chips and spring rolls, but wanted to make sure the optics were right.

'You read my mind – no more pumping today. They'll repair everything and start slightly later tomorrow morning,' I said.

'Station meeting?' asked Rhonda, noting it was Friday and we hadn't planned a meeting that week on account of the shift work.

'We'll do it at bar snacks at 1600. Mainly an update on where we're at and the week ahead.' I moved to the whiteboard and updated the daily total for hours pumped and wrote: 'Station meeting 1600 – Nina's'.

The ops whiteboard was the focal point of all information, but at times it became crowded with information or disinformation when things changed. On more than a few occasions in recent weeks, the team was getting increasingly vocal when shift start times were adjusted even slightly to work around weather or other factors. The best way to ensure the correct information required five steps: write it on the whiteboard; email everyone; send a message on the group chat; send a station-wide SMS to all phones; tell everyone I saw to check those four things.

Despite that, there were times when responses such as 'I checked the board yesterday', 'I don't use email on weekends', 'I muted the group chat' and 'I don't read those texts' were used, along with my all-time favourite, 'Nobody told me', when they were hiding in their room actively trying not to be informed. But it was my job to inform people so, despite internally fuming, I'd simply take the moment to endeavour to improve the existing systems and move on. The best way to reach everyone, though, was a station meeting.

As everyone gathered at Nina's bar for the station meeting, I noticed that the atmosphere was more relaxed than usual. 'Alright. What a week!' I began. 'We've pumped a total of forty-one hours over ten days, with an average of about ten hours a day when it all went well and a fair bit less when, like this morning, it didn't go so well. Thanks to everyone for their patience as we refined the way to get it done. It's now a pretty smooth routine.

'We've also decided that, despite theoretically being able to pump overnight, we're going to abandon any plan for twenty-four-hour pumping and stick to the day shifts as we've done the last few days. Once the hose has been pumping for that magical ten hours, there seems to be a gradual ice accumulation that is only solved by thawing them overnight, so we'll stick to that, which is better for fatigue management as well.'

This cleared up the last remaining rumours of running nonstop or changing the shifts from four four-hour shifts to three six-hour shifts or any other permutation that might have been suggested. As always, there were many opinions and many ways to achieve the outcome. The plumbers were happy with the current shifts and that was good enough for me.

'So when does it end?' someone asked.

'Great question. It depends ... The best estimates are around eighty to one hundred hours.' I looked at Gaz and the plumbers, who weren't keen on putting figures on it, as they knew it could be longer. What they didn't know was that there was a group of increasingly agitated scientists who wanted to know when we would be finished with the tarn so they could redeploy their field teams. They needed an answer, no matter how vague.

With all three mechanics tied to tarn shifts, we couldn't deploy a mechanic into the field to respond to a breakdown, which meant no fieldtrips during the tarn work. This wasn't news to anyone and had always been the plan, but after a solid week's work and some long hours and frustrating moments along the way, there was a growing sense of impatience.

It wasn't just the four-hour shift that was the problem. As always, the Antarctic factor had to be taken into consideration. As we'd be standing around outside for four hours in minus 15 degrees, we wanted to be well fed and well layered with clothing, which meant we'd start getting ready at least an hour before the shift started. On the morning shift this meant waking up at about 5am. Because we only had three teams and four shifts, every third day we'd each work both the set-up shift and pack-up shift with an eight-hour break in the middle and then a late start the next day. That was if the shift even ended at the four-hour mark. There were many occasions when we would work well into the second shift to help fix an issue or cover for someone who was called to their primary role.

Also, when we weren't on shift, we'd generally still do our normal jobs, adding another five to six hours to our days. On at least two occasions during the week there had also been the need for an 'all hands' emergency pack-up, so even if we weren't on shift, we would make our way outside to help. The kitchen kept running and turning out extra meals to meet the end of each shift, which meant additional helpers in the kitchen when we had a spare moment or were simply given a tea towel or cleaning cloth by Rhonda and 'voluntold' to help. Add in an hour for the gym, any phone calls or video meetings back home and our four-hour shifts had become a pretty jam-packed and exhausting day.

I'd started filling in on the shift teams when others couldn't make it and enjoyed the simplicity of the role, as well as chewing the fat while standing around discussing aspects of the system that could have been better or worse.

'Do you reckon we should change to three shifts a day? Then you'd only work one shift per day, but it'd be six hours instead of four,' I put to Jimbo as we wandered along the hose, tapping it with rubber mallets to break the ice accumulation along the way.

'From what we've seen this week, I think we've proven four hours is about as much standing around in the cold watching a hose as the human spirit can endure,' he replied. We agreed to stick to four-hour shifts.

* * *

Day 358: 16 October 2020
Temperature: -13.4°C to -5.5°C
Maximum wind speed: 50 kilometres per hour

We were now seventeen days into refilling the tarn and morale was up as we approached the end. I was proud to see people bonding again after the earlier squabbles. There was also fresh news that the first Adélie penguin had been spotted down on the sea ice that morning. They were beginning to return from their winter at sea to their courting and breeding ground.

With constant assessment and monitoring by the plumbers, relaying information back to Kingston about the level of the tarn, the consensus was now that 'we're getting close'. With good weather forecast for the next two days, it made sense to keep pumping and make sure the station was well set up for the uncertain time ahead.

By now I had joined a specific team after one member had to return to their primary role too often to be reliable. As I approached the tarn to replace the earlier shift, I noticed that no one was there. Figuring they were walking along the hose back to the pump end, I sat down on the snow bench that had been carved over the last few weeks and watched the hose.

With four hours of staring at the hose ahead of me, to be broken up periodically by walking up and down the line as we rotated through our watch, I sat quietly with my thoughts and remembered how peaceful it was to listen to running water for a change. Although a team, we were often spread out along the hose as we walked back and forth or went to check on the couplings or vehicles. The most important roles were the mechanic standing at the pump end, and whoever was watching the outflow at the tarn end.

Refilling the tarn had taken longer and been harder than we'd all pictured, but it was this kind of challenge I'd expected. As the job neared completion, I was encouraged by the practical jokes and friendly banter of the shifts, which had replaced the earlier bickering and expert advice on better ways to skin this cat. One by one, I mentally analysed where I felt everyone was at. One of the shift teams was even regularly playing hide-and-seek or Marco Polo–style games around the pressure ridges of the tide crack and rock formations along the shoreline.

The overwhelming majority of the team members had risen to the challenge – they had found ways to break up the days and weeks with fitness or study and were actively involved in community events or activity to some degree. They had professional relationships with all on station and, although not necessarily best friends, they were certainly friendly and engaging with one another. There were, of course, a few who had withdrawn from the community events and were increasingly short-tempered and unprofessional when asked to do even simple tasks. It was these few who worried me. What could we do to engage them better and reset the group for the last few months?

With the tarn nearly finished, operationally we had the most complex tasks completed. There was some critical maintenance over summer for the powerhouse and then firing up the plant to desalinate all this water we were pumping into the tarn, but nothing that wasn't relatively easy. The solution? Two parts, to follow the tarn job and a well-earned low-tempo few days.

First, we'd run a series of sessions to help everyone learn and understand each other's methods for managing mental health and physical wellbeing. 'Wellness week', as it became known, was the brainchild of Doc and me as we canvassed the community to stand up and run sessions based on their particular coping method.

The second part of the plan was to instigate a five-day work week and do away with Saturday-morning work for the peak sea-ice period from now until it broke down again in summer. This would give everyone a full two-day weekend to get out and enjoy the scenery and wilderness.

These concepts were generally well received, albeit with some scepticism from Gaz, who was worried we'd fall behind on station maintenance. Ultimately, many of us worked six to seven days a week anyway but, once again, it was about creating opportunity for people where possible and giving everyone a break.

As I was lost in my thoughts staring at the hose, Jimbo walked up behind me and sat down. Now we both stared at the hose pumping away and spraying water into the full-looking tarn in front of us.

'What are you thinking about?' he asked.

'Usual station leader stuff – how everyone is doing and how we can best cope with the last few months.'

'What did you come up with?'

'Well, I reckon it's all about motivation. Those of us who came here looking for adventure, either professional or personal, seem to have done a bit better through the difficulties compared with those who may not have had a clear reason for signing up,' I said.

'Deep,' laughed Jimbo. 'Mate, you've had too much time to think while staring at that hose.'

'Well, what do you reckon, then?' I asked.

'Everyone has dealt with it their own way. I agree, there are a few that maybe didn't contemplate what can happen when you head down here,' replied Jimbo, standing up as the cold of the ice bench started to penetrate his layers.

'I mean, I never quite expected to get stuck on an Antarctic station for a year and a half, watching a global pandemic, during the one year in thirty our country doesn't have its own icebreaker and our planes can't get through the now-closed international borders … it was hard to predict,' I said.

We both started laughing at the bizarre turn of events that had unfolded to leave us in such a predicament.

Noting it was time for a walk, I slowly stood up to take my turn walking along the hose and I wrapped up the conversation. 'Given all that, it's incredible we're doing as well as we are.'

'Well, it's not like anyone can quit,' said Jimbo as I wandered off, picking up a rubber mallet I noticed was Bunnings home brand, to knock the ice off the couplings as I walked along.

'Typical government operation, cheap mallets,' I said. I laughed to myself as I daydreamed of the multitude of DIY projects that awaited me whenever I got back home to my half-renovated house.

* * *

That evening, sitting in the lounge with a few members of the team, enjoying a cup of tea and staring out the windows towards the icebergs, as had become the tradition, the mood was good. We'd just confirmed tomorrow would be the last day of pumping as we'd hit about 120 hours total, to be followed by a day off before the long-awaited 'Tarn Party', which had now blended into Oktoberfest. We marked the occasion with a cake and the best homebrews we'd produced over the last month as part of a competition.

The living quarters lounge is a half-level higher than Nina's bar, which sits on a mezzanine level between the mess and other lounges above. This means you can hear the noise of the bar if someone's getting a bit loud. I'd noted people were at the bar as I sat down, so nothing was out of the ordinary, but the noise level seemed a little elevated for a school night.

'He's one of them, typical boss.' My ears pricked up. It wasn't uncommon to hear people voice their opinions, but this sounded a bit too direct. The hairs on the back of my neck stood up as I realised who he was talking about. 'He knew all along and chose not to tell us! Made us sit there through dinner and then – *boom!* – the next day, you're all staying!'

That confirmed it – I was the subject. I was sick of this conversation, which I'd had a hundred times with more than one expeditioner over the previous few months, about our extension and the circumstances around it. I stood up and walked towards the bar and head-on into the verbal tirade directed at me.

'Right, what's your beef?' I said, taking a seat directly across the table as I noticed the empty pint glasses of our finest homebrew and the empty packet of chips.

'You are! You knew all along we were staying,' fired Fred.

'I'll leave ...' Gaz, the only other customer at Nina's, sheepishly offered.

'Na, stick around. This will be fun,' I said to Gaz, with a look that suggested it would be beneficial to have someone impartial involved in what was going to be an interesting exchange. I turned to Fred. 'First of all, I didn't know. I could see like the rest of us it wasn't looking good, and I made my peace with staying as long as they needed us to, but I found out the day you did.'

'I never signed up for this long!' continued Fred.

'Like I said the other day, when you sign up to go south it's open-ended until you get home. It has been that way for a hundred years. Things down here don't always go to plan, with ships running aground, engine fires, sea-ice breakouts, horrendous blizzards and, this year, a global pandemic. We don't have an icebreaker or any planes, so there's not much we can do about it.'

'Well, what are the Chinese and Indians and all them doing?' said Fred, pointing towards the Larsemann Hills stations 100 kilometres away, past the glacier we could see on the horizon out the window of Nina's.

'They're all staying too, in fact. I was speaking to the Indian station the other day – they might have to stay for a second winter, and if the French can't get a plane into Antarctica and up to Concordia then they'll also be staying another winter.'

I was trying to balance the tone of this conversation and give him some perspective. The conversation was heated beyond what I would have liked, but at the same time, I was sick to death of rehashing the same conversation and giving the same answers.

Every time I listened to expeditioners complain about the situation that I was equally impacted by, I tried to be understanding and empathic, but I'd finally had enough.

For the first time since arriving in Antarctica, my brain engaged a mode of operation that had long been dormant, and that was not within my current leadership handbook. Against my better judgement, I let my emotions get in the way as I told Fred exactly how I felt about the situation and his reaction.

'I can't pull a plane out of my arse. We're all here until that ship gets here next year, and you can either sit here and keep complaining about it or you can come up with a plan, get involved, do your job and go home safely. Just like everyone else has done.'

I sat back in my chair. It felt good to finally voice what I'd been bottling up inside to confront the ongoing complaints, and I waited to see if this Hail Mary would work and get him back on track.

'Yeah? Well, I quit!' said Fred as he stood up and walked off.

'You can't just quit.'

'Can, and just did. See ya,' smirked Fred as he kept walking towards the accommodation, smug and seemingly proud of his actions.

I'd tried everything. Since the extension, I'd explained the situation more times than I could remember. We'd adjusted work routines, allowed days off, approved every request for recreational fieldtrips, run the community college, won the film festival, arranged a second gym, organised wellness week, offered professional development programs, celebrated birthdays, Zoomed into weddings, funerals and anniversaries, watched as the world changed. As I sat there I wondered how on Earth I would deal with this new situation, until I remembered a daydream I'd had about the ill-fated Trans-Antarctic Expedition.

After abandoning their ship, the *Endurance*, when it was trapped by pack ice, Shackleton, the expedition leader, and his crew camped on the treacherous sea ice of the Weddell Sea. But one member of Shackleton's expedition famously quit and refused to work. So I wasn't the first to have such a bizarre scenario play out in extreme circumstances … but that was a hundred years ago and this was now. Was there a process for this? I asked myself: what would Shackleton do?

I was lost. We had tried everything and nothing worked. This was beyond management and leadership problems, this came down to fundamental human motivation and ethos. From the moment I'd signed up for the Antarctic program I felt a sense of having joined a club whose founding members had hauled sleds across ice and snow while surviving on frozen rations and staring death in the face. Those days were long gone, but this was the legacy of Antarctic expeditions. It was a role that attracted people looking for a 'hazardous journey, small wages, bitter cold, long months of complete darkness, constant danger, safe return doubtful, honour and recognition in case of success'.[20] To me it meant that once you set sail south towards Antarctica, no matter what happens and what challenges you face, *quitting is not an option*.

* * *

I walked over to my office and called Rick. 'Funny story. I've had

---

[20] An alleged advertisement by Ernest Shackleton in the *Times* for the expedition.

one of the team quit,' I said after excusing the late hour of the call. I wanted to make sure he heard it from me first and could arrange the response from Kingston's end.

'Alright, don't stress. It's actually happened before. Standard procedure is generally everyone cools down on both sides and we'll get him back to work in a day or two,' said Rick calmly. He'd noticed I was a bit worked up and was perhaps considering the possibility I was the problem.

'Okay, cool, that actually helps. I'm just sick of explaining the whole story and taking the heat for the extension.'

'I hear you. We'll try to take the heat off you. Technically he can't resign to you anyway, and would need to formally resign to Kingston, so let's just see what he says tomorrow and go from there. Try to get some sleep and hang in there! The boat will get there eventually.'

Just before I hung up, I sensed Rick's humorous disbelief at the ridiculous situation we were now both in.

* * *

I didn't really sleep that night as I replayed conversations and meetings in my head over and over again, searching for a way I could have avoided this scenario. In the early hours of the morning, I resigned myself to being awake all night rather than pretending to sleep. It made more sense when I remembered what I'd said the day before, watching the water flow into the tarn: 'It's incredible we're doing as well as we are.'

There isn't a perfect way to deal with this situation, I told myself.

Everything I had done was working to keep the team together and focused on the tasks at hand. It was the situations beyond our control that were breaking us. So no matter what we did to manage ourselves and the team through this challenge, it was now so far beyond what any of us had expected or signed up for that maybe this was unavoidable. When you push things beyond their limit, they break.

I'd always wanted to be a leader. I enjoy it and have never been shy in seeking opportunities to lead, but this was the first time I'd ever felt like I was failing spectacularly. As I lay there looking at the ceiling, searching for guidance, I recited 'If' by Rudyard Kipling in my head, a poem I'd had on the back of my door while completing officer training that I thought embodied the qualities and attributes of what leadership was.

One line seemed particularly familiar: 'If you can keep your head when all about you are losing theirs and blaming it on you.'[21]

But 'If' wasn't enough to rally me. What I was feeling was beyond simply 'keep calm and carry on', so I kept searching. I finally found the words that resonated with how I felt at this moment: the loneliness, the criticism, the mistakes, the setbacks, the challenges. I'd probably heard it before, but it had never been as true as it was right now – a speech by Theodore Roosevelt given over a hundred years ago.

'It is not the critic who counts; not the man who points out how the strong man stumbles, or where the doer of deeds could have done them better. The credit belongs to the man who is actually in the arena …'[22]

But I wasn't in an arena. I was stuck on an Antarctic station,

---

[21] Rudyard Kipling, 'If', in *Rewards and Fairies*, 1910.
[22] Theodore Roosevelt, 'The Man in the Arena', 23 April 1910.

leading a team that was falling apart and with at least one member who no longer wanted to be part of it.

* * *

As we gathered for a station meeting to wrap up the tarn and congratulate the plumbers and everyone for a job well done, I also had to address the elephant (not) in the room, as we were one man short at the station meeting. Rumours spread quickly so everyone knew what had happened – and everyone was more than happy to stay out of it, as I explained the plan to get Fred back to work.

Sure enough, after a few days of back and forth between Kingston and Fred, we were getting closer to a solution. I knew that, regardless of process and contracts, I had to reset our communication on station and re-engage. I hadn't spoken to Fred since the bar but knew vaguely where I could find him and, sure enough, while everyone else was at work and the chances of interruption were low, I found Fred in the lounge.

'How you doing?' I asked.

'Not great. That's not quite how I wanted this to go,' offered Fred.

'I agree, not quite what I was looking for either.' I was relieved we were both open to moving past this.

'What do you say about coming back to work? We want you back.'

'I want to work, but not how it was – I don't think I can do it.' He was flat, and his body language and tone said more than the words coming out of his mouth.

'I know you're talking to Kingston about it all, and I can't change your contract or have a situation where we don't know what you're doing on station, but if you come up with a plan to work independently or different hours or whatever, I'll support it. We need all the help we can get to run this place.' I gave him some options that were the only obvious ones left if he didn't want to return to his original role.

We sat around a bit longer making idle chat over a cup of tea in the cramped shipping container used as a lounge away from the main lounge – a good place to hide for video calls or a game of poker or cigars. Eventually we developed a plan for him to return to work with a few changes to his role and a different reporting structure. But I could tell his heart wasn't in it anymore. This guy had signed up for a one-year adventure that should have been over soon; instead it would be months until we were home, and all we could do on station was help manage him and everyone else through to the end.

* * *

Having someone move from their original team on station and into a new role wasn't unheard of on Antarctic stations during the winter, as personality clashes evolved, boredom set in or priorities changed. With everything going on, this was the best option. Fred was happy to just chip away at the odd jobs we gave him and work independently while we all counted down the days and did what we could to keep ourselves going.

But how had it come to this? I felt responsible for the whole situation, as did Fred's team on station, Rhonda and even Doc, but each of us continued to work as best we could from our own professional positions to help not just Fred but everyone else get through this.

The formal station leadership group in winter was about half the station, so these meetings were focused mainly on operational matters and plans that the other half of the station wouldn't be interested in. So we saved all the community and broader station decisions for the weekly station meeting. But every so often Rhonda, Doc and I would find a moment to work something out as a smaller group, often focused on mental health or stress-related situations.

As a trio we couldn't have been more different in our backgrounds and experience, but that's what made it work. Between us, we had a common goal to get everyone through, and offered the community three different avenues for communicating issues or resolving conflicts. If someone didn't want to talk to me about it, they had Rhonda or Doc, and if someone had an issue with either of them, they could talk to me.

With everyone else at their workplaces, we quietly met in the cinema, surrounded by racks of DVDs and old-school video-game consoles and some fitness gear for those who used the cinema for yoga. We closed the door, sat down on the comfy leather swivel chairs and laid the facts out.

'I feel like it's falling apart,' I said. 'I don't want to end up with twenty-four people on different contracts working their own hours and only talking to a few people. I need to know from your points of view what we can change or how we do the same thing differently to get everyone to the end.'

Rhonda and Doc sat silently for a second, and I could tell that they sensed I was not quite myself.

'I don't think it's that bad,' said Doc.

'I agree, we've done everything we can,' added Rhonda.

'We've done a lot, but I still feel like it's not quite hitting the mark and the group is splitting a bit beyond repair,' I said, looking at Rhonda's and Doc's tired faces staring back at me. Eventually they agreed something was off and there were more noticeable divisions developing.

'Maybe there isn't an answer, but we have to keep going,' I said. 'The plan for November is to get out and enjoy the ice while it's there. Hopefully that cheers a few people up and drags the rest with them,' I added, trying to focus instead on what we could do.

There is nothing more challenging than an Antarctic winter as an isolated community, and we'd been pushed to the limit. It was starting to show on all of us – eyes sunken and bloodshot, as many of us struggled to sleep properly, haircuts and beards unruly, conversations terse and borderline unprofessional at times. Between the three of us in that room, with our collective experience, we failed to find a silver bullet but committed to keep going, and keep trying, because that was our only option. It was our best chance at success.

'You know it's the anniversary today?' said Doc.

'Did I miss our wedding anniversary again?' I joked, trying to lighten the mood.

'One year since we left,' replied Rhonda. 'That could explain the moping around – the fact we would have been going home about now but still have months to go, that this just never ends …'

I exhaled, struggling to find hope.

'Wellness week, let's do that now, reset a few heads and go from there,' said Doc, reminding me of next week's plan, which had taken a back seat while I dealt with the shock resignation.

'Of course – I'd forgotten. Hopefully everyone is still keen and we'll have some fun.' I wrapped up the meeting with renewed enthusiasm.

* * *

Wellness week was long overdue, having had a few false starts, but was exactly the creative and physical outlet we needed. We all had our own approach to wellbeing on station and this week we'd share them with others through a series of classes and sessions each afternoon. There were more classical options such as group fitness and yoga, along with a session on mindfulness and then tai chi or wu for a truly different approach. I was well known for loudly attacking the boxing bag in the gym and doing my own creative MMA-style workouts, so I decided it was time to start my own dōjō and run some group sessions.[23]

The problem was that I was a bit rusty. I muddled my way through a few techniques, but they didn't quite go to plan. The overall effect of letting off some steam by punching something and breaking a sweat has always worked for me, and even though it was clear I should probably stick to my day job, I got good reviews from those who attended the classes.

Wellness week wasn't just about fitness and meditation, though,

---

[23]   MMA is 'mixed martial arts' and dōjō refers to a hall or place for immersive learning or meditation, traditionally used in martial arts.

and Rhonda outdid herself yet again with an amazingly healthy range of meals for the week. At one point, when I got a message from a mate back home asking 'How's life down there, pretty tough?' I replied with a photo of my cos lettuce salad with pine nuts and grilled chicken. 'Yeah, it's rough.'

By the end of wellness week I was feeling better. I'd slept well for the first time in a long time and there was an energy about the place that seemed to lift everyone's mood. It prompted me to appreciate the incredible team we had and how, even this far into our trip, we were still learning things about each other and could come together when it mattered.

It's hard to not focus on the negative aspects of leadership and management in a situation like this. But I was determined to reward positive attitudes, and the overwhelming majority of the team had risen to the challenges we faced. As we looked ahead to November, with the sea ice at its peak and the weather improving, those who wanted to get out and enjoy everything Antarctica had to offer were given the keys to the Häggs and offered flexible work hours to make it happen.

Chapter 9

The Last Days of Sea Ice

Day 405: 2 December 2020
Temperature: -3.3°C to -0.06°C
Maximum wind speed: 69 kilometres per hour

With the temperatures up and the sun shining, summer was returning to Davis. The bleak winter days were behind us and we were getting a sense that the worst of it was over. More information evolved about the voyage plan and eventual resupply at Davis in early 2021. The end was in sight.

I was intent on making the most of the last of the sea ice and, after letting everyone get out and adventure in November, during our lower tempo month, it was time to have my own fun. I did enjoy a few recreational trips with different groups during the year but it was always a bit weird when teams had to decide if they wanted the station leader on their fieldtrip. The best way to solve the problem was to just do the fun work trips, which had the added bonus of being on the approved list of quad-bike activities.

By this late stage, everyone had been out in the field dozens of times and had the routine down to a tee. A quick check of the weather at breakfast and a reminder of what time to meet at the bikes and you were set.

On this day, I headed off with our resident engineer and award-winning film producer, Dan, down to a small island towards the Sørsdal Glacier known as Kazak Island, where there was a time-lapse camera and automated weather station that needed a service before the ice broke out and they became inaccessible again.

'I've got the recovery kit and sea-ice drilling kit,' I said to Dan as he arrived in the shed to start loading the bikes.

'Perfect. I've got a trunk full of spare parts and gear that'll take up all my space,' replied Dan.

He'd learned well through the season to take pretty much everything you might need, as on more than one occasion he had to return to station for extra parts or tools to repair the instruments and equipment he was responsible for.

'I'll go turn the tags and meet you outside the living quarters?' I said, firing up the bike.

'Done. See you soon,' said Dan through his helmet, and gave me a thumbs-up signal with his giant mittens.

I was grinning as I headed to the mess to turn the fire tags. The short ride from the vehicle shed had a small rise over a culvert that had created a spectacular morning view. I turned our tags to red but before I could get out the door, Doc grabbed me. 'Can I have a quick chat before you go?'

'Sure, no worries,' I said, as we made our way into the cinema and closed the door for some privacy. Doc was dressed in his usual board shorts and scruffy T-shirt, and I was kitted out ready to rock and roll on the quad bikes. One of us was overdressed. 'So, what's up, Doc?' I asked.

'We've got a relatively serious medical issue with one of the team. We're looking at treatment options on station and we think we can manage it until the end, but I have to run a few more tests and speak to some specialists back home,' said Doc.

'Alright, I'll let them come forward and inform me in their own time, but let me know what you need and if there is anything we can do,' I replied.

It was the trickiest of situations for Doc. For patient confidentiality reasons, he couldn't give me any more information unless the patient agreed, and it appeared there were still a lot of unknowns about the situation. The only good news was that Doc was confident the patient could be treated on station, and everyone knew we wouldn't be home until April.

'I'll chat to you a bit more tonight after I'm back from Kazak Island,' I said.

I left the cinema and walked down the stairs and out the door as my mind scrolled through all the possible medical conditions Doc could be dealing with. I hoped we could treat it. It clearly wasn't as simple as a broken leg or appendicitis, which we could treat on station or set up to operate if needed. Our medical clinic was well equipped, but it was nothing compared to a real hospital, and any advanced treatment would require evacuation back to Australia.

As I came down the steps of the LQ back to my quad bike, Dan arrived and the two of us rode off into the distance.

As we rode along the sea ice, something strange happened: I soon realised I was experiencing a sensation I hadn't felt in months – I was hot. Having almost frozen to the pegs of the quad bikes in winter and been bitten by the cold finding its way through any gap in my clothing, I'd overdressed.

We both stopped about ten minutes in to open a few vents on our jackets and work out a better way to reduce the fog in our sunglasses. These were problems I simply hadn't had to deal with since last summer, and they were glorious problems to have.

Arriving at Kazak Island, we had to be careful. Recent satellite imagery from the area showed the sea ice had broken out on the coastal side of the island and towards the Sørsdal Glacier's tongue, which floated on the sea and broke the sea ice as it moved up and down with the ocean. Summer was coming. So we slowed down, drilling the sea-ice depths to ensure it was still safe to keep going as we made our way through the islands and to our destination.

We dismounted, grabbed our field packs and started the short hike to the far side of the island. We wandered through a few penguin rookeries of Adélies as they squawked and stubbled around the rocks and ice. They were now all back on land and into the start of their breeding season.

The weather station was perched high on a hill and had a spectacular view back down the glacier. I knew this would be my last trip to this area and made sure to take it in. The wildlife had returned in force, and we watched the southern giant petrels circling and swooping around, getting ready to take advantage of any unattended penguin eggs or chicks. I took my camera out to capture the scene. I was enjoying photography again after losing my passion during winter when cameras kept freezing and lighting was dim.

'If this is the vibe for the last few months, we'll be alright,' I said to Dan as I passed him tools or rolls of duct tape while he worked on the equipment.

'Everyone seems to be doing a lot better lately,' replied Dan.

'The end is still too far away to get excited, but you just get the sense now it's close enough to see the light,' I said.

'That's it! Done,' said Dan as he closed the pelican case that housed the instruments and got ready to leave.

'Took us an hour to get here for that?' I said. I'd expected at least a day's work away from my desk.

'Yeah, it was easy, just a memory card swap and firmware update,' said Dan, also surprised that it had gone to plan.

We packed up and headed back to station. Along the way we followed some emperor penguin tracks across the ice in the hope of finding a few to photograph on such a lovely day, but they were long gone.

Riding back towards station across the sea ice, I knew the days were numbered before we had to close access. The ice was still over a metre thick but was fast decaying from the bottom and would soon be unsafe for vehicles or foot travel. This would mean for the rest of the summer we'd be confined to the rocky areas we could access around Davis itself, and could no longer access Whoop Whoop or land a plane on the sea ice in the event of an emergency.

Crossing the tide crack and returning to station all but confirmed it; navigating the large cracks with the quad bikes was a challenge and it took us nearly half an hour to find a safe route back onto the beach. There was just one last thing we needed to get done on the ice before I closed it officially for the season.

* * *

There was one strange positive to come out of our extension that I was keen to take advantage of. With just the two dozen of us on station, when ordinarily by December there would be teams of field scientists flying in to collect samples and study the environment, it was up to us to fill in for them. Just as the Weather Magician had done throughout the winter season as the substitute lead scientist, we did what we could as citizen scientists.

'Dave, we need you to undertake some benthic ecology work,' said the head of underwater science back in Kingston over the video link.

'Sure. Remind me again what that is?' I said. There had been a team on station last summer as part of this project.

'It's the study of organisms that make up the seabed. The team from last summer need some comparison photos of the areas they studied then to see what's changed.'

I was confused about how we could accomplish this.

Last season they had a state-of-the art suitcase-sized remote-operated vehicle that looked like a bomb-disposal submarine from the future. 'How exactly can we replicate their work without the ROV?' I asked.

'Up to you. They'll send through the grid references and requirements. See what you come up with – thanks!'

We certainly didn't have the sophisticated robot but, when we distilled the requirements and looked at what we had available, the solution was simple. All the robot enabled was an easier way of navigating around under the sea ice to find locations of interest and take photos with the multiple GoPro cameras mounted on it. We already knew where to look, and with solid sea ice we could just drive to the location, drill a hole and put the camera down. Simple!

The next day, Bob and I jumped in the Hägg loaded with every GoPro battery and additional charging pack we could find, plus the all-important 2-metre cane we would attach the camera to, and headed off onto the sea ice. In the freezing-cold water, the batteries would only last a few minutes, so we had to change the camera each time, but by the end of the day we'd successfully taken photos of the seabed at each of the fifty sites.

As I uploaded the photos that evening, I was surprised to see just how many fish and sea spiders lived just out the front of the station under the sea ice. You never know what's lurking in the ocean ...

Chapter 10

A Christmas Miracle

Day 417: 14 December 2020
Temperature: –3.5°C to 0.7°C
Maximum wind speed: 43 kilometres per hour

With Christmas fast approaching, the only thing on my mind was making sure we got the right balance of work and rest over the upcoming Christmas–New Year break. With Kingston on holidays, there would be less work coming in from our technical bosses and we could afford a few quieter days to relax.

I had long planned to give the office a makeover and repaint it from 'stale purple' to a more vibrant 'dull yellow' colour, of which there were sufficient leftovers in the dangerous-goods shed. The mechanics had just completed the annual maintenance of the main powerhouse, which left us with just the desalination plant to fire up after Christmas to start making water. The finish line was finally in view.

'Can I come see you?' said Doc as he rang to confirm I was in my office.

'Yep, come on over,' I replied. I double-checked I didn't have an upcoming video meeting or phone call, and assumed we were going to discuss his application for the role of Santa Claus.

His mood was flat as he closed the door and got straight to the point.

'What are the options if we have to get someone out of here right now?' asked Doc.

He knew it was above my pay grade to make such a decision. However, as station leader, I was the only one on station who was tracking the operational movements of all maritime and aviation assets from other nations in Antarctica to enable mutual support for emergency requirements and search and rescue over the vast distances.

'What are you talking about? You know as well as I do there are no real options until the ship arrives,' I said, switching one of my computer screens to the live tracking map.

Resembling a flight tracker, it showed a few dots scattered across the Antarctic continent and the Southern Ocean. Twelve months earlier, at the peak of summer, this map was littered with dots and route plots as the icebreakers, cargo vessels, research ships and tourist yachts navigated around the coast, and various planes and helicopters leapt between stations. Right now, it was bare.

'All I'm aware of is the American plane at McMurdo, which they're sharing with the French and Italians to access Concordia station far inland, but that's 5000 kilometres away. In terms of ships, the Chinese icebreaker is somewhere between New Zealand and Antarctica, but there's no chance we can get either of those unless its critical. What is going on?' I suspected this was not a hypothetical scenario.

If there were planes sitting around on Antarctic stations with nothing to do, they would have come and taken some of us home. With only a few planes out of the dozens in a standard Antarctic summer making it to the icy continent, they were working at full capacity for critical cargo and passenger transfers to inland stations, making sure no one endured a second winter.

'It's bad. Remember the situation I told you about a few weeks back, when we thought we could treat something on station? Well, they won't make it until our ship gets here with what I've got. So how do we get this happening, the things with the planes or ships and an evacuation back to Australia?' Doc stared at me until I fully understood that he was deadly serious.

'There's no guarantee. It's all theoretical and we'll have to move heaven and Earth to get approval from the other nations. And then we've got COVID-19 to consider. I'll need to know what to plan for and how to manage this operationally while you manage the medical side.' My mind started racing through the emergency procedures checklist.

Doc was in a tough position. He'd informed me a few weeks earlier there was a serious but manageable medical condition on station, but clearly it had taken a turn.

'I can't go into details, but he needs treatment in Australia asap. Can you make the calls?' said Doc.

What was about to happen would be a fittingly unprecedented end to 2020.

'I'll hit the red button. What you're asking is nearly impossible and we just closed the sea ice, so we can't use the sea-ice runway or drive to Whoop Whoop. You'll need to get the Polar Medicine Unit back in Kingston to brief the director so decisions can be made there. I'll work with operations, and let's both hope for a Christmas miracle.'

Doc turned and left my office.

You've got to be kidding me, I thought. The timing couldn't have been worse. Just a week or two earlier and we could have scraped out an emergency runway right out the front on the sea ice. Now we'd not only need to find a plane we could borrow, but we'd need a way of accessing Whoop Whoop.

Thankfully, we'd sent one of the snow groomers back up to Whoop Whoop after it was serviced, so we had the capability up there to build a runway, but we still couldn't get to Whoop Whoop because the sea ice had decayed beyond safe use and would break out any day now. Or could we?

* * *

'You wanted to see me?' said Jarrod after I'd called him to my office.

'We might need to get to Whoop Whoop. I'll explain more later, but I need you to put a team together and develop a plan for a reconnaissance trip looking for an alternative route via rock and fjord to Whoop Whoop.' Pre-empting his next question, I continued. 'All I need now is the plan and who you'll take. I'll get you the approvals from Kingston and some advice from Mitch and anyone else we can find on old waypoints or different options to get there. This is real.'

I had engaged emergency mode and could see Jarrod computing the various issues and risks this would entail, but I needed him to stay on task. The overall problem wasn't his to worry about, and keeping people focused on their part in the emergency response was critical to the efficiency of the whole response. Right now, I needed to know if there was a snowflake's chance in Antarctica of getting a Hägg to Whoop Whoop with a mechanic to start building a runway.

Throughout the long history of Australia in the Vestfold Hills, numerous tracks and roads had been created, scattered around the hills and in unlikely places, so you could sneak a vehicle between boulders and across rocky areas we'd otherwise never use. We'd all seen the old-school maps hanging in the field huts, which showed historic routes out of the fjords and onto the plateau, although we usually accessed the sea ice from the front of station. But if we could access Long Fjord to the north and overland across the rocks, then maybe, just maybe, the ice inside the Fjords was still solid enough. Were any of these routes feasible with the ice conditions we had right now?

This was a unique situation, not a case of knowing there was a road from A to B like you would back home. This required an experienced set of eyes and comprehensive and regular testing of the sea ice and glacial ice. A route that was safe today in certain temperatures might be unsafe tomorrow if temperatures were just a few degrees warmer.

The Häggs needed 60 centimetres of good sea ice to travel safely, and the quads were safe at 40 centimetres. There was a safety factor in their load limits, meaning you could get away with a few centimetres less than the regulations, but we didn't want to create more problems by dropping a vehicle through thin ice, so it was either good to go or closed.

I needed answers to the million questions running through my head.

After Jarrod left, I picked up the phone to make a conference call to all stations and hit the red button. 'We need to do an evacuation,' I said to Rick and the other station leaders after explaining the basic situation. 'The chief doctor of the Australian Antarctic Division should be walking into your office, or about to be. I'm initiating the station Incident Management Team and will brief the station immediately after this call.'

I still couldn't believe what I was saying and what was happening. I felt like I was on autopilot, watching myself run through the process and looking on in disbelief. Good luck trying to pull this one off in the middle of a pandemic, with no helicopters, no ships and none of the dedicated aviation teams you had during summer, I thought to myself. But back in Kingston no one batted an eyelid as they pivoted the operations team to emergency mode.

'Acknowledge all that,' said Rick. 'We've initiated the crisis management response team at Kingston and sent requests to all foreign nations with assets in the vicinity, declaring we have a medevac situation with more details to come.' We went through the formal but critical processes of pivoting both the station and the division to crisis mode.

The other stations were informed they were now on a go-slow to reduce the chance of a secondary incident, and additional resources were made available to me back at Kingston to help support the team at Davis. Importantly, I needed a team helping Jarrod plan the field routes and search and rescue contingencies before anyone went out testing alternative routes to Whoop Whoop. I also needed a team from aviation to get in touch with the mechanics on station, who would have to prepare an emergency runway.

'Copy that. We'll get those teams together back here and start feeding you the plans and options as they develop,' replied Rick without hesitation.

We were already in the midst of the greatest challenge we'd faced in recent years, with a global pandemic hampering the delivery of a new icebreaker and prohibiting aircraft access to Antarctica. But with yet another crisis added to the mix, our only option was to face the challenge head-on.

* * *

It was time to brief the station. We'd had a series of drills throughout the year, dating all the way back to our arrival, to test the Incident Management Team. After a few tweaks to the teams for the road ahead, I walked into the cinema to brief everyone.

'From right now we're in a station incident management situation to enable a medevac. Doc is currently with the patient. He'll be okay but we need to get him home asap. Doc will update you a bit more later on. All three other stations are on a go-slow and this is the AAD's highest priority until completed.'

I took a breath and watched the faces around the room. I felt the full attention of everyone on station for the first time in a long time during a meeting.

'The plan isn't certain and there are significant risks and issues to work through before this goes ahead. There is no guarantee this is even feasible with the ice and weather conditions. The plan right now is to send a field party to Whoop Whoop, either by land if the route is safe or in a foreign helicopter if one is in range. We're also working to get the US plane across from McMurdo via Wilkins to here. Because the US plane can't fly to Hobart, we'll then get the patient back to Australia on the A319 out of Wilkins.'

I took another breath. 'Jarrod's recon team will head out shortly and I'll speak to a few of you separately on key roles after this. The other factor is fatigue. This might drag on for a week or more, so if you can rest, then rest. There will be some long days ahead.' I exhaled again as everyone took a moment to digest the situation.

There was one question everyone wanted to ask. It wasn't quite the right time to ask, but it was also absolutely the right time. One brave soul put up their hand on behalf of the team, knowing this might be their only chance.

'Will there be other seats on the plane? Asking for a friend.'

'I don't know. Anyone who wants to nominate for the stand-by queue will have to speak to Kingston. Our job is to make the medevac happen.' At some level, everyone was interested in those spare seats, but for now we all had a job to do.

* * *

'It's simple. Scomo calls the president of China and asks for a helicopter. He then calls the president of the USA and asks for approval to use their plane. Done,' joked Jimbo as we walked out of the cinema.

He wasn't wrong. It was technically that simple, but making it happen without creating more risks or endangering lives or aircraft was another issue. Oh, and remember the Australia–China trade dispute of late 2020, when the two nations weren't talking officially and were imposing tariffs and embargoes on each other's goods? Yeah, this was right about then.

While ordinarily an operation like this could be coordinated through the three nations' Antarctic programs, with COVID-19 and strict quarantine requirements, our request for an emergency medevac would indeed end up on the desk of the prime minister of Australia and the president of China for final approval. I'm not sure if it made it to the White House.

* * *

After I made the decision to push the red button, I worked remotely with teams in Kingston and Canberra to organise and plan the operation from start to finish and cover every single risk and contingency to make sure we didn't miss anything or make the situation worse. There were only twenty-four of us on station but dozens more back in Kingston directly assisting us. To match the work hours of those back in Australia, this meant I was awake from about 0200 to 2200 hours each day as we developed the plan and jumped through hoops.

One major hoop was checking the airworthiness of foreign helicopters. The team back in Kingston was required to check that foreign aircraft met Australia's Civilian Aviation Safety Authority maintenance standards, to ensure the safety of our expeditioners and patient. This was something that usually took weeks, but that the poor team back home would have to achieve in a matter of days.

Once the plan was developed, we met as a team and agreed that the plan was sound, the risks were acceptable and, despite all the paperwork, meetings and planning, we could actually do what was needed.

* * *

Day 421: 18 December 2020
Temperature: -2.0°C to 0.6°C
Maximum wind speed: 35 kilometres per hour

'We're on.'

The words hung heavy in the air after the AAD's aviation operations manager gave me the final green light that the governments of China and the USA had agreed to make assets available to support the operation within strict COVID-safe requirements and limited operational windows. It had been a week of frantic planning, thinking, stressing and worrying but now, seemingly out of nowhere, we were about to put together one of the most complex medical evacuations ever from Davis.

Soon a helicopter from the Chinese icebreaker *Xue Long II*, nearly 100 kilometres away from Davis at the Chinese station of Zhongshan, would lift off and fly to Davis to collect a team of five expeditioners and transport them to Whoop Whoop, where they'd spend five days preparing the runway.

The helicopter would come back later to transport the patient from Davis to Whoop Whoop, where it would meet an American aircraft from McMurdo, which now was still 5000 kilometres away, waiting for a weather window to get to Davis. It would then fly the patient to Wilkins, where he would be transferred onto the Airbus A319 and flown back to Australia.

If anything went wrong and the helicopter couldn't return to Whoop Whoop, the team would have to walk some 50 kilometres back to the station over glaciers, rock and snow. Nobody wanted to walk home: it was an arduous journey at the best of times, but with the added weight of failure of the whole operation, it would be abysmal.

To make the medevac happen, we needed suitable weather at no less than five separate locations across a huge slice of the Southern Hemisphere. The final piece of the puzzle would be Australia's intercontinental Airbus A319 flying from Hobart, which would transport the patient back to Australia from the Wilkins Aerodrome, near Casey, once we could get him there.

Optimism was high throughout the team, but we all knew there were still a million things that could go wrong, most of which were out of our control.

From down the hallway I heard a phone ringing at the unstaffed communications console. The console was a hive of activity in the summertime, attended almost constantly to coordinate and log all air traffic and operations throughout the station operating area, but it had been dormant for almost a year. Surprised to hear it ringing again, I answered the phone and realised it was the Chinese operations coordinator on the *Xue Long II* setting up the ground communications.

It was a relief to no longer have to go via Canberra and Beijing – now it all felt real. This was the first ground-to-ground conversation of the whole operation and, hearing the eagerness of the Chinese team to support our operation eased my nerves.

Across a patchy satellite phone connection, the Chinese had just one question: 'When would you like our helicopter?' asked the coordinator.

'Asap! But the weather is bad today, so tomorrow we'll confirm go or no-go after the morning forecast and expect the first flights around 1300 Davis time,' I said, looking out the window at the low clouds and strong wind.

I looked up at the four clocks above my head – Davis Local (UTC+7), UTC,[24] Kingston (UTC+11) and Zhongshan (UTC+6) – and tried to calculate in my head while on the phone and writing down key details for the flights. My desk at this point was covered in sticky notes, draft after draft of the overall operational plan, the risk assessment for putting Aussies on a Chinese helicopter, the field risk assessment, the manifests for the flights, the passenger details and equipment lists, and the COVID-19 plan. Thankfully, the AAD had initiated its Crisis Management Response team for this and dozens of experienced expeditioners back home were working on these problems with us, as we would never have been able to do this alone.

Oddly, this was the most connected to the real world I had felt in a long time.

* * *

Day 422: 19 December 2020
Temperature: -2.2°C to 1.1°C

Like all good plans, ours was broken into phases. Phase one: get the team of five to Whoop Whoop.

The results of Jarrod's reconnaissance trip across the rocks and

---

[24] UTC refers to Coordinated Universal Time, or Greenwich Mean Time (GMT). All Antarctic stations seemed to run on different time zones to suit their own programs or national capitals.

fjords had shown us that this route was impassable. What we needed was a helicopter and, in a stroke of luck and good timing, the *Xue Long II* was currently resupplying the Chinese Zhongshan station and had two helicopters on board to transfer cargo and passengers. With some high-level discussions, and helped by an enduring Antarctic friendship between Australian and Chinese stations, the Chinese had agreed to lend us their helicopter before the ship departed the area and headed to other Chinese stations across Antarctica. One week later and we would have been out of luck and on our own.

The airband radio down the hall from my office came to life. 'Davis station, Davis station … This is Chinese helicopter Seven Zero Charlie Zero … requesting clearance for landing.'

The Chinese pilot spoke with the exact cadence of an aviator informing you to keep your seatbelt fastened while seated. I smiled again at this curious similarity.

'Chinese helicopter Seven Zero Charlie Zero, this is Davis station, you are cleared for landing on helipad two. Welcome.' I stepped out of my office to see him approaching the station and quickly walked the 100 metres to the helipads.

My mind wandered again to the irony of adhering to the strict air control requirements when everyone on station was fully aware of the incoming chopper and the nearest other air traffic was probably 3000 kilometres away.

As they approached pad two (the helipad that didn't have cranes and bulldozers parked on it), each member of the ground team went to their posts and looked skyward with anticipation. The fire team had spent the days before running through emergency procedures and equipment and stood ready with extinguishers and rescue gear.

The mechanical team had positioned all the refuelling gear and fuel to support the Chinese team.

Those onboard the incoming helicopter waved as they completed a loop around the pad and confirmed the wind speed and direction (a perfect 10–15 knots from the north-east). We watched on and hunkered down as the wash from the powerful twin-engine Augusta AW-169 started kicking up stones and dust from the Davis helipads that had been dormant for nearly a year.

* * *

As they touched down and the aircrew jumped out to complete shutdown procedures, we donned our N95 surgical masks and gloves over our Antarctic layers and prepared for the moments ahead. This would be the first contact with anyone under the now-global COVID-19 procedures but, for us, it was all new. These were the first people we'd welcomed in nearly twelve months and our first interactions of the COVID-19 era.

'Welcome to Davis,' I said, greeting the Chinese team as they approached. I carefully remained 1.5 metres away and offered a strange wave emulating a handshake.

'Thank you. It is good to be here. We are here to help,' their chief aviation ground safety officer replied as he returned the awkward air-handshake gesture and informed me he had actually spent a summer at Davis as part of an exchange program a few years earlier. Fittingly, much like our own AGSOs, he was stylishly dressed in Chinese Antarctic Program aviation gear.

Time to get down to business. We were all wearing a mask for the first time, complete with gloves, a bottle of hand sanitiser each and an ounce of confusion. We had to keep it COVID-safe while I conducted the briefing, which would be outside in the cold and 1.5 metres away from each other when possible, which was not always maintained. I very quickly received a reminder from Doc to space it out a bit.

To lighten the tense mood, Polar Medicine Unit had advised us that morning that the N95 masks we had on station were less effective with facial hair, so those of us directly involved in the medevac would need to shave our beards. Many of us had been growing beards for the better part of the year and so, as you can imagine, this was met with firm resistance. I soon learned that arguing with doctors during a pandemic is tricky, so we shaved and got a good laugh out of how young and silly we all looked with cuts and dried blood on our cheeks and necks from our last-minute shaves.

For the briefing we'd positioned a table outside near the helipads and I'd made A3 laminates of the weather report, aerial photos of Whoop Whoop and the required flight path from the station. The flight also needed to include a reconnaissance of Platcha Hut along the return walking route for the field team, in case the helicopter couldn't return or, in the worst-case scenario – a downed aircraft – as a safe refuge halfway between the station and Whoop Whoop.

The briefing continued, using mostly hand signals, as I pointed to the maps and the white horizon some 40 kilometres away in the direction of Whoop Whoop.

'We need you do a fly-by of the walking route in case you cannot return. Jarrod here will guide the rest of the Whoop Whoop team and he needs to see the area for crevasses,' I said.

'Oh, that's a long walk. But, okay, we can do the fly-by,' replied the pilot.

The pilots and I completed the paperwork outlining the flight plan and manifests before it was their turn to brief our team. I was nervous. It had been nearly a year since we last ran through this process with our own pilots and, back then, I had an experienced team around me of Brian, Mitch and Sam, but today, on this cold and windy helipad, was starkly different from the warm operations room with a cup of tea, and there was nothing routine about this flight.

The Chinese pilots came prepared with a laminated notebook outlining the emergency procedures and seating arrangements on their machine (sadly, no in-flight movie) as our team looked on, dressed head-to-toe in disposable coverall suits, masks and goggles. It was possibly one of the most serious yet hilarious moments I'd ever witnessed. I made a point of setting up a quick team photo before they left – the team of five, me and the Chinese crew in front of the chopper. It was almost a year to the day since we stood on the same helipad with eighty-odd expeditioners on station for the Christmas party.

As the team boarded the chopper and crammed as much gear as possible inside, there was a great sense of amazement that we had come this far. Just days earlier there was no plan to have any contact with the outside world until early next year. Yet here we were welcoming a helicopter and sending a team to Whoop Whoop about to evacuate a patient. Just how had we gone from sitting around waiting for a ship in a few months to this in the space of a few days?

The team of five was the bare minimum, with each member as essential as the next. Two mechanics and a plant operator would build the runway and move the fuel drums to refuel the plane when it landed. Jarrod, as the field leader, would guide the walk back in the worst case and a weather technician and observer would set up the weather instruments vital to safe air operations.

'Have you all got your passports?' I asked the team sitting inside the Chinese helicopter surrounded by bags of food, glacial travel gear, radios, batteries and anything else we could fit.

'Make sure they come back and get us – I'm not keen on that walk!' replied Jarrod.

Of all the contingencies, walking back from Whoop Whoop was the worst scenario in terms of safety, and would be physically demanding. The reason we'd told them to take their passports and be prepared not to return to Davis was that, if the Chinese helicopter couldn't return but we could land the US Basler aircraft at Whoop Whoop, then all five of the Whoop Whoop team would be flown to Casey. This was unlikely, but with everything going on we had to be ready for anything.

'Good luck, gentlemen. See you back here for Christmas,' I said as I watched the pilot flicking switches and heard the familiar whir of the ignition sequence beginning while the Chinese AGSOs removed the wheel chocks and double-checked the cargo doors. I stepped back and walked to the edge of the helipad to watch it depart.

'Davis station, Chinese helicopter Seven Zero Charlie Zero requesting clearance for take-off for flight to Whoop Whoop with five Australian passengers on board. Over.'

'Cleared for take-off. Godspeed and thank you,' I replied via the handheld airband radio as the noise of the rotors grew louder and dust started to fly off the ground.

As the chopper lifted off and faded into the distance towards the Antarctic Plateau, a wave of emotion hit me. This was it, now, in the middle of nowhere. With a team of exhausted yet experienced expeditioners, we would have less than a week to build a runway, coordinate the aircraft from the US, Chinese and Australian programs to link up across the Antarctic continent, and evacuate our expeditioner. Nothing was certain, and tensions ran high as the Chinese ship with its chopper had a hard deadline to depart the region and manage their own challenges getting to their stations. Within the next week, we would either achieve one of the most daring and complex medical evacuations or be left isolated for another four months wondering why we failed.

Oh, and the weather forecast was bad. For the next week, howling katabatic winds would roll down from the Antarctic Plateau that could deliver frostbite to exposed skin in just minutes, while visibility and blowing snow meant struggling to see a brightly coloured building metres in front of your face. This scene was one that would see anyone else hunker down inside with a cup of tea as they watched the weather rage outside – but, for us, it was the last Sunday before Christmas, and we had a job to do.

* * *

Days 424–425: 21–22 December 2020
Temperature: -2.4°C to 1.5°C

From the minute they arrived at Whoop Whoop, the ground team got to work. With clear weather conditions for the first day and night, it wasn't long until the crew had scraped out a basic landing area, and they would now continue to enhance it until everything else was in place.

But after that, the weather deteriorated. With blizzard conditions hampering their ability to venture outside and see the runway area in front of them, they were forced to sit inside. Nature has a cruel way of reminding you who is boss in Antarctica, with all your work clearing snow for days undone in a matter of hours. The harsh Antarctic winds can deposit enough snow to bury vehicles and buildings overnight.

* * *

Day 426: 23 December 2020
Temperature: -2.9°C to 2°C

Crunch time. For seventy-two hours the team of expeditioners up at Whoop Whoop had done their best with the limited equipment and short weather window to scrape out a 1-kilometre runway for the US plane to land, and everything was more or less ready to go. A groomed Antarctic runway looks similar to a freshly groomed ski trail at a resort anywhere around the world except for one fact – it's flat. To make the edges of the runway, the team filled black garbage bags with snow so that a stark line of black dots could be easily seen from above on the white wasteland of the Antarctic Plateau. We were ready for phase two: patient transfer.

There was one problem – the weather was still terrible, with low cloud over Davis precluding any flights. After many sleepless nights and early starts, I was beginning to feel the impact of collective stress. Returning to my office that morning, I noticed a small Tupperware container marked 'brain power snacks', containing the last unsalted cashew nuts on station, secretly delivered by Rhonda to keep me going as I struggled to eat properly and stay sharp that week. What a legend. We'd recently started desalinating the salted cashew nuts but they tasted a bit weird after being washed. Still, raw cashews were now hot property.

For some, supporting this operation was easy; for others, it was tougher. For a range of reasons it had been decided that our patient would have a chaperone on the journey home. Theoretically, this would have been a doctor or paramedic but the station couldn't operate without a doctor. It was time to deliver some good news to someone for a change.

Grabbing the VHF radio in my office, I put out the call. 'Copy Fred, or anyone who's seen him – can you send him to the station leader's office?' I said, using a radio call usually reserved for bad news. The reply came back quickly.

'Copy copy, we'll send him up, copy.' As was customary, someone else jumped onto their radio and added an extra 'Copy that, copy copy.' It was reassuring that with everything going on, humour was still present on station.

A few minutes later I heard the loud clunking of the doors to the operations building opening and someone completing the rigmarole of taking off boots and jackets and gloves and beanies before knocking on my door.

Fred smiled as he entered my office. 'I think I know what you're about to say.'

'Yep, call your wife. You'll be home for Christmas, but I want to be 100 per cent clear. This whole operation still hangs in the balance. Any number of things can go wrong and then no one goes anywhere, so don't get your hopes up,' I said.

Fred was also one of the few expeditioners with kids back home, who he spoke to every night, and naturally he was desperate to get home to see them. The icing on the cake was that Fred's role on station had redundancy, so, if we sent him, there would be minimal impact on others' workloads.

'You'll have a role to play, though: Doc will talk you through a range of specific medical requirements and you'll have a lot of work to do helping with the patient's gear plus all the COVID-19 rigmarole for the two of you, but, all going well, you'll be home in a couple of days.' Fred was elated but cautious as we stood and shook hands. 'Don't thank me until it's done,' I said.

And so a golden ticket was handed out that would see a second expeditioner whisked away and safely back home by Christmas – or stuck at Casey waiting for the ship to arrive there around New Year's, which remained a very real possibility. With two doctors and an international airstrip nearby, Casey was a better place for our patient to be stuck.

What did it mean to the rest of the team? How do you watch on as your mates are magically transported home but you're still here, isolated, alone and staring down the barrel of another four months until you're able to see your own family? As much as we all knew this operation had to be successful and the patient needed to be evacuated, after over a year away and everything we'd been through, our minds started to wander. The collective mood was to see this through to the bitter end and ride home on the ship as a team, whenever that would be, which left just the patient and Fred going home.

With the morning's forecast suggesting a night-time operation had the best chance of success, I did the only sensible thing and called Kingston. 'We're standing down until 1600. Don't call, don't bother us. It'll be a long night and we need a break.'

I told the station to do the same. 'Rest up and be ready for a long night ahead.' I'd see them back in the Incident Control Room at 1600 hours.

I went to my room and stared at the roof. Realising sleep was not going to happen, I did a lap around the station. It was blowing about 25–30 knots, there was cloud in almost all directions and you didn't have to be the Weather Magician to know it was terrible weather for helicopters.

My mood dropped. It was summer. Davis was known as 'the Riviera of the South' for its unusually good weather – but of all the moments when we needed a blue-sky day, this was the weather we'd been handed. I wandered around and made idle chit-chat with those floating around. We all knew the weather looked rubbish, but optimism told us that it would clear up, as forecast.

We convened the Incident Management Team at 1600 hours and got an updated weather brief. It still looked bleak out the window but was forecast to clear around 2300 hours that night, creating a window of clear skies across the continent and all the way back to Hobart. If – and it was a pretty big if – the forecast was right, we were on.

The pilots of the Basler, now just 1000 kilometres away at Wilkins after the hop across from McMurdo, were sceptical, though, and delayed their take-off. They wouldn't launch until we had visual confirmation from Whoop Whoop that it was clearing.

The Chinese were keen and were soon on the phone. 'Are we go or no-go for the helicopter? We have good weather at Zhongshan. We want to come now,' said the Chinese ops coordinator.

'We are on hold for one hour. It's too cloudy at Whoop Whoop but forecast to clear later,' I replied, hoping he didn't say it was now or never.

'Okay, we'll come as soon as you say.'

I got the sense they were keen to get it done sooner rather than later. So now I had a Chinese helicopter 100 kilometres away champing at the bit, an isolated team at Whoop Whoop 40 kilometres away in poor weather, and suitably cautious American pilots 1000 kilometres away waiting on our update before they would take off. If the four analogue clocks above my head could have synchronised and told me what time it was, they'd have undoubtedly agreed. It was crunch time.

The absurdity and pressure of the situation was not lost on me. As the incident controller, I was in control of all tactical decision making and planning, but the team I had around me was incredible. We were exhausted, but that exhaustion was the accumulation of a year's worth of Antarctic experience for all of us.

Up at Whoop Whoop was the man building the runway, well known across the Antarctic program for his attention to detail and commitment to building runways efficiently and to a high standard. He was the man you wanted in the snow groomer that day. The others up there supporting him were all experts in their fields and worked as a team to make sure everything had been done correctly (including the important task of making of tea and warm food for those outside).

Then, as I waited for the hourly observation to be radioed through, it would come down to the human eyeball of a seasoned Antarctic weather observer to provide the updated weather report, which would then be sent to the pilots, who would make their own judgement about taking off.

The weather observer cracked open the mic and gave me the news at 1900 hours. 'It's clearing up to the east, over,' he said, adding to the required technical reports on wind speed and cloud cover.

While not a precise weather report, this comment, on the back of the technical readouts, was exactly what we needed to hear, and once we passed word along to the US pilots waiting at Wilkins, they were out the door and airborne in less than an hour. As they took off, I was on the phone to the Chinese team, giving them the go-ahead to fly their helicopter up to Davis and get ready to take the patient to Whoop Whoop once we had the plane on the ground.

It was on. This was what it all came down to – days of planning and years of experience all leading to this.

In the background, the final piece of the puzzle, the A319 from Australia, took off from Hobart and started making its way to Wilkins to wait for the US plane carrying the patient from Whoop Whoop. The balls were all in the air – except these balls were all expensive international aircraft from the Chinese, US and Australian Antarctic programs, all working together with a common goal.

I made a flurry of phone calls, sent a bunch of emails and text messages back to all the relevant players in Kingston and other stations to update them. The replies were reassuring and made me realise just how many people were involved in making this happen. At this point it was nearly midnight back home, but evidently not much sleep was being had by the AAD's crisis management team overseeing the whole operation.

I then mentally shifted focus – from now on it was all tactical. By the next morning I would send back reports of either success or failure.

I donned my high-vis winter Carhartt jacket, clipped the required radios to my belt (one for station ops, one for aviation ops and one for comms to Whoop Whoop), stashed some spare batteries in my jacket, along with my mobile and a satellite phone, and headed for the helipads.

Eerily, this routine felt comforting. In my previous lives there had always been similar moments before stepping outside the door and into the unknown, when forgetting even the simplest of items could have dire consequences. With that thought and a dozen memories flashing through my mind all at once, I smiled, and reassured myself. *We got this.*

The hours ticked by as final preparations around the station were made for the patient transfer and operation. The Chinese helicopter returned to Davis and sat patiently on the helipad, ready for the word to transfer the patient to Whoop Whoop once the plane landed. Almost everyone had a specific role directly supporting the operation or was helping out where they could – a great sense of purpose for all.

Finally, at 2330 hours, the word I was expecting to hear crackled through the airband radio I was carrying around. The Basler was on final approach to Whoop Whoop and was happy with visibility. The

Chinese pilots waiting at the Davis helipad heard this and started readying the chopper.

'Wheels down,' came the call from Whoop Whoop.

It was time to load the patient and Fred onto the helicopter to begin their journey home. A final briefing from Doc saw the end of formalities before the patient and Fred departed their home for the last year.

'Thanks again,' said Fred as he put his jacket and gloves on to step out of the hut and into the cold.

'Merry Christmas and I'll see you back in Hobart next year sometime,' I replied, shaking his hand. I looked across at Doc, who was intently speaking to the patient as he readied him for transport. 'I hope it all goes well, all the best and Merry Christmas,' I said to our patient.

'Thanks for all this,' he replied, his mind on more serious matters and the various worst-case scenarios that lay between departing Davis and being safely back home.

As they boarded the chopper and prepared for take-off, it was just Doc and me sitting in the hut, listening as the rotors gained speed and the downwash started to kick up dust and pebbles.

'I hope this all goes to plan,' I said to Doc over the noise of the helicopter now above us.

'We've done everything we can, but yeah, fingers crossed, hey!' said Doc, switching back to the lively Doc I knew.

I wasn't on the ground at Whoop Whoop to see the transfer, but a full change of COVID-19 protective gear between the Chinese and US aircraft for the two passengers was required to make sure there was no chance of exposure. Both ground teams remained separated as the party boarded the US plane and flew off towards Wilkins.

The weather gods had smiled and given us the window we needed to achieve the operation. With the Basler in the air and on its way to Wilkins, time was of the essence to deconstruct everything and get the team back to Davis before the weather turned sour.

'Whoop Whoop party, Chinese helicopter is on its way back to get you. Put as much and as many on that chopper as you can and get yourselves back here asap. Over,' I directed them.

'Copy that. We're not walking home!' replied Jarrod. As the chopper returned to Davis with half the Whoop Whoop team, the lateness of the hour was written on our tired faces. Although the sun never set at this time of year, there was a dim twilight in the early hours of the morning that gave the helipad an ominous vibe. There were still expeditioners at Whoop Whoop who I needed back on station immediately.

'Whoop Whoop, this is Davis, the next flight will be the last. Forget anything you can't fit on board and leave it in the huts for the next season to worry about. Get your butts back here.'

'Copy!' They didn't argue.

The Chinese were keen to get this finished too: they needed to fly back to Zhongshan, finish their own resupply and sail off to the next station. As the helicopter returned to Davis that final time, they didn't shut the engine off or even get out to say goodbye. As our last expeditioners jumped out, we waved and said farewell via radio.

'Thank you very much for your help. We couldn't have done this without you.'

'No problem. We are always happy to help our friends down

here,' replied the pilot as the helicopter lifted off and disappeared into the distance.

In the silence that followed the retreat of the helicopter, I went over to the Whoop Whoop team, who were loading gear into a ute for the short drive back to the station.

'Well done, team, epic work, and welcome back,' I said looking at their tired faces and mountain of gear in the back of the ute.

I walked back from the helipads to ponder everything that had just unfolded. When I got inside, everyone was sitting on the couches exhausted and starving as they reheated food or made coffee. I sent a few emails back home and to the station and voyage leaders from the US, Chinese and Australian stations, who had all supported this operation. The messages were short and simple.

'We cannot thank you enough. Merry Christmas from Davis Station.'

I found a quiet corner and poured a beer, stared out the window and glanced at my watch. It was 0300 on 24 December 2020. Tired, exhausted and emotional, it was done, an operation for the history books of Davis and the Australian Antarctic Program, during a season like no other before it, or likely to be seen again for many years to come.

I walked downstairs to the noticeboard, removed the multitude of weather forecasts, operations plans, manifests, incident team allocations, rosters, COVID-19 plans and 'how to wear a mask' signs, took a step back and looked back at the bare whiteboard. I then stepped forward and simply wrote 'Station Population: 22'.

* * *

Day 427: 24 December 2020
Temperature: -0.9°C to 0.8°C
Station population: 22

Those who slept woke to our second Christmas eve on station, while the patient and Fred were now home safe and well in Australia and would spend the holidays with their families. A bittersweet emotion of success and despair hung in the air. Christmas mark II would be a low-key affair, an experience so unique that I struggle to describe it.

As we sat down for dinner, no one really wanted to be there; everyone wanted to be home, and should have been. But here we were, sharing another Christmas as a family of isolated and exhausted expeditioners. Few would ever know the feelings we experienced that day, and few leaders would ever experience the challenges and obstacles I'd had to overcome during these weeks to ensure success and make it happen.

Even though the medevac had been successful and, professionally, it was the most dynamic and audacious operation I'd ever been involved in, I was flat. I was torn and I felt more alone than ever as I shared a quiet drink with Doc. As the only other man on station who knew the whole story of what had just happened, and what it had taken to achieve the impossible, we sat in silence alone at Nina's.

We turned to each other and raised our glasses.

'Merry Christmas, Doc.'

'Merry Christmas, indeed,' replied Doc, as our glasses clinked.

Part III

SUMMER II: THE SEQUEL

Chapter 11

The Waiting Game Sucks

Day 435: 1 January 2021
Temperature: -2.3°C to 1.7°C
Maximum wind speed: 48 kilometres per hour

For the week between Christmas and New Year everyone was finally able to take their foot off the accelerator in their own way. While work continued, there was now a sense the end was near – and surely, after everything we'd been through, it would be a smooth run to the finish line.

Raising morale was the fact the MPV *Everest* had arrived at Casey station and was completing their resupply before it would return to Hobart and gear up for the voyage to Davis that would take us home in February.

I needed to reset my own wellbeing after the stress created by the evacuation. I was professionally proud of what we had achieved this late into our season but it was hard to celebrate, and there were certainly mixed emotions around station. So how do you unwind when you're still stuck in Antarctica with the same people at the same station?

The first step was to paint my office and change the scenery around me. Kingston was on holidays and those who were at work were focused on the resupply voyage to Casey. Painting the office gave me a clear task with an easy process and sense of achievement, without any complexity or opinions on how it should have been done or which level of risk was acceptable. Just good old-fashioned renovating. I listened to the same radio station I did back home when working on my house in Melbourne – there was nothing Antarctic about it (if I didn't look out the window).

One of the other creative ways to take a mental break from Antarctica was only revealed to me late in the game, but was a game changer nonetheless. Once a month I'd volunteer to maintain the hydroponics hut for the week. The modest-sized container housed four rows of hydroponic crops with UV lights and a nice humid environment to supplement our frozen rations for the year. The hydroponics team consisted of about half a dozen regulars who kept it growing. A simple job, once a day you'd wander up to the hut to fill up the tanks, check the pH levels and taste the kale or lettuce. My favourite job was having to 'be a bee', using a paintbrush to pollinate the flowering plants to fill in for bees. On the handover day, I asked Jimbo if he'd checked on the hut that day wondering if I needed to start this afternoon or could wait until tomorrow.

'Sure have! Been up there dancing away and getting some UV on the rig,' said Jimbo joyfully as he danced.

'Why am I only just learning this secret now?' I suddenly realised that there were obvious benefits of working in the hydro hut: the UV lights helped your body generate vitamin D, of which we were all running low, and we were fast running out of supplements. Then there were the dopamine benefits of dancing around like an idiot.

Even if Jimbo had checked the plants that morning, it never hurt to double-check. There had been a recent incident where we lost a whole row of crops due to bad checking by someone on the team. I walked into the warm, humid air of the hydro hut, cranked the radio, ripped off my shirt and danced around for half an hour like an uncoordinated baby giraffe under the UV lights. It had been a long time since I'd been able to laugh at myself and just enjoy the moment like this. I'm sure the skin cancer guidelines would advise against such fun, but for half an hour I did not care.

Everyone was in a better mood by January. The gym was more crowded than ever, which caused a few niggling issues when people used equipment that someone else was planning to use. It was wise to always have a Plan B, C and D if you planned on a particular machine or area for your workout. The downside was that after the sea ice had decayed and broken out, we were confined to areas we could access by foot for recreational trips. But by now everyone had seen everywhere they'd wanted to, and there were few requests to leave the station on weekends. Everyone had turned their attention to home. After-dinner conversation topics had changed from local issues to life back home and ways to pass the time while we sat around and waited for the ship.

After dinner, with a dozen or so of us sitting around the lounges scrolling through phones, playing chess, reading books or casually drifting in and out of the group conversation, we lobbed up ideas for what to do that evening and in the coming days.

'Any new movies?' questioned the crowd.

'Not really. COVID hasn't been a good year for movie releases, and it's been downhill since *Tiger King* and *The Witcher*,' replied

Dan, our award-winning producer, as everyone returned to looking at their phones and lounging around.

'We should do another art show,' the Weather Magician said.

'Good idea.' I looked around to gauge responses and noticed a collective nod.

Back in the first summer season, just after Christmas, as a way to display the amazingly creative gifts from Secret Santa, we'd hosted an art show. Complete with canapes and bubbly, the night had been a hit. So why not make it a new annual tradition?

Once the art show was announced at the next station meeting, everyone got to work. As I walked around the station, each room would have a secret project shrouded in garbage bags or behind closed doors with 'do not enter' signs, as we all strove to outdo each other in creativity and humour with our artwork. With supplies running low, especially paintbrushes and good-quality timber, it was slim pickings from the scrap bins.

When the night came for the second annual Davis Art Show, the collection was magnificent. An artistic splotchy acrylic painting of the station, colour-coded to the distinctive buildings and only recognisable to the trained eye, would go on to sell for an undisclosed amount to one of the team, who in a suitably artistic tone remarked, 'I simply must have it!' Other displays included ornate chessboards, photos of all of us out in the field, and authentic movie props from *Totally Cooked* and other films from the festival.

To commemorate the unique Anzac Day ceremony from April, I'd flown a brand new flag that morning and kept it aside to frame and hang in the operations building. This was my submission; it now hangs in the ops building on permanent loan.

As we toasted the artists among us, it was clear we were all doing better. I sat back watching the crowd mingle and discuss the artworks, just as they would back home. I saw expeditioners who had been bickering now laughing and sharing cupcakes (thanks, Rhonda), others reminiscing about the trips out in the field and moments along the way. It may have been an art show, but it was also a trip down memory lane as we looked back at what had been an incredible year and a lifetime's worth of stories.

* * *

Day 458: 24 January 2021
Temperature: -1°C to 5°C

'Big news! Congratulations to all those who have bought new houses this week!'

Prior to our year in Antarctica, online auctions and video inspections of houses in Australia were not commonplace, but with COVID-19 restrictions and the rapid uptake in video calls and remote sales options, expeditioners were getting their feet into the property market back home. This was another strange way in which the pandemic actually bought us closer to home – it didn't matter if you were interstate or in Antarctica when you had to use Zoom in lieu of face-to-face meetings.

I announced the news at the station meeting and gifted the new homeowners some of the last bottles of cheap 'champagne', which I'd found in the almost-empty 'Fort Knox' liquor cabinet when I'd audited it ahead of the upcoming handover.

I gave a brief update on the *Everest* voyage, but a healthy level of scepticism remained around what date it would arrive at Davis after it became apparent from the Casey resupply that the *Everest* wasn't quite as fast as the *Aurora Australis*.

The planned departure from Davis was late February. There was a renewed focus, however, on the sea-ice conditions off the coast of Mawson station. Once the *Everest* completed the Davis resupply and picked us up, we'd spend another few weeks on the ship as we sailed to Mawson and completed their resupply and changeout. The good news was we'd be able to relax on the ship without much to do, but we'd all learned over the year that boredom is rarely your friend.

'What's the plan at Mawson, then? Can we go ashore? Do we need to be on the resupply rosters?' These were the big questions without any firm answers, and a few among the team (me included) were keen to complete Australian Antarctic station bingo by setting foot at Mawson.[25] Luckily, I'd been speaking almost daily with the Mawson leader, Matt, and the voyage leader of the *Everest* – Chunky, the same VL who had been on the *Aurora* for her last visit – and we all supported shore trips and a joint resupply roster for any of the Davis team who were keen to get involved, as well as those who were happy to stay on the ship and relax. Everything was shaping up well, except the sea ice.

Following the conclusion of her winter field science role, the Weather Magician had returned to her full-time forecasting job and would be continuing the role once we boarded the ship.

---

[25] Davis, Casey and Mawson are the three Antarctic continental stations, not counting those at Macquarie Island or Heard Island, which are sub-Antarctic.

After looking at the latest satellite image of the Antarctic coastline between Davis and Mawson, I wandered over to the BoM building to look at it in more detail on the big screen.

'Did you see the latest satellite image?' I asked the Weather Magician.

'Not quite what everyone is hoping for. Looks pretty solid.'

'Is there a more detailed assessment of why it's hanging around?'

'The theory is that the giant iceberg that's been floating past slowly over the last month is disrupting everything,' she said.

Each year the sea ice grows around the Antarctic continent in the winter time, and after reaching its peak starts to decay in the summer, and by February or March there should be an open water passage into Mawson station. As the fast ice breaks away from the landmass and the sea ice breaks up, it rafts together and is known as 'pack ice'. From the satellite image we were looking at, there was pack ice blocking the access to Mawson for hundreds of kilometres in every direction a ship could approach from. If it didn't clear in time, the *Everest* would not be able to make it into Mawson.

'Okay, side note – are you happy working on the voyage?' I said. 'It's been a long year, and surely they could have found another forecaster for the ship.'

'I'd rather be working than just sitting around on the ship all day,' she said. 'It's not too hard.'

It reminded me of just how incredible the team was. She wasn't the only one who stood up and volunteered to play a key role on the voyage home, when after so long away and everything we'd been through we were simply exhausted.

'See you at sweat session this arvo, then, thanks,' I said as

I left, realising I needed to walk all the way back to get changed for the group fitness classes we'd been running in the afternoons. They'd seen a resurgence in popularity ahead of the voyage home, as we knew we'd have limited exercise options on the ship.

* * *

I entered the green store that served as our main warehouse and cargo preparation area. It had been rearranged to create an indoor cleared concrete space about the size of a basketball court, which we used for the 'sweat sesh' fitness classes. I noticed just how crowded the space was as the preparations for resupply were well underway, with pallets of our personal effects and other equipment and scientific samples now labelled and ready to be containerised.

The group was moving rubber mats and weights down from the gym mezzanine above us and setting up the circuit as our two gym instructors (a plumber and an electrician) started briefing the group on the combinations of push-ups, burpees, dead bugs, squats and shuttle runs we'd be doing.

I'd never truly found a good gym routine on station over the year, and had even Zoomed into an online session of my gym back home once to break it up. My weekly chin-up competition had been the only consistent routine: I'd film my max reps each Monday morning and send them to my mentee, who would send theirs back to me, as we challenged each other to squeeze out 'one more rep'. I peaked at around ten but had lately slid backwards, with a few gains around my belly weighing me down again. As I moved between the stations of the circuit, my mind wandered to the comfort zones we'd all created for ourselves, and the routines we had set and adjusted along the way.

Coming home is often the hardest part after an expedition or deployment, and I'd certainly seen that over the years. Few other groups besides astronauts had spent this long without any interaction with the outside world. How would we adjust? As Jimbo wandered over to stand on my feet during a sit-up and crunch station, I brought him into the conversation I was having with myself.

'What do you reckon will be the hardest part about going home?'

'Besides crowds and COVID and all that? Probably explaining what we went through,' replied Jimbo.

'What's your plan?'

'First, get as far away from everyone as I can, to get myself right and chilled out, lay low at the farm and hang with my dogs.' After living with twenty-three others in an isolated community, many of us felt the same way. We craved privacy and anonymity, away from others. Humans are social creatures but we also need our space, and down here, despite being the most sparsely populated continent, we felt like we were living on top of each other. Breaking out of our new comfort zones would be the real challenge. I heard the 'beep' signalling it was time to move stations.

* * *

Day 478: 13 February 2021
Temperature: -7.1°C to -2.3°C
Maximum wind speed: 50 kilometres per hour

Few people ever get the chance to visit Antarctica; even fewer have the chance to winter on the continent. Since the heroic age of exploration, your status as someone who has 'wintered over' has defined the true Antarctic experience.

It had been over six months since we celebrated joining this club with our mid-winter's dinner. In honour of the *Everest*'s departure from Hobart on its way to Davis bringing to an end our Antarctic adventure, this evening we would sit down and commemorate the rare opportunity we had been given as a team to have completed such a long expedition. This would be our final formal dinner and, with resupply preparations in full swing and an anxious team awaiting the arrival of the ship, it would be a low-key but memorable night.

'What's for dinner?' I asked Rhonda. We were running low on the more exciting options, but maintained a good amount of frozen meat and a carefully managed stock system that accounted for the worst-case scenario of the ship not making it and us staying another winter.

'We can do all the favourites. There's one pig left and enough steaks, plus cakes and vego options, of course,' replied Rhonda, running through the amazing range of meats and veggies we'd be enjoying, before asking me about the wine situation to accompany the meal.

'Surprisingly good. We've still got the emergency shelf of bad "champagne" and goon[26] for winter mark II, if it came to that, but with a lot of people trimming down before the voyage, we've got enough for one last good party. Then the shelves will be bare as the ship arrives.'

'Excellent!' We both smiled.

---

[26]   I'd ordered this cask wine initially for mulled wine and cooking, but once we were extended, it was moved to a 'break in case of second winter' emergency shelf.

Ordinarily for a formal dinner we'd decorate the lounge and drape international flags of Antarctic partner nations but no one was in the mood for that. The set-up was straightforward – iron some tablecloths, move the tables upstairs and set up the cake table. Of course, our one dedicated expeditioner would make fancy napkin arrangements, as always, to give the table a bit of class.

With a bit of a break before dinner, I decided to go for a walk to reflect on everything that had happened and what lay ahead.

The end was certainly near, but we had a number of complex tasks to complete before we handed over. Even then, the voyage would have to go via Mawson station, and the sea-ice conditions were not looking favourable for an easy passage into Mawson and the famous Horseshoe Harbour used for anchoring the ship and resupplying the station. There was a Plan B for the resupply, however, and as I wandered up to the heli-hangar, I opened the door to check on the two helicopters that would be the backbone of that Plan B.

Right at the end of last season, as the *Aurora* was getting ready to sail back home, a decision was confirmed that, for the first time in the Australian program, the helicopters would remain on station over winter. Without any wintering pilots or engineers, though they were useless.[27] The HeliRes team had sent a giant pressurised balloon that could be temperature and humidity controlled and would house the two choppers after they'd been stripped down a bit and squeezed as close together as possible to spend the winter. It had been a weekly task for the mechanics to check the fluid levels.

---

[27]   It takes considerable support to run Antarctic aviation and would mean at least four additional personnel for the entire winter to have kept the helicopters operational. Their storage at Davis for the winter was to allow for the exact contingency that unfolded.

The electricians had wired the sensors and heaters into the station's building management system and nothing had gone wrong besides the odd power outage, but there was no Plan C.

Our operating procedures required that the helicopters must operate in pairs when outside of station operating areas and beyond the search and rescue range of other aircraft, so if we did indeed have to fly from the ship to resupply Mawson, they would both have to work – and that meant that these two helicopters, which had now joined the club of 'winterers', would need to fire up perfectly and be ready to work flat-out for however long it would take to do a 'fly-off' resupply from the pack ice. I trusted the HeliRes team and the manufacturers, but when you're one 'check engine' light away from failure, it can be hard to remain optimistic.

The other worst-case scenario we had to be prepared for was the unlikely but devastating situation where the ship could not access the station and we would remain at Davis for another winter. Technically, we would be okay – there was sufficient emergency food supplies, and with rationing and efficiency we could stretch the fuel supply through until the next summer – but the human factor would be devastating. Everyone knew this scenario could happen. We did our best not to dwell on it, and just focus on the tasks at hand for the far more likely and positive scenario of the ship arriving as planned for a smooth handover and resupply.

I returned to my room, pulled out my tuxedo, which I'd worn just the once, at the mid-winter dinner, and got ready for our final celebration. I'd had the tuxedo tailor-made in Islamabad, Pakistan, when I was posted there, and I'd been much fitter than I was right now, having twice finished sixth in the Islamabad Ironman triathlon[28] in consecutive years. I had to breathe in as I strained to button up the pants, but you can never be overdressed, they say, and it was 'fitting' for the occasion.

It had been 478 days since we'd left Hobart, and we were every bit as exhausted as you would expect, both physically and emotionally. With recent attitudes and tempers flaring, I was blissfully surprised that pre-dinner snacks and dinner itself were an upbeat and positive affair.

I gave a short toast and handed out awards to everyone, not based on their work, which everyone had done professionally and diligently right to the end, but for their contributions to the community and team. These were the virtues and characteristics that set Antarctic expeditioners apart from being just employees.

'What makes an Antarctic voyage so unique is the people,' I said to the assembled team who had started the journey as strangers. 'From the quiet achievers to the hardest workers, to the barber, to the best slushy, from the brewers to the trip leaders, the barbequers and teachers, the botanists, the pianists and violinists, adventurers and bookworms, here's to the team of the Davis 73rd Australian National Antarctic Research Expedition: Summer … winter … summer.'

* * *

Day 488: 23 February 2021
Temperature: -3.0°C to 0.4°C
Ships sighted: 1

---

[28] An annual social event, with an 800-metre swim, 16-kilometre cycle leg and 8-kilometre run, held around Islamabad's diplomatic enclave.

I'd been up since 4am and had spoken to the captain in the early hours of the morning, so I knew today was the day. With a small crowd of eager eyes loitering around the binoculars and telescopes turned to see the ship come in from the best viewing point in the LQ lounge, spirits were high. But, with a lot to prepare for, I couldn't just stand around all day trying to be the first to see the ship emerge on the horizon through the icebergs.

It was a beautiful morning and brilliant sunshine danced off the icy waters as I made my way over to my office, only to hear the elated radio call almost the moment I turned my back to the sea: 'SHIP!' echoed loudly across the airwaves at 0715 hours.

I stepped back outside onto the balcony with a pair of binoculars and saw it. The oddly shaped vessel we had so long dreamed of was now carefully navigating through the icebergs to the Davis anchorage.

As I entered it into the station log, I noticed the date, 23 February, the same day when, in 1998, I'd last seen my father alive as he dropped me off at the train station on our way to school. And here I was, twenty-three years later, waiting to be picked up by an icebreaker. Would he ever have imagined I'd end up here?

'Davis station, Davis station, this is the MPV *Everest*. Hello!' said the captain over the radio, excited to finally arrive.

'Hello, MPV *Everest*! It's great to see you out there! Let me know when you're anchored and tell the voyage leader to call me when he's ready,' I said back.

'Will do. Out.' The end was here.

My phone rang shortly after with Chunky's familiar British accent on the end of the line – he was back again for another trip as voyage leader. Now they were in range of the station, we could talk over the station's mobile phone network.

It was slightly strange how our phones worked down here just as they did back home, thanks to a lone mobile phone tower installed on the station for local use only. It made communication much easier than through a VHF radio or satellite phone in situations like this, as we could chat through the plan clearly and precisely for the first time since the ship left Hobart.

It would be a tempered start to resupply. With the ship having only been at sea for twelve days, we would run on 'COVID amber' settings. A dozen new arrivals were segregated into different accommodations, with food delivery allowing them to operate independently until we reached day fourteen and could integrate freely. Critically, we needed the helicopter engineers and watercraft operators ashore to establish the two capabilities as soon as possible. Most other tasks and handovers could wait until 'COVID green' began in earnest, with outdoor, socially distanced interaction allowed until then with the limited number of those who came ashore for key roles.

As the ship lowered its inflatable rubber boats into the water later that morning, I began the slow wander downhill to the wharf to greet the first arrivals. Oddly, the team of engineers and watercraft operators were also the last faces I'd seen depart the same wharf a year ago, with the HeliRes team and Mitch. They were here to operate the station's watercraft, which were currently stored in the boatshed, ready for use during resupply.

'G'day,' said Mitch in his familiar tone.

'Good to see you all again,' I said to the gaggle of humans. They all looked the same in the ill-fitting faded-red Mustang flotation suits and bright-yellow life jackets we'd worn on the boats. With a biting wind flicking icy-cold water into their faces, most were covered with buffs and goggles, so it wasn't until they removed their outer layers that I actually recognised anyone, while of course remaining 1.5 metres away.

Everything was set up for them. I pointed the HeliRes team to their ute, which was loaded with everything they'd need, along with the phone numbers of those who would assist with meals or equipment. Then they were on their way to the heli-hangar.

The station's boats were assembled and waiting on the trailers to be launched by the watercraft team. They set to work quickly, taking the boats back out to the *Everest* to begin ferrying people ashore in greater numbers. Once everyone was focused on their job, I had a quiet moment to chat to Mitch.

'How was it?' asked Mitch, knowing full well how rough the extended stay had been for the team.

'We're cooked. It's been incredible but it was tough back in October–November. Seeing that ship out there this morning has lifted the mood a million times for the better, but just be careful – tempers and patience are short. How was 2020 back home?'

'You didn't miss much being down here!' Mitch said, laughing. It was time for him to jump on a boat and time for me to get back to work.

This statement became one of the most common phases I would hear for the next few months as I returned to life back home. Although we hadn't missed much, it certainly hadn't been smooth sailing being the 'lucky few to miss 2020'.

For the next few days we gradually increased the pace, and as more and more people came ashore we moved to 'COVID green' and could socialise and begin handovers. I was able to start delegating things to the incoming station leader and resupply coordinator, who'd be managing the specific cargo and logistics elements around the station.

There were a few teething problems, like when I was accused of missing a briefing, which I would never do. It was all in good humour, though, and a simple miscommunication about who would run the morning pre-start meeting. My team were smiling and laughing again as they showed their replacements around, and the bustle gave the station a festive vibe.

I too was in good spirits, but I had one odd outburst to remind me that, after a longer Antarctic season than I'd bargained for, I was still a tired and a pretty cranky individual.

One evening I saw an expeditioner I didn't know start removing panels from the ever-temperamental and noisy post-mix drink machine that was the fountain of all things fizzy and an important part of morale I didn't want damaged.

'What are you doing? Don't touch that!' I snapped. He was in fact a fridge technician and knew exactly what he was doing, and had me eating some humble pie for dessert. There are more than twenty-two people in the world, I reminded myself.

* * *

Day 492: 27 February 2021
Temperature: -9.8°C to -2°C
Flights: 7

Before we could fly the helicopters out to the ship to be packed into their specially designed containers on the back deck of the *Everest*, they needed to be tested, especially if they were to be used as workhorses for a fly-off resupply over the pack ice to Mawson.[29] The more testing and hours we could give the pilots, the better. They'd spent the last year barely flying and then weeks of hotel quarantine and the voyage twiddling their thumbs.

As I opened the air task paperwork, I noticed the last entry in the book was signed by the pilots of the Chinese helicopter I'd briefed with my giant laminated photos and sign language back in December. I was thankful to be back inside the warm operations room with our own pilots and routine again.

The weather was perfect for a long day of back-to-back flights but we were expecting strong winds and poor visibility for the last few days of resupply, so today was the day to get a few things done. We organised a team of mechanics to be flown back up to Whoop Whoop to show the new team the remote camp and pick up everything we'd left behind from the medevac. This included all the glacial travel equipment we would have needed if the party had walked back to the station over the plateau, along with some food.

Also on the list of priority flights would be to take the incoming station leader on a guided tour around the hills to show her the key sea-ice danger locations and discuss the various leader-specific field decisions, like when I'd opened and closed different passages as the conditions changed throughout the year. She'd been a station

---

[29]   Unlike the *Aurora*, the *Everest* did not have helicopter hangars onboard and could not travel across the ocean with helicopters on the deck so this solution was the only way to do it. Thankfully, the helicopters had been left at Davis for the year to enable this solution.

leader before, at Mawson, and had even briefly visited Davis, so our handover was focused on specific Davis details rather than having to explain how I managed the slushy roster.

I enjoyed flying around one last time, narrating as we flew over all the locations I'd seen from the ground and the air, bringing back memories of an incredible year. You'd think after so long I'd have known the area backwards, but I still managed to mis-identify a lake until corrected by the pilot, who had certainly flown around the hills many more times than this muppet. I just laughed and pointed out the next lake along, the infamous Deep Lake, a hypersaline lake that, even in the depths of the Antarctic winter, would never freeze – a great daytrip from the station.

I knew this would be my last flight over the station, and the view of the ship out the front and the barges ferrying cargo back and forth was spectacular. I'd miss Antarctica, but it was time to go home.

* * *

Day 502: 9 March 2021
Temperature: -5.5°C to -2°C

I woke up earlier than usual and gathered my thoughts for my last day in charge. I'd moved out of my wintering accommodation and was now staying in the transit accommodation attached to the ops building, which meant I could walk to my office in pyjamas to check the overnight emails.

Putting on some more appropriate clothes, I left the building to complete my first daily task of raising the flag. But before I reached the flagpole, I realised I had the wrong flag. I looked at the tattered and faded flag in my hands, neatly rolled just as I'd been taught in the army many years before, the same flag that had flown over Davis every day since the handover ceremony. I walked back into the ops building, grabbed a brand new Australian flag from its packet and laughed at the bright colours and neat creases compared to the almost grey flag that now represented everything the Davis 73rd ANARE team had been through. I raised the crisp new flag, stepped back and looked up as it caught the breeze.

As my gaze lowered to the horizon, it settled on the MPV *Everest* sitting, idle in the still waters off station, and I wondered which porthole I'd be looking out of tonight.

We gathered in the LQ as we had done at the handover ceremony well over a year before. There was cake and snacks for everyone to enjoy as we eagerly awaited confirmation that we had completed the handover checklist and the incoming team were ready. This meant that the on-call trades had handed over their phones, the new doctor was prepped and the new fire team had their gear ready and had rehearsed a call-out. With those tasks completed, the moment came to hand over the key to the station.

After 473 days in charge of Davis, being responsible for the safety of all operations and expeditioners through the longest continuous expedition in Australia's modern history, I handed the ceremonial key and station leader radio to my replacement and wished her and her team all the best for the winter ahead.

'Davis 73rd ANARE, out.' I walked towards the cake, shook a few hands, shared some reflective moments with others from my team and enjoyed the last moments on station.

Full of cake and memories, we donned our bright-yellow survival gear, turned our tags for the last time and walked down the hill to the wharf. Despite specifically telling the team not to souvenir their fire tags, I saw a few of the team pocket theirs on the way out – classic.

I was sad to be leaving behind what had become my home and would be forever etched in my memory, but I was done. I was starting to feel that I could let go. The handover had gone smoothly and the new team were experienced. While we had certainly developed a sense of ownership of the station, it was not ours, and we had to leave it to the new team to make their own.

I was determined to be the last one onto the barge. This turned out to be an easy task, as the dozen or so others couldn't have climbed in quicker, throwing their bags down from the wharf and stepping down the cold steel ladder onto the jet barge for the voyage to the *Everest*. I sat near the bow as we crammed onto the starboard side so we could look back up at the station as we pulled away from the wharf. We waved at the team standing on the shore and called out our final good wishes and jokes.

'Don't believe anything they say about when you'll be going home!'

'Bon voyage!' the new leader said, waving as we pulled away from the wharf.

The jet barge was fast, and as the rocky shoreline faded behind us, I turned to look at the *Everest* preparing to depart. Its anchor was raised and it was stationary. The *Everest* had an advanced dynamic positioning system, which can hold a ship in an exact position. This is critical for saturation diving and risky underwater operations, but today it would save us time. Once we were transferred onto the deck, using a bizarre but fun cage that was lifted with a crane, the barge would be lifted and stowed, and we'd be away.

It was all smiles as we boarded, collected our keys, found our cabins and reported for induction and tours. I'll admit that at this point I paid about as much attention to the briefings as you do on a flight from Melbourne to Sydney. I noted which muster station I was assigned to, along with which life raft and the general emergency procedures, but this was a near new polar-certified vessel with an experienced crew and a captain who had the right mix of seriousness and humour to reassure you that if anything went wrong, he'd know what to do – in classic sea-captain style. For the first time in well over a year, if something did go wrong, I wouldn't be in charge.

Feeling a strange sense of relief, I went back to my cabin and turned on the TV, which I'd soon learn was showing James Bond movies twenty-four hours a day, for some background noise. I lay down on my bunk and fell asleep.

Chapter 12

What Do You Mean, Yet?

I slept almost constantly for the first two days, waking only for meals and the occasional coffee or chat. The ship didn't have much of a social scene like the *Aurora Australis* had; this was a working vessel. The crew focused on their jobs and we stayed out of the way.

We were welcomed on the bridge but were required to maintain strict silence so as not to distract the watchkeepers, a task that was rather difficult for the talkative Australians we were. I wasn't the only one to be politely reminded to shut up with a stern look from the ship's officers.

There was a loophole, though – Jaimie, the chief ornithologist on board, required someone to help with birdwatching, as part of an ongoing science program. Volunteers would enter data into the laptop as she called out what she saw. Many of us enjoyed the low-stakes challenge, and Jaimie was always up for a chat.

As I looked at the pack ice around the ship; it was becoming clear that we wouldn't make it through to Mawson. It was late in the season and you could see the sea ice regrowing around the ship as we negotiated the pack ice and tracked out to sea and back towards Mawson, trying to find a path into the station. I asked the watercraft operators their thoughts on whether we'd make it to Mawson for an over-water resupply. I asked the helicopter pilots their opinion too, and both groups seemed confident it would be their services that would be required. Ultimately, the Antarctic pack ice would make the decision for us.

'It's a fly-off,' said Chunky to the crowd gathered after dinner in the mess. 'We can't get any closer than about 90 nautical miles, which is around the same as Bass Strait. We'll set up the helicopters for operations from tomorrow and will need helpers to start de-stuffing the containers and prioritising cargo to go ashore. It's a game of weight and sea,' he said, playing on the words. 'Weight will be critical to each flight with only internal loads. At this range we can only fit so much in, and if we're lucky we can do about three or four round trips a day. I can't say how long this will take. We'll stay here until we can't stay here any longer due to sea ice or the ship's endurance.'[30]

'What's a few more days?' said Gaz as we sipped a cup of tea and pondered how long it would take. We'd been expecting this once we saw the thick pack ice and got a feel for the ship's capabilities. For us, after so long away, it wouldn't change too much and would give us something to do. We'd be helping to rearrange the cargo from being in 20-foot containers designed to be barged ashore over water to internal payloads for the small helicopters.

Our enthusiasm got the better of us when more helpers showed

---

[30] A ship's endurance is a calculation of food and fuel. There are strict maritime laws dictating fuel reserves and distances from nearest ports. When you're this far away from land, it's *very* important to know you can get home.

up than were actually needed, which made working on the cramped and icy decks tricky. So, after a few days, we settled into a rotation. I'd generally help out early in the day, chipping ice off the back deck before they rolled out the helicopters, or late in the afternoon for the final run of the day.

Rhonda was there seemingly twenty-four hours a day, triaging food and supplies going ashore. As a former wintering chef at Mawson, she knew the station well and had discussed with the ingoing chef what they'd need for the year ahead – another example of just how dedicated the chefs are to morale and the wellbeing of the team. Without the two chefs coordinating this, the team may well have ended up with only potatoes and flour for a year.

The humans were the most important cargo, though. The Mawson teams of just under twenty were swapped out efficiently in the first few days so that, if anything went wrong and we had to leave, no one would be staying a second winter. This meant that my nearest peer for the last year, the outgoing Mawson leader, Matt, was now aboard and we could vent about the unique stresses and frustrations of being an Antarctic station leader.

My routine became comfortable on board. Wake up nice and early for breakfast, help out with cargo or de-icing if needed. If not needed, nap for a bit, then work on my end-of-season report or chase reports from my team. I had plenty of time to work so didn't feel too rushed. I did some wildlife photography in the afternoon if there were whales or seals floating around, and chatted to the captain or first officer on the bridge if they were in a good mood. Maybe I'd get into the gym if it wasn't too crowded (which it was, most of the time), then enjoy dinner and get an early night. Life was easy being just another expeditioner hitching a ride home, and I found myself becoming increasingly interested in the role of voyage leader for a future season.

The weather was favourable and we were getting through the cargo, slowly but surely, towards a point that, if we had to leave, the team ashore at Mawson would have enough to get by.

* * *

Day 525: 1 April 2021
Average temperature: -1°C
Days at sea: 24

As the days sitting off the coast surrounded by sea ice and Antarctic wildlife blended into one long day, we were starting to get the sense it was time to go. The ship would track around in circles each night to keep open water around us, and allow the ship space to ram ice out of the way if needed. The pilots were reporting that large areas of previously open water had now refrozen as sea ice. The season had changed. Winter was coming, which meant, for our non-icebreaking vessel, it was time to get going.

Icebreakers like the *Aurora* and *Nuyina* are designed to drive up on top of sea ice and break it with their weight. Ice-strengthened ships like the *Everest* are designed for polar travel, and can push sea ice out of the way but cannot break it. If the sea ice froze around the ship, it would become trapped. If you want to know what happens then, ask Ernest Shackleton.

* * *

'We're on the way home!' said Doc as he passed me on the stairwell, having just come from the bridge and confirmed we were motoring north. For the first time in a long time, we actually had an arrival date we could start planning for. It would take about twelve to fourteen days to sail back to Hobart, which meant everyone was now frantically using the abysmally slow wi-fi to contact friends and family to plan their arrival.

Rumours were running thick and fast about what the homecoming process would involve and what level of celebration would be appropriate, with everything from a royal visit to 'just go to the nearest pub'. What we didn't want was an overly stage-managed and formal affair – people didn't want to hang around waiting for some dignitary to give a speech. As much as we'd feel honoured to be recognised, people just wanted simple pleasures, like kicking off their shoes to find some green grass to stand on and hugging their families. But it was real: we'd be home by the middle of April and our journey would finally be over.

I was relieved and excited as I went back to my cabin and started lashing down loose items in my cabin for the rough ride ahead as we left the safety of the pack ice and ventured north into the wild seas of the Southern Ocean. Any voyage through the planet's roughest sea carries some risks, but this was a new ship with a good crew. After everything else that had happened to us, we had no reason to expect anything to go wrong – until it did.

* * *

Day 529: 5 April 2021
Average temperature: 2°C

I'd got up early for breakfast and enjoyed a couple of sunny-side-up eggs on toast and some porridge with honey before bumping into the captain on my way to the coffee lounge

'All going well?' I asked.

'Ja, all good, back in Hobart soon enough!' said the captain as he headed up the stairs to the bridge.

I entered the coffee lounge and sat down for my first of two regular morning coffees and chatted to the voyage leader and resupply coordinator about anything and everything related to the polar resupply operations. I eventually decided I'd apply to become a voyage leader for the next season, even before I was home.

I don't get seasick but I don't necessarily sleep very well when the ship is pitching about 30 degrees each side. This ship had an incredible roll, and holding on was a must when walking around. Luckily, it was a bit calmer this morning than it had been overnight, so I wandered back down to my cabin to catch a few hours of sleep before lunch and an afternoon of playing *Age of Empires* with the computer club we'd set up in the conference room.

I flicked on the TV expecting Bond, James Bond. I was surprised to find a rather entertaining dramatisation of London's 1980 Iranian Embassy siege. With a bunch of bad accents and over-the-top cliches as the SAS retook the embassy from the Iranian gunmen, I drifted off to sleep ...

* * *

'FIRE, FIRE, FIRE! Fire in the engine room; not a drill, not a drill!' said the captain, as the announcement echoed through the ship at 1100 hours. Are you kidding me, a fire? I sat up and hit my head on the bunk above me. 'Ouch,' I said, still in denial. I flicked the light switch – nothing. Not a drill, no power, let's roll.

With my eyes adjusting to the dim emergency lighting and the gravity clear in the voice of the captain, I knew this was serious. I fumbled around for my Antarctic survival bag and immersion suit, threw on my heaviest Antarctic jacket, shoved my feet into my Sorel boots, which were held together with duct tape, and made my way to the muster point one deck below in the enclosed focsle.[31]

The muster point led out to the lifeboats and, as I made my way down, I could taste smoke and fumes wafting through the decks. I could not believe what was happening, and neither could those around me. The mood was surreal. The crowd was deathly silent as VHF radios barked orders for crew members to join fire response teams and account for everyone.

I crouched through the small watertight door to the focsle and moved my tag across on the board to show I'd made it to muster. The crowd steadily grew as we filtered in through the small doors, all carrying survival bags, life jackets and immersion suits like old grandmas with too much baggage at an airport. I moved through the crowd to the back. This let me see everyone and kept me out of the way of those still arriving, so I could take stock of myself and those around me. That was when I saw the face of Rex, an ordinarily upbeat and loud member of the team … he was silent, and white as a ghost.

---

[31] Historical term for 'forecastle'. On the MPV *Everest* this was a large enclosed space in the bow of the ship sheltered from the spray and high above the waterline but not heated beyond the residual heat of the ship's engines.

'How you doing?' I asked.

'I saw it. It was massive. We were just standing there looking out the window and then BOOM! A fireball erupted,' said Rex, replaying the event with hand gestures and wild facial expressions. He still looked shocked and was trying to understand what had happened.

It turned out there had been a fire in the port-side engine room, disabling the ship and creating a spectacular fireball from one of the air intakes. It had been powerful enough to incinerate the two rubber boats sitting on the deck next to the intake and turn them into rubbery goo. When I saw them later, the scorched outboard motors were the only thing identifying the goo as having previously been boats. One of them had been the boat I'd enjoyed cruising around icebergs and chasing penguins in at Davis last summer. Farewell.

We discussed who was up on the bridge at the time of the fire. I wanted to know who from the Antarctic teams had seen what happened. It seemed it was mainly crew and some round-trip expeditioners, all of whom were safely now down here at the muster. Ships are a rabbit warren of corridors, rooms, doors and compartments. It was easy to get lost even with lights on. If the crew and expeditioners couldn't be located, it would impact the captain's ability to deploy fire control systems or close bulkhead doors and risk trapping those unaccounted for.

'Alright, be prepared to speak to the captain or anyone who asks about what happened, but for now, put some warmer clothes on and stay ready,' I said. I'd noticed Rex was still wearing shorts, and he would soon experience an adrenalin dump from the shock.

This was as real as it gets in terms of ship emergencies. There were people around who had never been this close to real danger, and it was written on their faces, whether they knew it or not. I knew the voyage leader and captain would manage the response, so I decided the best thing I could do was to help those struggling. I started talking to the small groups around me to get a sense of how people were feeling.

The focsle was sheltered from the freezing cold outside but there were large openings where the anchor chains fed through the ship's hull, as well as a number of other panels and hatches that allowed the bitter cold of the Southern Ocean breeze to circulate. There was also smoke still lingering, so we finessed the right balance of ventilation and warmth as we huddled together like penguins.

We were clear of the sea ice and had crossed north of 60 degrees latitude, which designates the Antarctic region, but we were still days from the coast of Australia. Where were we? It dawned on me that cramming into the lifeboats was a very real possibility. If the ship's crew could not get the engines restarted and steer the ship into the oncoming waves, it would endanger the ship. Without engines or power, we were dead in the water.

Although the captain and crew were now fighting the fire and had accounted for everyone, there were some worrying signs and radio traffic telling me that it was far from over.

'Muster complete. We're trying to fight the fire, but it's not time to go to the lifeboats yet,' said the captain, updating us over the intercom.

'Yet?' we mouthed in unison. Was it just that the captain's English was a bit rusty sometimes and he'd thrown in an extra word?

Or was it now a fact that the engines were destroyed, and we would abandon ship, just not … '*yet*'.

I spotted the Weather Magician and, knowing she'd been forecasting for the ship's path, thought she'd have a good idea where we were this morning.

'Where's the nearest land? Any other ships on the tracker this morning?' I asked as she stood there with a few others, now much closer to the door leading to the lifeboat deck.

'No ships anywhere near us. Heard Island is somewhere out that way but certainly not close, maybe two to three days away.' She pointed in a generally north-westerly direction.

'Well, everyone always wants to go to Heard Island,' I joked, trying to lighten the mood.

Heard Island is managed by the Australian Antarctic Division and is Australia's most remote territory. It's uninhabited, but over the years various field camps have been set up, though nothing permanent that would be seen as safety, and the approach is notoriously difficult. I remembered that Heard Island is part of a chain that includes French external territories and a station at the Kerguelen Islands, but they wouldn't have any rescue ships or facilities to handle all of us. The nearest land of any real help was the Australian mainland, nearly a week away. So it was up to the crew to get this ship going.

Plan B in the lifeboats was not looking good. Unless there were any illegal fishing vessels out there searching for Patagonian toothfish, we were on our own. Once again, I felt the true meaning of the word 'isolated'. At least this time we had a few more people than just the twenty-two of us at Davis – there were around a hundred people in total between the crew, the Davis team and the Mawson team we'd picked up. Those lifeboats would be very cramped indeed.

As the adrenalin wore off, people started putting on extra layers of clothes, and chatter reduced to a minimum as we huddled around waiting for an update. The voyage management team arranged blankets and extra jackets to be brought out to those who'd underdressed for the situation. Finally, there was good news.

'The fire is out. You may go back to your cabins, but stay alert and keep your bags with you,' said the captain, now back to his normal cadence and tone.

This was good news, but we weren't out of the woods, *yet*.

* * *

There is nothing quieter than a ship with its engines off. You get used to the continuous background noise and feel an eerie sense of fear when they're off. We were in the middle of nowhere, the ship was now swaying from side to side as the 5-metre waves crashed into the ship, unable to steer into them to soften the impact. Some stayed in the focsle, unwilling to return to their cabins, but most made their way back and added a few layers of clothes and essentials to their survival bags, things they now realised should have been in them all along.

The mood was different. Until now, people had sat in their rooms with doors closed and headphones on, watching movies or reading books. Not today. As hour after hour passed, we sat there in silence, hoping the crew could get the ship going again. Doors were propped open, and tea and coffee rooms were crowded with small groups seeking out company and some form of assurance that they were not alone.

Others, of course, managed their response in their own way. For some on board the *Everest*, this wasn't even their first scenario like this. Stories were told of what had unfolded on the *Aurora Australis* in 2016, when she broke a mooring line during a blizzard at Mawson and ran aground in Horseshoe Harbour. It was a harrowing tale of the expeditioners having to abandon ship to Mawson before the crew could refloat the ship and limp home to Fremantle.

Would this be the sequel? Would we divert to Fremantle? Would they send a rescue ship? These were the questions floating around our minds as we floated around the Southern Ocean.

By late in the day, the ship's crew had restored some power, but it was clear that the port-side engine room would be out of action. This left just the starboard-side engines to do all the work. All in all, it was just over six hours from the time the fire began until the crew could safely restart propulsion. Although it was tempting to solve the problem immediately, rushing to start the other engine room before knowing what caused the first fire was a recipe for a second disaster – we certainly didn't want to jeopardise the good engines we had left.

* * *

Suddenly everyone was a lot more attentive to every change in the ship's systems, from the noise of the starboard engine room now chugging away and driving us home to the ship's track as we navigated our way north. We were still being hit side-on by the westerly waves as we inched closer to the safety of Australian waters. The after-dinner briefings were now every night and the crowd listened attentively for any updates on our predicament and planned arrival.

Following the initial response from the ship's crew and voyage leader, we established a formal Incident Management Team comprising a who's who of voyage members who could fill a variety of roles on board; included many members of my team and the team from Mawson who were willing to assist. This included both station doctors and members of the fire and emergency response teams, who would remain on higher degrees of readiness in the event of another emergency. We were no longer just passengers hitching a ride home; we were now in the midst of an ongoing emergency.

Matt and I were able to assist by providing a single point of contact for our teams to help the voyage leader manage communication between individual expeditioners and Kingston, which enabled the incident team to get on with managing the situation while we took care of some of the human factors as they emerged.

It took me a day or so to realise the uniqueness of what we were experiencing. Most crises or critical incidents are over in a flash. I replayed moments throughout my life where I'd been shot at, had dodged explosions by mere moments or watched tragedies unfold in front of my eyes, but these had all been more commonplace experiences, where the time between the 'flash', 'bang' and 'calm' is often so brief, you struggle to realise what has happened before it's all over and the scene returns to relative safety.

This was different. We knew the fire was out and the ship was now limping home on the one good engine, but we were a long way from safety. We were in an unusually long lull between the incident and the aftermath, and it was impacting some people in ways they didn't even notice. While I discussed the case study of the *Costa Concordia* incident with one of the watercraft operators over a cup of tea, a number of other expeditioners began eavesdropping as we delved into the complex human responses in moments of crisis. We soon realised there were many who wanted to understand what had just happened in terms of their own emotions and reactions. The time for investigating the fire would come later, and was beyond my technical expertise, but helping expeditioners understand how to manage their own fears when faced with a crisis – this I could do.

We'd been running after-dinner talks, as was traditional on AAD voyages, about previous polar and global adventures, so I hijacked one of these sessions and turned it into a seminar to talk about my experiences living and working in conflict zones.

For years I'd been trying to understand the fundamental elements of how individuals and teams face our fears – a subject that fascinated me. The Australian Army Parachute School lives by the motto of 'knowledge dispels fear'. From my first deployment to the Solomon Islands as a twenty-two-year-old platoon commander on a peacekeeping mission, I soon learned that humans have no idea how to actually manage fear until faced with it. So, in a crowded cinema, deep in the bowels of the *Everest* as we limped our way back home, I told the story of my first real experience with fear, how I'd felt my body reacting to the situation around me and what I'd learned about how to embrace fear.

* * *

As a peacekeeping force on the Solomon Islands back in 2007, we rarely went on the offensive and spent most of our tour doing random patrols and supporting the local police with various odd jobs in the villages. Our primary role was to provide the last line of defence in the event of large-scale riots or unrest but, late in the tour, the local police, aided by the Australian Federal Police, decided it was time to track down and arrest two prison escapees.

It was believed they were hiding in a small village a few hours outside the Solomon Islands capital of Honiara, where we were based. My platoon would provide the security perimeter around the village to allow the police to safely enter and conduct the arrest. This would be a textbook 'cordon and search' operation, straight out of the infantry tactics handbook; it was the dream of every young lieutenant to navigate their platoon through the pitch-dark jungle to arrive in silence, surround the targets, leaving them with no escape, and pounce. This was what we had trained for.

'You alright?' asked the platoon sergeant. We were waiting in the staging area for night to fall before setting off into the jungle with only our night-vison goggles, GPS and a compass to guide us.

'I just threw up,' I replied, confused by my own response.

'You going to be okay?' he asked, bemused.

'Maybe ... just give me a minute. I feel weird,' I added, waving him off while I tried to compose myself.

Moments later, the call came through on the radio to set off. As soon as I had a job to do, I was fine. As we patrolled through the jungle, step by silent step, towards the village, I realised it was the accumulation of stress and fear that had disrupted my stomach, heart rate and body as I mentally prepared for what lay ahead that night and the consequences of failure or mistakes. I knew I could trust our training and my soldiers, but there were a lot of unknowns with the local police force, the village itself and the guys we were looking for. We knew there were some weapons still floating around in the community. The chances of a firefight were very low, but not zero.

As we slowly surrounded the village, I smiled, realising we had achieved the first part of our mission flawlessly. All was still and silent as, one by one, the team radioed through. They were set and it was time to 'go loud'.

'Bang, bang, bang!' The rapid-fire noise of the flashbang grenades broke the tropical jungle silence as the assault force moved into the target house. Almost immediately, as we all focused on the target, I heard the radio traffic from the perimeter team about 50 metres away from my central position. 'Weapon! There's someone headed your way carrying a gun,' said the solider to his section commander.

'Can't see it, your call,' the reply came back.

I felt my entire body tense up and the whole world slow down as my brain instantaneously recalled the months of training and lessons on rules of engagement, the endless scenarios we had rehearsed, the grey areas, the morals, the ethics, the realities. I even recalled that what I was experiencing was known as temporal distortion, and that it's common in these moments as your brain goes into overdrive.

'Stop! Put the weapon down!' I heard the verbal warning over the top of the noisy raid going on in front of me. My mind narrowed to a level of alertness I'd never experienced. The assault force was yelling and screaming at the occupants of the house right in front of me but my hearing became superhuman as I listened for the distinctive 'click' of the safety catch on the soldier's rifle still 50 metres away. I waited for what seemed like eternity for the sound of the trigger being pulled and gunfire to echo through the jungle.

'Got him,' I heard over the radio after another soldier leapt from his position in the darkness like a velociraptor to tackle the man to the ground, disarm him and secure the weapon without firing a shot.

'Well done that man,' I said as I opened the mic and relayed a classic army adage, before turning to the platoon sergeant and sending him to supervise the arrest and the recovery of the weapon. Never in my life had my brain computed so many things in the space of a few seconds, and never had I been so impressed by the actions of a team working together in the pitch dark of the jungle to achieve a peaceful solution.

* * *

So, what did all this have to do with being stuck on a ship in the middle of the Southern Ocean struggling to get home? Well, on that night I learned, clear as day, that you may be in control of the situation, the response and the team, but you are *not* in control of your body. And it will do all sorts of weird and wonderful things when pushed to the limits of fear.

We went around the dark room in the bowels of the ship and, one by one, relived the moments on the bridge where the expeditioners had seen the fireball, understanding the clumsy movements through the doorways into the focsle, the odd choices of clothing, the nervous banter, the inappropriate jokes, the blind optimism and the denial. This was the full range of human reactions to fear and it played out right in front of our eyes. Once you can understand what is happening physiologically to yourself and others, you enter a whole new level of operating in the face of fear.

I was backed up by some of the incredible experience in the room. Mitch joined in the discussion about the 'Cooper conditions' that break down the fight or flight response into a traffic light system, aligning almost perfectly with the heart rate training zones. Everyone knows how uncoordinated you are when physically pushed to your limit as your heart struggles to get enough oxygenated blood to your muscles and brain. Fear can deliver the same effect instantaneously without a gym.

For the few who had seen the fireball erupt from the ship and the moments that followed, I felt this helped them understand what they had been through. I was glad I'd found a way to help in the short term until we all made it home safe to fully unravel what had happened.

Later that night, the word came through that we would divert to Fremantle, as it was a few days closer than Hobart. A support vessel had been arranged to shadow the *Everest* back into port and would arrive in the area in the next few days. We were finally about to get home.

Chapter 13

Home

Day 537: 13 April 2021
Temperature: 11.8°C to 21.8°C

I sat alone on the starboard-deck wing of the *Everest*'s bridge, looking out across the waves as we paralleled the West Australian coast on the approach to Fremantle. It was a beautiful sunny day and I could smell the salt air and feel the warmth on my face as I sat there in just a T-shirt and shorts, trying to get some much-needed vitamin D from the sun's rays on my ghostly white skin.

We knew there would be a rigmarole getting ashore, and from the moment the pilot was ferried out to guide the ship into Fremantle, we donned masks and would be required to adhere to Australia's strict quarantine requirements until we all passed a temperature check and were cleared to enter Australia.

There was some last-minute anxiety that the Western Australian Government, which had the strictest border rules in Australia, would deny us entry and we'd have to stay on board and sail back to Hobart, but this was quickly quashed after the government realised how long we'd been at sea and that the unique circumstances warranted a rare exception from WA's mandatory fourteen days' quarantine on arrival.

Matt and I sat around a phone, trying not to slide away from the table, as the ship rocked side to side. The ship still seemed to be struggling in the swell even in the smoother Australian waters.

'What's the final plan with flights and hotels and so on?' I asked the AAD team who'd just flown into Fremantle.

'We're not expecting you off the ship until late afternoon so we'll put everyone up for the night in Fremantle and then disperse from there. People can return to Hobart or home as they choose. But they'll need to complete border crossing applications and download the different COVID apps for each state,' said the head of HR.

'Brilliant, but also, what?' I said, confused. Each expeditioner would have the ability to decide their own travel plans to accommodate a visit home before going back to Hobart for debrief. But when it came to navigating our way around Australia, we would be faced with the challenge of crossing state borders at our own risk.

On one hand, this gave us the very thing we had lost, control of our lives. On the other hand, none of us had ever lived in an Australia with anything other than open borders, so we were confused beyond belief at the prospect of navigating who could go where and what flight routes even existed in this new world. All we wanted to do was get home, but trying to understand what travelling looked like in the COVID world was overwhelming.

As we rounded Rottnest Island, home of the quokka, and turned east towards Fremantle Harbour, I moved to the top of the heli-deck for the incredible view as we sailed in past the large cargo ships sitting at anchor. Craning our heads skywards to look at the buzzing news helicopter circling above us, which was trying to get footage of the fire damage to the ship, we all made idle chit-chat about where might be the best place to enjoy a beverage once finished with the formalities of the welcome.

I squinted and looked up and down the coast, trying to spot Cottesloe Beach. I reminisced about the last time I'd been there, staring out at the ships and relaxing on the sand. I couldn't wait to feel the sand between my toes, or the blades of grass under my feet. I was desperate to find some peace and quiet away from everything ships and Antarctica.

As we sailed through the heads of the harbour, a small number of locals who'd parked their cars along the banks were waving at us as we took in the sweet smell of civilisation and the harbourside ambiance on a picture-perfect Fremantle afternoon. It was only then that I remembered that the last members of my family to sail into Fremantle were my grandparents and father when they immigrated to Australia in the 1950s. What had changed since then?

With the background sounds of mobile phone messages pinging away now we had reception again, I made a few calls back home to work out the plan to get back to Melbourne the next day. It was hard to think about anything except getting through the next few hours of what would still feel like work until I was free.

With the diversion from Hobart and Western Australia's strict borders, there were very few AAD staff there to welcome us, except for the essentials from operations, shipping and personnel, along with the director himself. After a slow but expected immigration process on board, we were bussed to a hotel and welcomed by a crowd of families and staff.

It was overwhelming and confusing as some rushed in to hug and shake our hands to welcome us home, while others awkwardly stepped back and offered fist bumps or a muffled 'Welcome home' behind a mask. Evidently, those of us who'd recently arrived in Western Australia had different rules from those who lived there. We'd been expecting some level of uniformity.

There was a short welcome ceremony to be held in an upstairs function room, but between that room and the gaggle of expeditioners was the hotel bar. For one last moment I was forced to be the 'bad guy', as one of the team refused to head upstairs for the ceremony.

'I'm not going,' he said, comfortably holding a beer and propping up the hotel bar.

'Just go upstairs, collect your COVID welcome pack of masks, sanitiser and paperwork, receive your pin and then you're done,' I said, and I walked off, not expecting him to appear upstairs. I rounded up the stragglers and headed upstairs.

This was clunky. But this was the COVID world. We'd soon learn everything had a clunky and frustrating overlay – nothing would ever be the same as it was before we left, nearly a year and a half earlier.

I don't remember much of what was said at the ceremony as the director handed out the pins awarded to each expeditioner. We also received a special edition patch along with the two pins to acknowledge our contribution to both the 2019–20 and 2020–21 seasons, which was nice.

I'd handed out the wintering medallions at the handover ceremony on station, which was the real memento of our season (along with my kazoo), so I wasn't in the mood for ceremony. Neither were most of the crowd, I realised as I eyeballed the freshly made Australian pizzas from my position up front.

I chatted to a few families and other expeditioners as the party dissipated, then I made my way back to the hotel lobby, where the bulk of the crowd was now happily enjoying a beer and relaxing.

We were keen to get out of the hotel, and rumours started spreading of a nearby pub that met two criteria. First, it was open until midnight and, second, it had live music. With that hot bit of intelligence, the expeditioners and crew from the *Everest*, made up of all nationalities of the high seas, descended on the one pub and gave them a Tuesday night to remember. It wasn't until I was reaching over the crowded bar, passing cocktails back and forth between groups of expeditioners, that I had a thought: 'Should we have checked in or done some sort of COVID thing on arrival?'

One of the locals laughed. 'This is Western Australia, mate – we don't do COVID over here!' We clinked glasses and jokingly toasted the Republic of Western Australia!

Eventually I did the old fade-away and went back to the hotel to get some rest. My brother-in-law had sent a welcome gift of a bottle of whisky for me and bottle of champagne for Rhonda, who I knew had a similar flight the next day, so I'd have to find her in the morning. With the collective exhaustion of our time away hitting me, I fell asleep on top of my bed, out like a light.

* * *

I woke to my phone buzzing: someone was trying to call me. 'Yep, what's up?' I answered, realising as I tried to speak that my voice was probably still at the pub.

'Wakey, wakey. The press conference is on for 9.30, so get

yourself prettied up and downstairs asap for the pre-briefing,' said the AAD's media rep, reminding me I'd agreed to a press conference that was planned for the night before but then rescheduled. It was now set for 9.30am the morning after my first night back in Australia in 537 days. Great.

As I sat in the small hotel meeting room with bright lights and the director and others looking fresh faced and well attired in AAD-branded jackets and polo shirts, I was distinctly aware how shabby my hair and beard were, along with my 'nice shirt', which was the same shirt I'd worn to most special occasions on station for the last year and a half, so was a bit faded and not as fancy as it once was. Somehow, Matt looked immaculate, but I figured I at least *looked* like I just got back from Antarctica. That would sell papers.

The press grilled the director and general manager of operations about the fire on the ship and other aspects of the season, but by the time they got to me it was mainly about life on station, missing the pandemic and our favourite penguins.

We filmed some additional footage of Matt and me getting a coffee and learning how to check in and stand on the footprints 1.5 metres away but, once again, it appeared Western Australia didn't really seem to care. Others in the cafe looked on, confused about why this was newsworthy, but I got a free coffee so that was a win.

* * *

'Have you seen Rhonda?' I asked Lewis at the airport as I made my way anxiously through security and the largest crowd I'd seen in a long time. I used to love airports, but having travelled around the world continually for work and pleasure, I was surprised how overwhelmed and confused I was now as I tried to remember what to do.

'She's on my flight so should be at the gate,' said Lewis as we parted ways. He went to pick up some souvenirs and I went searching for Rhonda. Luckily, it's a small airport and I found her soon enough.

'I couldn't have done this without you,' I said. 'Thank you for everything you did for me and the team.' We sat down for a final farewell. I handed her the champagne and a small present I'd made on station for this exact moment.

'Thank you. I'd follow you through that again any day,' she replied. 'What a year!'

We hugged, knowing that finally, after everything we had been through as a team and as the leadership duo of the station, it was over.

I meant every word of what I'd said, from day one to day 537. Rhonda was the glue holding the team together and we all knew it. Recognition would come later as she was awarded the Australian Antarctic Medal in 2021 for service during our season and her many seasons before ours. If there was one member of the team that embodied everything an Antarctic expeditioner should be, it was her.

'Safe travels and enjoy the new farm,' I said. We parted ways to rush to our flights. I knew Rhonda was excited to see the farm she'd purchased online but had yet to see.

* * *

My brother met me at Melbourne airport for a low-key arrival back home, and we went for a quiet dinner near my house. I was inundated with messages and welcomes but was not in the mood. I turned my phone off, ready to sit down with my brother and eat a chicken parmigiana in peace.

'Inside or outside?' the waitress asked.

'Outside,' I replied. I was wearing shorts and a T-shirt in the sweltering Melbourne heat.

'Inside, please. He's a penguin,' said my brother, more sensibly attired in jeans and a jumper for the 12-degree autumn evening.

Listening to the stories about what had happened back home in Melbourne as they endured some of the strictest lockdowns, along with home-schooling young children while working from home, it was clear it had not been smooth sailing for those back home.

'How'd Mum go with it all?' I asked.

'It's been rough. She's bored and frustrated with everything going back and forwards all the time like the rest of us.'

'I'll go see her tomorrow. It will take time to readjust to all this. I've got such little patience left in me after everything that happened.' I sipped a pint of fresh beer and realised just how much better it was than our homebrew on station.

'Join the club. We're all exhausted too,' he reminded me, bringing me back to Earth.

* * *

Waking up in my own bed felt like I'd never left. I noticed the noise of the neighbourhood birds and construction trucks beeping and bustling past my house in inner-city Melbourne, and realised how quiet it had been on station. The constant background noise of the ship's engines had been more uniform.

I was keen to wander around and enjoy some freedom. I took off my shoes and roamed across the freshly mown grass around Albert Park Lake and looked back at the city skyline. I couldn't believe I was finally back.

I met up with one of my best mates, Drew, later in the day and stood on the beach looking south as his dog ran around chasing seagulls. 'I feel like a lost dog wandering around the city not knowing what to do,' I said.

'You look like a lost dog with your mullet and shaggy beard,' he said. 'You're also about ten years older,' he added.

'Ease up, tiger!'

It reminded me of what I'd thought when I first met Simon on the helipad back in 2019.

'Are hairdressers normal? Do I just wander in?' I was confused – every shop seemed to have a different system and everyone else knew how to do COVID except me.

As we approached a small cafe to grab a coffee, I was scolded by a patron standing near the door.

'Excuse me! There are already *four* people inside and I'm next,' said the patron as I backed slowly out of the shop.

'Sorry, I didn't see the sign,' I said as I noticed the 'Maximum occupancy FOUR people' sign in the window.

'Watch out for Karens,' said Drew.

This was the new world. Getting a coffee or doing anything now involved layers of bureaucracy and admin, and I kept getting into trouble. I was also appalled by the decision to abandon reusable cups in favour of non-recyclable takeaway cups that were now strewn all over town, along with discarded face masks and rubbish everywhere.

'Has the world become so fixated on COVID-19 that we've given up on the environment?' I asked.

'Yep, there is one news story and one conversation, COVID, it's exhausting. You've at least got something to talk about,' he said.

'Maybe that's what I'll do then, talks, become one of those guys,' I mused.

* * *

I'd first done presentations on Antarctica to a few different groups via Zoom while I was still at Davis, but the offers to present my story and what I'd learned from the experience came in thick and fast as I settled into life back home.

I'd been on leave without pay from my old job while I was away on my 'twelve-month sabbatical', but returning to that would mean a move to Canberra to manage a desk. I couldn't think of anything I'd rather do less, so I joined the 'great resignation' that was sweeping the UK and making its way to Australia. I did the maths and calculated I could survive a year without a job to decide what to do with my life. I was lost and I needed something to focus on.

Renovating my house was my immediate solution. I dusted off my toolbelt and got stuck into renovating and exploring the daydreams I'd had while away. I was in my element – a clear task, no distraction, full creative control (within Australian building regulations and with local council approval, of course). It was just what I needed as I gradually reconnected with my friends and family, but I was different. It was hard to find joy and I couldn't relate to those back here.

To my young nieces I was a novelty. Their teachers thought they were lying when they said their 'uncle lives with penguins', but then I arrived at their school to present to the 'big kids' on the Antarctic environment and run a 'penguin Q&A' with the younger kids. I wasn't sure who was having more fun as I recounted the sounds and stories of nature's most hilarious creature to a captive audience of five-year-old kids and a few teachers, who were equally fascinated. The questions were different when speaking to some of Australia's largest corporations and firms, but often the penguin photos were just as popular in the corporate offices as in the schools.

* * *

Having arrived back home in April, Anzac Day was the first real event since returning. Heading out on the town with lads from my tour to the Solomon Islands and running into mates I'd worked with in Iraq and Pakistan was an annual tradition, and despite all the lockdowns and COVID-19 rules, the event was relatively normal, although not quite as busy as in other years. I had started to appreciate how 2020 had impacted everyone back home.

By midyear, I arranged a week up at the ski fields on the border of New South Wales and Victoria with some mates from Canberra. You'd think after a year and a half surrounded by ice and snow I'd want a beach, but I was oddly looking forward to *enjoying* the snow

– riding down it on my snowboard instead of digging it out with a shovel so I could move the Red Hägg to get to the Pink Hägg so I could take the quad bikes.

The snow was patchy but the company was good. The village was a different story, and there was no 'après-ski' vibe under the clunky but now commonplace COVID-19 rules around venue capacities and masks. It wasn't the holiday I was craving – rules and restrictions had ruined it.

As the week came to an end, my fears of a return to lockdowns and limited social freedom came true as the COVID-19 Delta strain took hold across the world and Australia. Victoria announced the border would close within twenty-four hours and I was left with a choice of returning home or staying on someone's couch in Canberra while it all blew over.

I'd learned from history that these lockdowns always dragged on, so I quickly made my way home and went into a forced fourteen days of home isolation, having travelled from the 'hot spot' state of New South Wales, despite there being no cases anywhere near the ski resorts. I would finally get to experience what everyone else had been through while I was away. After I arrived back in Melbourne, I had nothing to do except sit at home, isolated and alone once again.

It all felt familiar. I was well equipped to keep renovating and using my home gym and reading books, but it was the bigger picture disinformation that got me. On station, I'd always sought to be clear with the team, and when rules or regulations didn't suit the circumstances we adapted them or were able to explain the 'why' behind the rule and move forward. What I was now seeing with the daily news briefings, newspaper articles, social media, Department of Health messages and the rumour mill was that, with too much information and too many inconsistencies as the population *tried* to do the right thing, the government was losing control.

I lay on my couch watching Victorian premier Dan Andrews in his North Face jacket answer a barrage of questions about hypothetical scenarios and excruciating details within the COVID-19 plans. I laughed as I related to what he was going through.

'I know how you feel, Dan. Don't worry, the ship will get there eventually.'

* * *

After weeks and months rolling on and blending into one, the light finally shone at the end of the tunnel towards the close of 2021, and once again social events were allowed indoors after the novelty of picnics in the park had worn off. I'd been reluctant to attend large events or crowded venues even before the latest round of lockdowns, but sometimes you get a good offer.

'Knoffey, dinner tonight with Dave Sabben, suit, medals and so on, 6pm. Be there,' came a phone message out of the blue from and old army mate who knew I wouldn't pass on the opportunity.

Dave Sabben was a living legend. As a lieutenant during the war in Vietnam, in 1966 he commanded 12 Platoon at the Battle of Long Tan, when Australia's Delta Company from 6 Battalion Royal Australian Regiment had fought a decisive battle while outnumbered by the enemy. It was a battle only fully recognised for its significance years later and recently immortalised in the film *Danger Close*, which we'd actually watched in the cinema at Davis during the year. I'd always wanted to meet him and hear his stories, as well as catch up with other veterans and characters you'd find at an evening such as this at a Returned and Services League (RSL).

As Dave spoke, it wasn't his tales of feeling the ground shake as artillery landed metres in front of him or watching the battle unfold around him as they faced the grim reality of being overrun that hit me. It was when he answered a question from the group.

'How did Vietnam change you once you got home?' one of the many experienced servicemen in the room asked in a loud voice to help Dave hear due to the aforementioned artillery's effect on his hearing.

'It aged me terribly,' he replied. 'I went to Vietnam listening to the Beatles and came back listening to Beethoven.'

I felt the same way. While nothing compared to what happened in the jungles of Vietnam or at Long Tan, Antarctica had aged me. Since I returned I hadn't wanted to socialise, I didn't want to go out, and I didn't want to return to full-time work. I wasn't interested in meeting new people and I was pushing those away who tried to connect with me. I wasn't quite myself and I felt like an old man.

There was another question I needed to ask. As the dinner wrapped up I found a moment to speak to Dave before he headed off. 'How did you go keeping in touch with those from Long Tan?'

'Some of us are still close to this day, but others didn't want anything to do with me or what happened,' said Dave.

The younger me would not have understood this, but right now it made perfect sense. What was playing on my mind was exactly what Dave described. I had caught up with a few of the team from Davis in Melbourne when they were passing through, and I had spoken to Rhonda a few times on the phone. I kept in touch with Doc and had spoken to others on mid-winter's day in June, but there were one or two who never replied to emails or returned phone calls, and it hurt.

Why did it matter? We all got home safely, we achieved more than we ever imagined as a team, we made it through more challenges and setbacks than we ever expected, and at every turn and at every stage I'd done everything to ensure everyone made the most of the opportunities. I'd run the station with a balance of professional and social activities, and more than half of the team had reapplied to return in future seasons, or at least to 'keep a foot in the door' to return down the track. So why did I care if one or two never spoke to me again? I did, and I couldn't let it go.

At least, not until a conversation around an outdoor table on a balmy summer's night in Melbourne. Sitting in a driveway carport with peers who'd led corporate teams through the challenges of 2020 –21, it dawned on me. Everything that happened down there was happening back here. Throughout the pandemic, people had quit, teams had fractured, leaders had stumbled and leaders had risen, communities were torn and the nation was exhausted.

The burden of leading through a crisis? Well, at the end of the day, being hated and questioned and challenged and doubted and alone … well … That's the price of leadership.

* * *

'You should write a book' was something I heard at least once a week as I caught up with everyone and was invited on a few podcasts to discuss what returning to normal life was like after our journey. I wasn't convinced. But as Melbourne returned to lockdown and I ran out of renovation projects that could be achieved, I turned my mind to how to tell this story.

I grappled with the emotions it would stir up in me as I relived some of the darker moments, and the conflicting opinions of the team as to how the story was told. There were twenty-four of us in the winter team, with twenty-four opinions and versions of this story, all of which have a different lead character.

I didn't reconcile myself to writing until I started rereading books about other moments in history, such as the Apollo 13 story *Lost Moon* by Jim Lovell and Jeffrey Kluger, and the Mount Everest story *Into Thin Air* by Jon Krakauer, where groups had set off on one adventure and been given another. As I relived the moments in our story through the highs and lows, the darkest moments and what it was like to come home to a different world, I knew that this was a story worth telling.

* * *

'It was good to see the *Nuyina* finally arrive in Hobart,' I said to Charlton, the AAD's general manager of operations and safety, while catching up over the phone in late 2021.

'We're always looking for good voyage leaders,' he replied, 'and after last season, we're leaving nothing to chance. We'll have three ships operating and one of the busiest seasons ever.'

Due to the disruptions of 2020, although all personnel had been changed out and the stations continued to operate, there was unfinished business. The fly-off over the pack ice at Mawson meant the station hadn't been refuelled, and it would desperately need this to be completed in the 2021–22 season. Also, the helicopters had only delivered a small portion of the cargo.

'Do you want to lead the cargo voyage to Mawson and Davis for early 2022?' he offered.

'Absolutely.' I didn't hesitate for a second.

I'd been offered jobs in Melbourne running operations and consulting, but these were nothing compared to the opportunity to once again venture south across the seas to Antarctica as a voyage leader.

* * *

You're going back again? After nine months at home readjusting and contemplating my options, I would return to Antarctica as the voyage leader to Mawson and Davis in February 2022 on the chartered vessel *Happy Dragon*. It wasn't an icebreaker, but this time we had a second vessel, the *Aiviq*, in support, which was a full-strength icebreaker and could lead a path through the ice into Mawson if needed.

I wasn't the only one who returned so soon. A number of the Davis 73rd ANARE team were already back down south for the summer of 2021–22 at other stations, and Rhonda would return to Mawson in 2022 for yet another winter.

Finally setting foot ashore at Mawson and returning to Davis once more, I felt like I had finished the journey that I had started back in October 2019. And when the *Happy Dragon* docked in

Hobart after a successful season that saw Australia's stations all fully resupplied and back to normal capability, there was a collective sigh of relief. I never got to step on board the *Nuyina* while she was in Hobart, but she still owes me a lift!

So why do people keep going back? The answer is simple. There is no wilderness so untouched, no landscape so remote, and no place quite like Antarctica. Once you set foot on the icy shores at the end of the Earth, you will always long to return.

Image Credits

Acknowledgements

This book would not have been possible without the help and support of the following people and organisations:

The Australian Antarctic Division – Director Kim Ellis, Charlton, Robb, Deepy, Don, Matt, operations, shipping, Nisha, Mark and the media team, infrastructure and everyone else who makes the Antarctic program run.

Affirm Press – Martin and Keiran, for taking a chance on an unknown author without a manuscript, and Armelle, Kerry and Natasha, for polishing it up.

Kelly from @Goodcontentkel and the Expert Author Academy for guiding me along the way.

And all the test readers, photographers, fans and others: Ally, Dan, Donna, Will, Rhys, Dylan, Ez and Raye for looking after my house, Jules, Linda, Steve, Peter N, Dave S, Lake Jon Swim Team, the Boat of Chiefs, Sasquatches, Cobra, Coco, Skydive GT, Monash airport lounge crew, Dave at St. Ali coffee, Waffle and Ziggy.

And, of course, the wintering team of Davis station's 73rd Australian National Antarctic Research Expedition – it may not have been what we signed up for, but we were all in the same boat.